SIMULATION AND GAMING
In Social Science

SIMULATION AND GAMING in Social Science

Michael Inbar and Clarice S. Stoll

THE FREE PRESS
A Division of Macmillan Publishing Co., Inc.
NEW YORK

COLLIER MACMILLAN PUBLISHERS
LONDON

The Free Press
A Division of Macmillan Publishing Co., Inc.
866 Third Avenue, New York, N.Y. 10022

Collier-Macmillan Canada Ltd.

Library of Congress Catalog Card Number: 74-143527

Printed in the United States of America

printing number

2 3 4 5 6 7 8 9 10

To

JAMES S. COLEMAN

"A tout seigneur tout honneur."
(To the master, all honor.)

Preface

"Science progresses by some of the damndest methods," George Homans said. This book is about one of those methods, simulation, the what, how, and why of the technique.

We first thought about this volume as a result of our association with the Johns Hopkins games project. It was there we received almost daily requests for information on the "procedures" for designing simulation games. No useful literature on design was available, so we began to think about filling this need.

Given the nature of simulation, we realized that to discuss the problems of design would require extensive descriptions. We felt that we should not rephrase what could be said directly by the designers. Thus, we decided to invite designers to prepare case studies in the spirit of the volume edited by Philip Hammond *Sociologists at Work*. We used the simulation developers to describe, especially for this volume, the actual construction process itself.

It was clear that the book should discuss simulation in general, not just games. We believe that there is a continuity across modes of simulation that is lacking in much of the literature. Often computer simulation people and man simulation people have remained segregated from one another. We wanted to demonstrate the commonality across the modes, as well as consider the special advantages and problems of each mode. If the amount of space paid to games in this volume suggests unequal emphasis, it is primarily because there are already several excellent volumes dealing with computer simulation techniques.

Preface

The book is addressed to both teachers and researchers in the social sciences. Thus sociologists, political scientists and social science educators should find the volume directly relevant to their interests. The economist, psychologist, or business reader with an interest in the behavioral aspects of their fields should also find many of the discussions useful.

In addition to being interdisciplinary, simulation is a multipurpose technique. We have therefore included examples of simulations designed for research, theory building, and teaching with both man and computer simulations. The volume should therefore be useful in courses in social science theory, methodology, and methods of teaching.

No work such as this occurs without the intellectual aid and support of others. Our first intellectual debt is to James S. Coleman, and for this reason we have dedicated the volume to him. Over the years he has given us an inordinate amount of encouragement and direction. At the same time he has always given us the freedom to make as many mistakes as we could manage, so he should not be held responsible in any way for those to be found here.

Another major debt is to the contributors who made the format of this book possible. They were remarkably prompt in meeting deadlines, and unusually cooperative in response to our editorial suggestions. One of our rewards is to have worked with them. Several contributions for reasons other than quality could not be included; we are grateful to their authors for their effort and good will, and above all for their understanding.

We would also like to acknowledge the contributions made by our Hopkins colleagues, and in particular those who are members of the Center for the Study of the Social Organization of Schools. In this connection we gratefully acknowledge the encouragement of its two directors, Edward MacDill, and later, John Holland. David Wirtz, Patricia Kraus and Christine Schulze typed the manuscript in its various forms and griped enough about some portions to force us to rewrite them. Among colleagues and friends who commented on portions of the text were: Donald Ball, William Gamson, Paul McFarlane, William Phillips, Cathleen Stasz, and Gerald Zaltman.

M. I.
C. S. S.

Baltimore, Maryland

CONTRIBUTORS

SARANE S. BOOCOCK, *Department of Sociology and Anthropology, University of Southern California* **SHLOMO BREZNITZ,** *Department of Psychology, Hebrew University of Jerusalem* **JERRY L. FLETCHER,** *Portland (Oregon) Public Schools* **WILLIAM A. GAMSON,** *Department of Sociology, University of Michigan* **FREDERICK L. GOODMAN,** *Department of Education, University of Michigan* **JEANNE E. GULLAHORN,** *Department of Psychology, Michigan State University* **JOHN T. GULLAHORN,** *Department of Sociology, Michigan State University* **MICHAEL INBAR,** *Department of Sociology, The Hebrew University of Jerusalem* **DONALD A. KOELLER,** *Educational Development Center, Cambridge, Massachusetts* **JIMMER M. LEONARD,** *Board of Cooperative Educational Services, Westchester County, New York* **AMIA LIEBLICH,** *Department of Psychology, Hebrew University of Jerusalem* **DAVID S. MARTIN,** *Newton Public Schools, Newton, Massachusetts* **PHILLIP D. PATTERSON,** *Envirometrics (Washington, D.C.)* **ROBERT B. SMITH,** *Department of Sociology, University of California, Santa Barbara* **CLARICE S. STOLL,** *Department of Sociology, Sonoma State College* **DENIS G. SULLIVAN,** *Department of Government, Dartmouth College* **GERALD ZALTMAN,** *School of Business, Northwestern University*

Contents

CONTENTS

SECTION B. MACHINE AND MAN-MACHINE SIMULATIONS

Part I

ANATOMY OF SIMULATION

"Truth emerges more easily from error than from confusion."

—Francis Bacon

Chapter **1**

Browsing Through Simulations

PART I. ANATOMY OF SIMULATION

Browsing Through Simulations

Traditionally first chapters are for definitions. Typically, though, definitions are abstract statements made by specialists about their field for the benefit of outsiders. As a rule the specialists do not need these statements and the outsiders do not always understand them. We shall try to avoid this pitfall by postponing an abstract discussion until the reader has had a chance to develop a *gestalt* for simulation. To assist the reader in this development the present chapter consists of various vignettes on simulation and its uses. The simulations presented are not a sample in any statistical sense; rather, they were chosen to illustrate the major forms and uses of the technique to date.

* * *

Consider the problem of managing money effectively in a credit-oriented society. There are many pressures in our society to purchase items for use in the present, while paying for them over a period of time into the future. There are a variety of ways to obtain credit, and the actual costs of borrowing on time, as well as the specific terms of the contract, can vary. Because a contract is required in order to borrow money, the borrower takes on additional legal responsibilities. Poor judgment on the part of the potential borrower can result in serious difficulties, as in the case of William R. Kratz.

Willie, as his friends call him, is earning an average income as a business machine repairman. His wife is a part-time saleswoman at a local dress shop. He was married one year ago and has no children. In setting up a new household much of his money was spent on basic items —kitchen supplies, furniture, linens. Willie managed well just paying cash until the day he started noticing what his friends had in their homes. He decided to buy some additional furniture and a washing machine on time. Since he was buying the items at various stores, he thought it would be most practical to get a loan from one source to cover all the expenses. Willie went to the Fort Knox Finance Company both because he remembered seeing its advertisements everywhere, and because he had heard that banks were tight with their money. Willie found the Fort Knox representative to be cordial and easy to deal with. He listed as collateral his basic furniture, which he had bought several months earlier. Willie was very pleased when his new purchases arrived —his house was then fully furnished. He had only to meet "small monthly payments."

Then the trouble began. Willie had unexpected automobile repairs one month. He talked to the man at the finance company, who agreed to overlook the failure to meet his payments. The next month his wife, who was now pregnant, was frequently ill and was forced to stop work. Willie now had a loss of income as well as some extra medical expenses. He again missed the finance payment, and nothing happened. He talked to the man at the finance company, who was understanding but pointed out that he couldn't cover for the missed payments indefinitely. Willie mailed the next installment two days late. That same day he came home to a half-furnished house. The finance company had claimed its collateral. Willie scraped together enough cash to make the payments and went to the company, but it was too late. They had sold the furniture (at a price well below its estimated value). Willie was now faced with the need to buy basic furniture again. But that wasn't all—there was still a balance left payable to the finance company, even after the collateral sale income had been subtracted from the bill. Willie decided to go to court. (One of his best friends was a lawyer so the legal fee was small.) However, he lost the case. The contract was unambiguous about the rights the credit company had over collateral. (In fact, they could have possessed his belongings several months earlier.) A dire situation, indeed.

And to make matters worse, a cousin of Willie's, who had had comparable income, spending habits, *and* unexpected bills, was doing satisfactorily! Willie vowed to talk to the cousin to learn why he had succeeded where Willie had failed.

Willie was ultimately fortunate, however. He was really a twelfth-grade student in a civics class that was playing a simulation game called Consumer (Zaltman, 1969). He had in fact started the game well and purchased several items with his available cash. His "neighbors" were fellow classmates in the game who had begun immediately by buying a large number of items on credit. The Fort Knox Finance Company was represented by a gregarious, enterprising fellow who posted signs all over the room and went about actively looking for potential borrowers. Willie heard that the bank was "tight with its money" from several other classmates whose buying habits presented poor credit risks. Willie didn't know that he himself was a favorable prospect for a bank loan, so he ignored the player representing the bank. The automobile repairs and his wife's illness resulted from the selection of chance cards which represented the intervention of unplanned life events upon financial needs. The purchased items, represented by pictures, were in fact taken by the finance office and auctioned off at a low price to other consumers in the game. When Willie called for a lawsuit, although he lost the case, he and the other consumers in the game learned the importance of reading contracts closely and taking them seriously.

Luckily, the game was almost over. Willie had not scored very high, but at least he had another chance, for the game would be played again the next day. Here is one reason why simulations are used in training—they provide an opportunity to repeat the situation. Whereas in real life Willie Kratz would have been spun further in the vicious cycle of financial difficulty, Willie Kratz, the game player, can terminate the activity and begin again.

Also, Willie can compare his strategy with his "cousin"—another player in the game. This successful player can show how he had managed in a comparable situation. For example, he had probably shopped for credit and found the lowest interest source. Then, too, he may have held off buying luxury items until later in the game. Also, the cousin would not have so burdened himself with monthly charges that he could not see himself through a financial emergency. This knowledge from others, along with the instructional experiences of the first game, should enable Willie to perform better the second time.

* * *

I have before me a plate with food. A strange bird flutters its wings furiously above the plate. I want to cut off its wings, but the bird escapes. I cannot eat—the plate is full of feathers. Suddenly I am in a hut. It is winter, and it is very cold. It is night and the hut is open. I am waiting for my boyfriend. Frightening lights are approaching and I see it is a horse with torches in place of eyes. It is going to overrun me! I am awfully afraid. Still my boyfriend does not appear. I am cold. Finally my friend arrives and asks me to marry him. While he is talking I see a snake crawling on the earth. The snake doesn't frighten me at all. I feel very friendly towards it, and am bored by my friend.

This passage is about a dream which, despite the appearances to the contrary, is not a natural night product but rather the product of Simdream, a simulation game (Breznitz and Lieblich, 1969). In this setting each dream is generated by a player who attempts to reduce his tension level by including as many tension-loaded ideas as possible in a dream of up to ten ideas in length. At the same time the player tries to avoid waking with a nightmare as a result of crossing his anxiety threshold.

In play, the ideas for the dream are drawn from a series of small boxes containing such themes as father, mother, animals, leisure, and so forth. Each box is marked as to whether the ideas within it are tension-loaded or tension-free. Both types have an anxiety score attached to them. Each time that a tension-loaded idea is vented, the dreamer earns a fixed amount of tension-release points, but risks accumulating anxiety points. The reason is that a random anxiety score is attached to the tension-loaded ideas. On the other hand, the tension-free ideas, although they do not earn tension-release points, have a random anxiety-*reducing* score attached to them. The dreamer may therefore elect to insert a tension-free idea in his dream from time to time in order to reduce his anxiety score (which has been building up while he was venting tension-loaded ideas) and move back from the awakening threshold. As a result of the selection process, dreams such as the one above are constructed.

Of much greater theoretical interest than the final dreams themselves are the hypotheses that this simulation has generated. For example, it happens that players almost always start their dreams by choosing a tension-loaded idea, because at the beginning there is little chance of passing the anxiety threshold and "awakening" after the first idea. Also, the longer a dream is—when its length is permitted to vary—the greater the number of tension-loaded ideas it tends to include. For real dreams, this would suggest that longer dreams possibly contain more strongly repressed ideas than shorter dreams and, more generally, that the way a dream *starts* is of paramount importance. Its ability to generate such hypotheses makes simulation a most useful, potentially powerful theoretical instrument.

* * *

By what means can the goal of racial equality in American society best be achieved? Would it be sufficient to eliminate occupational discrimination (that is, to assure that non-whites would receive the same occupational rewards as whites with similar education and skills?) If so, how long would it take to achieve equality? Which would be more effective in achieving racial equality: to subsidize the education of large numbers of non-whites, or to develop programs to give poor non-whites the benefits of family planning which rich and middle-income whites now enjoy? In the former case, better education for non-whites would result in greater earning power; in the latter case a larger share of family income would be available for the education of each child. These two strategies would have similar effects, but which would be more efficient? Are both necessary?

Today, questions like these can be answered by computer simulation. In fact, Sprehe and Michielutte (1969) are investigating this very problem—social mobility and racial equality. Because computer simulation requires precise definitions, they have defined "racial equality" to mean an equal proportion of whites and non-whites in each occupational category and on each level of education and income. The unit of analysis for this simulation is the household. Stored in the computer's memory is a set of data records, each of which represents a household and includes such information as the age, race, sex, occupation, etc., of each member. These records form a representative sample of households in the United States as reported in the 1960 census.

The computer's memory also contains the probabilities of various events happening to individuals with certain characteristics. For example, a white 25-year-old college-educated woman, married and having no children, has a certain probability of having a child during the year. For an unmarried woman identical to the other in all respects, there would be a different (much lower) probability. Similarly, the probability of a high school graduate's going on to college would depend on his father's occupation and income, the number of brothers and sisters he has, and so on. Like the sample of households, all these probabilities are derived from 1960 statistics.

On the basis of these probabilities, the computer determines what important events happen to each person in each household in the sample in a year. The computer then revises the records to take account of those events. If this process is repeated thirty times, the set of records will form a prediction of the characteristics of households in the United States in 1990 (thirty years after 1960)—assuming that the probabilities representing the major social processes remain as they were in 1960. By altering one or more of these probabilities (for example, the probability of a black, male child receiving a college education) and running the simulation again, one can predict the effects of the change. In this way computer simulations can be used experimentally to address questions of social policy.

* * *

There is a growing trend in the social sciences to translate verbal theories stated in discursive language into mathematical formulations. Often this is the first step toward developing a simulation. Many problems couched in mathematical terms defy analytical solutions either for practical or theoretical reasons—that is, we cannot afford, or don't know how to solve them "in general." This happens either where the equations are very complex or when the outcomes depend on sets of probabilities. This latter case occurs frequently in the social sciences where the mathematical models entail not deterministic but *stochastic* processes. In such processes events have a probabilistic rather than a definite outcome. Typically such stochastic models do not have an explicit simple solution. Instead it is necessary to make repeated trials of solutions of the model, to trace out the possible paths of the process. After repeated trials one can calculate the average outcome.[1] For example, the research

[1] The technique for solving these problems is known as "Monte Carlo." The name derives from the fact that the solution amounts to submitting the problem to a roulette wheel.

staff of a Canadian railway could find no analytical solution or equation for the most efficient way to schedule trains through bottlenecks on a line. So they simulated a concrete bottleneck in a computer and sent "trains" through it until the best way was found (Kruger, 1963).

Simulations, as a pragmatic device, are also very useful when time or speed are of great importance. This is the case, for instance, with simulations of voting behavior which predict nationwide outcomes on the basis of limited returns.

In essence, a mirror image of the national electorate is stored in the memory of the computer. (See, for example, Pool *et al.*, 1964.) This electorate is classified into voter types defined by social characteristics such as age, sex, income, religion, region. Thus a voter type could be "West blue-collar rural male Protestant Republican." As early poll returns are fed into the computer, estimates of the influence on the ballot of the various social characteristics are computed by multivariate techniques. On the basis of these results a projection of the national outcome is made according to the distribution of voter types in the electorate. As more elections give a better basis for the estimates, the projections become increasingly accurate.

To the extent that a speedy answer is desired and to the extent that many formal models of social processes are unusually intricate—entailing probabilities, nonlinearities, and time dependencies—the social scientist with a bent for mathematical modelling will have to turn to simulation for assistance. Otherwise the systems of carefully defined equations will be of little use in providing concrete solutions in real time to specific social processes.

* * *

The foregoing vignettes were meant to show the range of questions which may be handled through simulation. In subsequent chapters the reader will be exposed to the process which leads to these research, pragmatic, and educational devices. But before commencing a technical discussion on simulation, let us take a brief pause to note its most apparent qualities.

First, simulations can have varied forms. They may look like games, such as Simdream or Consumer, or they may employ the computer, as in the models of social mobility or voting. Another form of simulation, illustrated in the next chapter, utilizes both people and computers in its operation. The generic term for all forms is "simulation." "Man simulation" emphasizes that the decision-makers are human actors. "Machine simulation" stresses the exclusive reliance on a computer. "Man-machine simulation" indicates that some decisions are made by computers. Whenever we use the term "simulation" without qualification throughout our discussions, the statement is meant to apply to any simulation regardless of mode, and regardless of whether or not it is a game.[2]

Next, a simulation is a representation and abstraction of something else. In some cases the "something else" may be almost purely theoretical, as in Simdream, while in other cases there is a considerable content or reality base, as with the computer simulation of social mobility.

Also, a simulation can be about almost any substantive problem. It is as much an interdisciplinary technique as statistics is. More accurately, it is a research and experimental setting whose justification rests on considerations related to experimental design, rather than on any substantive or disciplinary rationale (Campbell and Stanley, 1966; Webb *et al.*, 1966).

Simulations occupy both space and time. Spatially they may vary considerably in size. A computer simulation may have only two or three variables or it may be quite massive, as is an existing 400-equation model of the United States economy (Duesenberry *et al.*, 1965). A game may have only one player (Simdream) or several dozen players (Gamson's Simsoc, described in this volume). Similarly, the life of a simulation may range from several seconds of a computer run to a full year, as is characteristic of management games found in graduate schools of business (Cohen and Rhenman, 1960).

Being objects in action, simulations can be observed and measured over time. And because they are flexible objects it is possible to alter their components and study how differently they develop. One can change a game by simply inserting players with different types of social and personal characteristics, or by changing some of the rules. Similarly, the social mobility example showed how one can experiment with a computer simulation by changing the initial conditions or instructions from one run to another.

A simulation, then, is a special world of its own, resembling either the fictions in the mind of its developer or parts of the world as he sees

[2] "Game" adds the nuance of a formal winner. In the literature man and man-machine simulations are generally called games, although this is not always in accord with strict definition. In fact, from our own use of the term in research on the sociology of games, we would be forced to deny that "game" is an appropriate choice of words here. Games have three features: (1) a structure of more or less explicit rules about the constraints under which a goal is to achieved with certain resources; (2) players' psychological orientation that the goal is valueless in itself; (3) social consensus that the activity is inconsequential for the serious business of life (Inbar and Stoll, 1970). Not all man and man-machine simulations have these features. Furthermore, the proper terminology would in any case be simulation-game. "Game," however, is a much less cumbersome term, so we continue its application here whenever we emphasize that a simulation has formal winners, recognizing that it is an imprecise use of words.

it. It is not foreign or alien or isolated, but rather, accessible and receptive and responsive. Hence, it is an apt (thought quaint) metaphor that those working with simulation may be called social cosmologists. We hope that this book will direct the reader in creating a cosmology of his own.

REFERENCES

BREZNITZ, SCHLOMO AND AMIA LIEBLICH
1970 "The Unconscious plays patience: An attempt to simulate dream-work," *Simulation and Games,* 1, 5–17.

CAMPBELL, DONALD T. AND JULIAN STANLEY
1966 *Experimental and Quasi-Experimental Designs for Research.*

COHEN, KALMAN J. AND ERIC RHENMAN
1960 "The role of management games in education and research." *Management Science,* 8, 131–166.

DUESENBERRY, JAMES S., GARY FROMM,
LAWRENCE R. KLEIN, EDWIN KUH
1965 *The Brookings Quarterly Econometric Model of the United States.* Chicago: Rand-McNally.

INBAR, MICHAEL AND CLARICE S. STOLL
1970 Games in Learning. *Interchange,* 1, 53–61.

KRUGER, CHARLES
1963 "An overview of current and potential uses of simulation in sociological research." Document S. P. 363. Santa Monica, California: Systems Development Corporation.

POOL, ITHIEL DE SOLA, ROBERT P. ABELSON,
AND SAMUEL POPKIN
1964 *Candidates, Issues, and Strategies.* Cambridge, Mass.: M. I. T.

SPREHE, TIMOTHY AND ROBERT MICHIELUETTE
1969 "Simulation of social mobility: Toward the development of a system of social accounts." Paper presented at the annual meetings of the Eastern Sociological Society, New York.

WEBB, EUGENE ET AL.
1966 *Unobtrusive Measures.* Chicago: Rand-McNally.

ZALTMAN, GERALD
1969 *Consumer.* New York: Western.

REFERENCES

Chapter **2**

Commonality in the Diversity

PART I. ANATOMY OF SIMULATION

Commonality in the Diversity

Until the early sixties references to "simulation" were concerned solely with computer simulation. When man-simulations came into vogue, there was considerable disagreement as to whether they could be called simulations.[1] More recently it has been recognized that there are essential features basic to the three modes—man, machine, man-machine. This underlying similarity will be the focus of this chapter.

Simulations designed for operation by computers differ drastically in technical apparatus and appearance from those designed for human actors. There are special terminologies to learn and distinct technical skills to acquire in each case. Also, the constraints are different. Thus someone skilled in the design of simulations in one mode will not be able to design simulations in another mode without acquiring additional skills. Nonetheless, he will be competent in the principles of simulation as a method, for simulating a process is basically the same intellectual problem, independent of the means used. Indeed, theoretically all modes serve the same purpose; the same problems of interpretation apply; and the principles of design are similar. As we look closely at the anatomy of a specific simulation, identifying its components and their functions, this point should become clearer.

SIMULATING THE PARENT-CHILD RELATIONSHIP

Perhaps the simplest way to highlight the common features shared by the three simulation modes is to present the man, machine, and man-machine simulations of the same process. For this purpose we have selected a basic model of the parent-child relationship. This model has been incorporated in a game by Schild and Boocock (1969).

The main characteristics of the simulated process are as follows.[2] The investigators begin by assuming that the interdependence between parents and children is essentially an *exchange* process as considered, for example, by Blau (1967). They note that the various issues that create conflict between parents and children have different utilities for each party. It is important to parents that they be able to show their friends how well their child has behaved on certain issues. Similarly, the child wants to be able to show his friends how he has *his* way on issues

[1] For example, the three separate articles under the heading "Simulation" in the *International Encyclopedia of the Social Sciences* delimit the scope of the technique differently. The paper on economic simulation excludes games; the paper on political processes includes them; the paper on cognitive processes ignores them.

[2] The following discussion is based upon personal communications with the authors of the simulation, who have no written this theoretical material in prepared form. Rather, the game resulting from their ideas represents their position on the topic.

important to himself. Because opposing issues seldom have the same degree of saliency for both parent and child, accommodation is possible. Furthermore, there is an underlying rationality to the process of accommodation, that is, a best way to settle the confrontation. This "best solution" requires that each party forego the obvious attempt to maximize gains by getting his way on every issue. Instead, parent and child will each gain most in the long run by realizing that there is an optimal accommodation that will benefit each party highly.

The attempt to get one's way on every issue is unsatisfactory because the other person can strike back. When a child misbehaves parents can administer punishment and may increase supervision of the child. When parents insist on total compliance children can react through disobedience. Poor family relationships are marred by patterns of retribution that result in only temporary satisfactions for parent or child. Presumably, one sign of a well-functioning family is the presence of an accommodation process.

Schild and Boocock perceive this model as applicable in a very general way. They consider the identity of the parent to be unimportant; the model applies to mother, father or both of them acting together as one unit. Also, the sex and age of the child and the presence or absence of siblings are ignored. The model considers the family only with regard to parental control of children, ignoring all the other daily activities the family faces.

Given this highly general model of parent-child interaction, let us see first how Schild and Boocock incorporated the model into a game.

The Game

Parent-Child is a simulation of the relationship between a parent and an adolescent. It is played by teams of two, with one person taking the role of parent, the other the role of child. Neither role is specified with respect to sex. The game is played with several teams; each team is referred to as a "family." There are two winners: one from the set of child players, and one from the set of parents.

The structure of the game is as follows. There is a board listing five issues on which the parent and child have opposing attitudes. For example, on one issue the parent wants the child to be home by ten o'clock; the child wants to be able to stay out later. There are a set of five point-cards for each player, which are shuffled and placed randomly, one to an issue. These point-cards make each issue worth 2, 4, 6, 8, or 10 potential points. Due to random allocation of points, the parent and child may have similar or different point values for each issue.

During the first part of the game the two players of each "family" discuss the issues and try to reach agreements as to how the child is expected to behave. At the end of a specified time period, parents must give an order for each issue on which no agreement has been reached. Hence each issue has been settled either by a verbal agreement between parent and child or by a command from parent to child.

During phase two of the game parents must turn their backs to the game board. Children then place markers on the board to indicate their actual behavior on each issue. Children are permitted to obey or disobey on any issue. For example, if there was an agreement to come in by ten o'clock, a child can choose to obey it or not. Likewise, he can break orders. All moves on the board are covered so that parents cannot see whether the child has in fact obeyed.

Parent players can now "supervise" the child by removing the cover that hides the child's behavior for one of the issues. If the child has kept the agreement or obeyed the order, nothing happens. If, however, the child has broken the agreement or disobeyed, the parent can punish the child by subtracting up to seven points from the child's score. (The parent does not earn any points during this part of the game.) Parents do not have to punish.

Points are earned in the following way. For any one issue each player has a possible point value assigned. For example, a child may have 10 points assigned to coming home late, while a parent may have 6 points assigned to the child's coming home early. Only one of the players will receive points for the issue, and points are determined *by the way the child behaves.* In this example, if the child decides to stay out late, he receives 10 points and the parent receives none. If the child decides to come in early, he receives no points and the parent receives 6. Most importantly, points are assigned in this way whether or not the child has disobeyed or broken an agreement. Hence a child in the game could behave solely as he wants to for a total of 30 points,[3] leaving his parent with none, but the parent could punish and cut the child's score. Neither player would earn many points through this strategy. The key to maximum scores for both parent and child requires that the child be willing to act in the parent's interest in issues unimportant (worth few points) for himself. Accordingly, the parent must insure the child's cooperation; sometimes this can be achieved by showing good will and not punishing disobedience too severly.

Having outlined the basic structure and rules of Parent-Child simulation, let us consider the components of the game. Just what "language"

[3] That is, the total number of points received over the five issues equals the sum of [2, 4, 6, 8, 10].

have the designers used to go from their model of a parent-child relationship to the simulation?

The first and simplest translation is from the components of the model to ***roles*** in the game. The roles identify the system of decision-makers. Here the designers have assumed that certain features of a family's organization are not worth inclusion. There is only one child, because siblings are considered to be secondary for the process at hand. The identity of the parent is not specified because the behavior assigned to the parent is assumed to be true for both mothers and fathers.

Goals are assigned to each role to orient the actors' behavior in the game. Parent-Child provides each role with one goal: to maximize satisfaction points. The competition, though, is structured in an unusual way. Children compete with the other children in the game, and parents compete with parents. In doing this the game designers have simulated how family relationships are partly a function of family members' desires to look good in their respective peer groups. Children wish to show one another how they are allowed to have their way on important issues and are not punished severely or unjustly. Parents wish to display how well their children obey them on important issues without repeated use of punishment.

A third component of games consists of the ***resources*** assigned to each role to assist the actors in meeting their goals. Both roles are given a freely-defined access to use verbal bargaining skills during the first phase of the game in which agreements are made. Parents are allowed two unique behaviors: to make orders and to punish. Children are allowed to behave in any way that they wish. (thus determining the point assignments) out of the eyeshot of the parents. These behaviors are the only legitimate resources to be used in gaining points.

Several kinds of ***rules*** complete the translation of the model into a game. The rules of a game are often analogous to the physical, normative, and legal *constraints upon behavior found in real life*. Other types of rules, however, are necessary more for the smooth operation of the game.

Environmental response rules specify how the environment would behave if it were part of the simulation. These rules are particularly important because they encompass the probable response of that part of the environment that is not incorporated in the actions of the players. In Parent-Child one aspect of the environment is represented in the way issues are assigned to a scale of importance. Where in real life attitudes on issues will come from many sources (especially through opinions expressed by other parents and children in the community), in the game importance is determined randomly. More generally environmental response rules generate variations in resources, constraints, and goals deemed to increase the fit between the process as it occurs in the artificial and in the actual environment.

Procedural rules describe how a game is put into play and the general order in which play proceeds. In the Parent-Child game players are not permitted to use their resources at any time that they please. Rather, there is a sequencing of activities that ensures the smooth operation of the game. In this case play goes through several phases: discussion and agreement, orders, behavior decisions on the part of the child, supervision, and punishment. Another procedural rule in the game states that players must reshuffle their point cards at the start of each round. A subtype of procedural rules that games often have, the ***police rules,*** specify the consequences to a player of breaking a rule. Parent-Child has no such explicit police rules and relies instead on the moral force of players upon one another.

In addition to rules, roles, goals, and resources, games are composed of ***procedural materials.*** Parent-Child is played at a board. Plays are denoted by three different markers designed to represent the location of agreements, orders, and behaviors. Points are accumulated either through chips or on score sheets. Other typical game paraphernalia include spinners, dice, play money, chance cards, player rule books. Though apparently trivial at first look, procedural materials are not less important in the design of an adequate, playable game than the other components.

MACHINE SIMULATION

Another way to simulate a process is to use the computer to generate the sequences of behaviors which constitute the process. Analytically computers consist of three main parts: a memory unit, an operation unit, and a control unit.[4] The key to the whole process is the program of instructions which is stored in its totality in the memory at the start of the run. The memory unit also stores data for transfer and use as directed by the control unit. The operation unit performs the arithmetical and logical operations that it is instructed to carry out by the control unit.

[4] Sometimes computers are described as having five components; these include the input and output units, a reader and a printer, respectively.

Because all forms of instructions are contained in the program, computer simulation is essentially a programming task.

Let us now consider the components of the Parent-Child model as they would appear in a computer simulation. One part of the simulation will consist of data to be stored in the memory. The memory itself is partitioned into bits of space identified by numbers or addresses. Hence it is possible to store information in a flexible way and yet be able to retrieve it simply by calling the appropriate number. In this case part of the memory will contain information belonging to the child. Other areas in the memory may have no entries at the beginning of the computer run, but they will be partitioned off to store information at some point during the operations. For example, parts of the memory in this case could contain:

0001–0005	Parent's position on issues known as A, B, C, D, E
0006–0010	Child's position on issues known as A, B, C, D, E
0261–0265	Space to store amount of punishment parent gives on issues A, B, C, D, E

This partial list of the memory partition shows that some variables are entered as input (such as the issues), while other variables are calculated during the course of the simulation (such as the level of punishment assigned by the parent). The designer must consider both types of data in calculating the amount of memory the simulation will require. Most of Parent-Child's variables are defined after the initial input of the five labelled issues.

Just as human actors are guided by procedural rules, so also is the computer. The program, with its directions for performing operations, is analogous to procedural rules in the game. The nature of the computer is such that instructions must be sequenced in a rigorous, painstaking manner.

Chart 1 displays the overall sequencing of instructions for Parent-Child. On this level the phasing of activities is identical to that found in the game. Within each block of activities, however, the operations of the computerized individuals are not as easily kept similar to the behavior of game players.

During the first phase, assignment of interest points, the computer and game operations are directly analogous. In the game the interest point cards are shuffled and placed randomly on the issues. In the computer, instructions are written in line with the following: Randomize the set of numbers $\{2, 4, 6, 8, 10\}$ and assign them to positions representing issues A through E.

The instructions guiding other non-mathematical phases of the com-

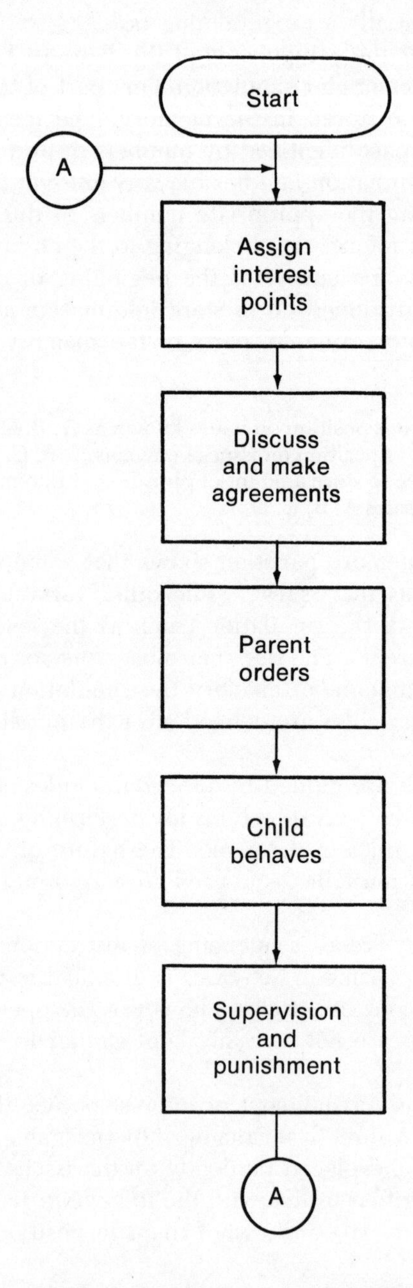

Chart 1: Sequence of parent-child activities

puter simulation are much more detailed than the game rules. For example, players can be told to "discuss and try to reach agreements about the issues." Either player may initiate the discussion· introducing any issue, with agreements being reached after complicated, subtle bargaining. On the other hand, instructions to the computer require precise programming as to how issues are introduced, how one player reacts to the offer of another, and how agreements are finally settled. Depending upon the intention and assumptions of the simulation designer, there are a variety of ways to make these instructions.

Chart 2 illustrates the flow of one possible way of simulating the discussion period of the game. Many assumptions were made to simplify the process. Both players are assumed to be rational in the sense that they will want agreements made in their own favor for those issues most important to themselves. Thus both parent and child begin by stating their most valued issue. If the issues are different, then it is assumed that either player agrees with the other. If both have their highest interest on the same issue, the child concedes and suggests his next highest issue as a trade. Since the issues under discussion now differ, a trade-off occurs. This process of offering the highest valued issue continues until the possible case that one issue is left which has equal value for both. In this case, the child, having no other issues to offer, must defer to the parent, who issues an order.

Obviously this model of the discussion-agreement period is grossly unrealistic. Only one order will occur any one round. Also, parent and child automatically concede to one another's choices wherever a trade-off is possible. Finally, it is a rare child indeed who gives up favorite activities because the parent is so strongly against them. A more complex, more realistic model is possible, so long as certain basic elements of the instructions are present.

Most important, the outcome of every decision in the model must be accounted for in the instructions. Consider the following possibility. The parent and child have raised and made agreements on four of the five issues. One issue is left that happens to be of equal value to both. Each raises the issue. According to the instructions the child is now supposed to introduce instead his next highest issue. But there is none. In this case the computer must have explicit orders as to how to settle the argument. According to Chart 2, this argument is settled by means of the parent's giving an order. If, however, the designer had not specified this direction, the computer would be left with an insoluble decision: to "store the agreement in favor of the player with the highest investment on the issue." Since neither player's investment is higher, the computer can go no further in its processing of the program.

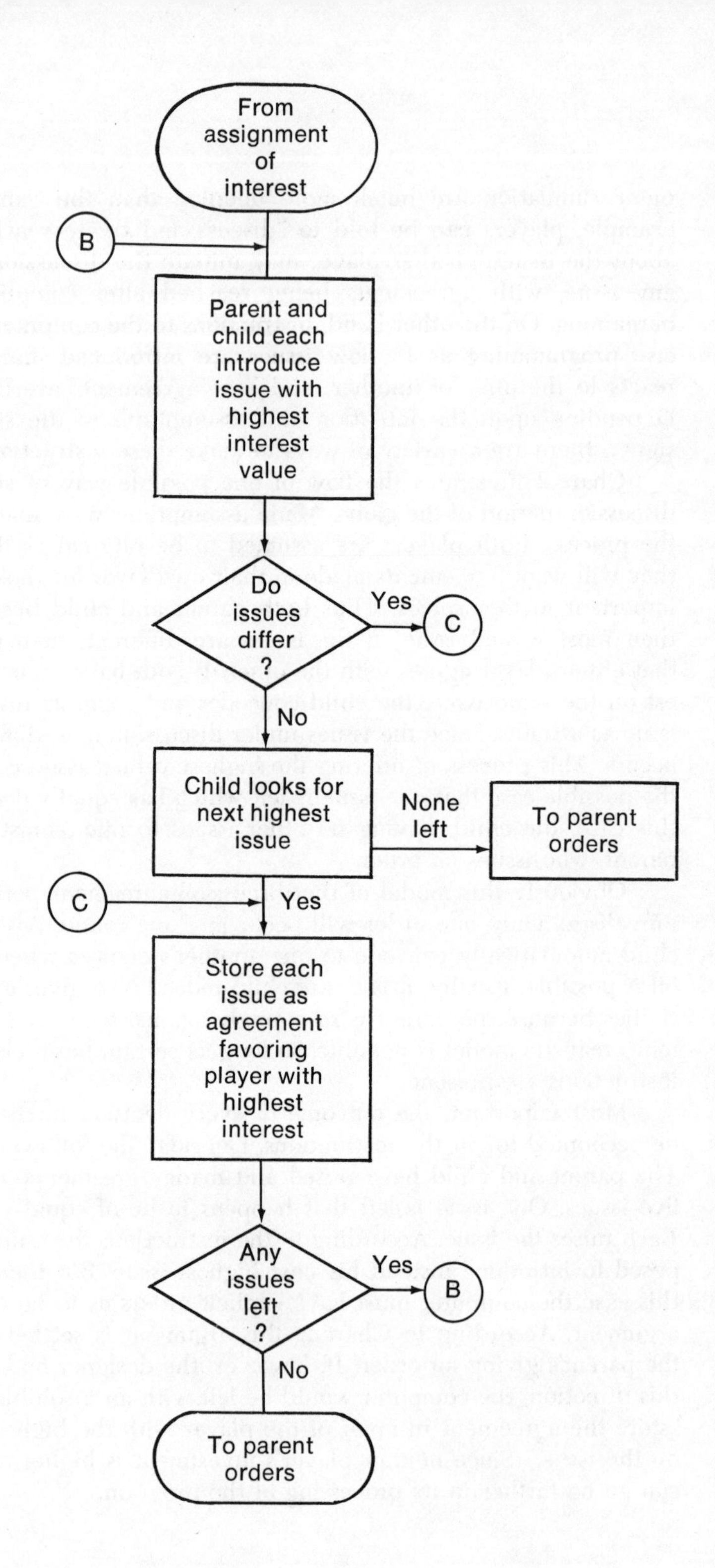
From assignment of interest
B
Parent and child each introduce issue with highest interest value
Do issues differ ?
Yes
C
No
Child looks for next highest issue
None left
To parent orders
C
Yes
Store each issue as agreement favoring player with highest interest
Any issues left ?
Yes
B
No
To parent orders

Chart 2

Although a flowchart assists in understanding the sequencing and instructions given to the computer, the actual instructions are written according to the rules of a special language the computer understands. Thus, for any one of the boxes depicted in the flowchart it is necessary to write numerous statements prepared precisely according to the grammar and syntax of the program language. This list of instructions is entered along with the input data.

Because a computer does exactly what it is instructed to do, it cannot take assumptions for granted. The design of a computer simulation is therefore more structured than the game design process. In our case, the roles (parent and child) and the resources (e.g., the number and value of issues which can be traded off; the right to punish or disobey) are identical. So is the goal—to get a high score. However, because everything must be specified in the program, whatever happens when the path to the goal is blocked must result according to rigidly predetermined strategies and subgoals. Consequently, both strategies and subgoals are more limited in number than those which occur in a real-life game. More strictly then, the goal of the computer child is really to "get his way on an important issue." (This restriction on behavior and goal shift is usually unavoidable when a man simulation is computerized.)

Once the designer has made a flowchart of the overall sequence of the process, he has in effect blueprinted the procedural rules of the simulation. The details will be inserted while the program is being written. The investigator, usually in assistance with a programmer, will find that program writing (like other techniques of formalization) requires extreme confrontation with the data and explication of the model. The flowcharting becomes more detailed at this stage.

Once a program is complete, error checks are necessary. This "debugging" process is usually lengthy and painstaking.[5] In addition the careless designer may discover that he has a problem akin to increasing the playability of a game. For example, computers vary in memory size and speed of operation. The more complex the process, the larger capacity the machine must have. The designer may have trouble adjusting the simulation to the needs of his machine.[6] Or a different type of problem may occur when the program language he has selected to use is not compatible with local equipment.[7] As computers and computer centers

[5] There is an informal law about programming which goes as follows: Estimate the longest possible time it will take to write and remove errors from the program. It will take twice as long to do so.

[6] For a full discussion of this type of problem, see Abelson (1969), as well as Chapter 16 in this volume.

[7] There are several variations of programming languages. Certain general purpose languages are tailored to algebraic manipulations (e.g., FORTRAN, ALGOL);

grow, the likelihood of being trapped by facility and capability limitations decrease. But this knowledge is small consolation to the hapless designer who encounters them.

MAN-MACHINE SIMULATION

There is yet a third way in which the Parent-Child model could be transformed into a simulation. In this case, the *computer game,* persons play the role of decision-makers, but the computer is also a participant, responsive to the players' activities. In this version of Parent-Child, an individual would take one role, and the machine would take the other. Let us assume that the computer plays the child. The player communicates to the computer by way of a typewriter or teletype connection; the computer can respond with a printout. (There are other means of communication, including a cathode ray device. In this case the computer displays a message or illustration and the player responds by touching a part of it with a special stylus.)

The components of a man-machine game combine elements of man and computer simulations. The player's instructions will resemble game rules. Thus the player in this case may be given the exact resources and constraints assigned to the parent in the game version. The computer player, however, must be programmed in detail so as to be responsive to any action on the part of the real-life player. There are several aspects to this programming.

One feature of the instructions will be to provide the computer with a *script.* Analogous to the dramatic use of the term, the script lists the messages conveyed to the player. Two kinds of messages are involved. One is a simple response to the player's actions. The other is instruction to the player as to the appropriate way *he* can respond to the computer. Computers only *appear* to understand English: care is needed to ensure that the player speaks the computer's real language. Here is a possible dialogue between the computer and the player, occurring during the discussion stage of the game. (Assume that the issues are identified by code names.)

COMPUTER: Let us discuss what you want me to do this week. Please select one issue you want me to agree to. Type in the code name.

others are tailored to special simulation problems (e.g., SIMSCRIPT; LISP 1.5); still others are intended for business (COBOL). For descriptions, see Green (1963); Naylor *et al.* (1966); Gordon (1969). Each of these languages must be translated into machine language by what is known as a compiler. The local computer facility may lack the appropriate compiler for the language a designer prefers to use. Or, it may be technically equipped to accept the program, yet lack staff who know the language and can solve problems when they arise.

PLAYER: Home early.
COMPUTER: I will come home early only if you let me forget housework. Do you agree to this or not? Type yes or no.
PLAYER: No.
COMPUTER: I cannot agree to come home early unless you let me forget housework. Is there another issue we can agree upon? Type in the code name or "No issue left."
PLAYER: No issue left.
COMPUTER: Okay, dad, you asked for it.

Note how the script structures the discussion. Parent's alternatives and the way to communicate them are precisely defined. If, for example, the player typed in "Oh, you think so, son?" following the final spunky message from the computer in the above illustration, the computer would then probably type "Error in format. Please remember to type in only messages as described by me." (Or more simply, "That does not compute.")

The flexibility and the "humanity" of the computer's verbal behavior is merely a reflection of the facetious mood of the programmer. Once the computer has determined after a rigorous computing procedure that it will disobey on an issue, it can as easily be made to print out the result in the form of a dollar sign, the word "disobey," or the last sentence in the foregoing parody.

In the script a set of instructions similar to those outlined in Chart 3 may have been operating. That is, the parent player suggested that the computer child agree to an issue worth six points or more to itself. At this point the computer has instructed to search for another high-valued issue and offer it as a trade-off. The computer located such an issue, offered it, and was refused. Then it was instructed to ask that a new issue be introduced, provided the parent had one. The parent had none, and in the exit instructions for bargainings ending with no agreement the computer was told to print, "Okay, dad, you asked for it." Had the player originally introduced an issue worth less than six points the computer would simply have accepted the player's suggestions. Thus the computer in this case has been programmed to look out for its own interests on high-point issues and be complaisant on low-point ones.

This particular choice of instructions is not the only appropriate one for this game. Indeed, one can see the computer player having several sets of instructions based upon the intention of the game user. During the Child's Behavior phase, for example, the computer could be given instructions to behave recalcitrantly (by breaking all agreements and orders), independently (by breaking only high-valued issues), compliantly (by obeying all agreements and orders), or nonsensically (by

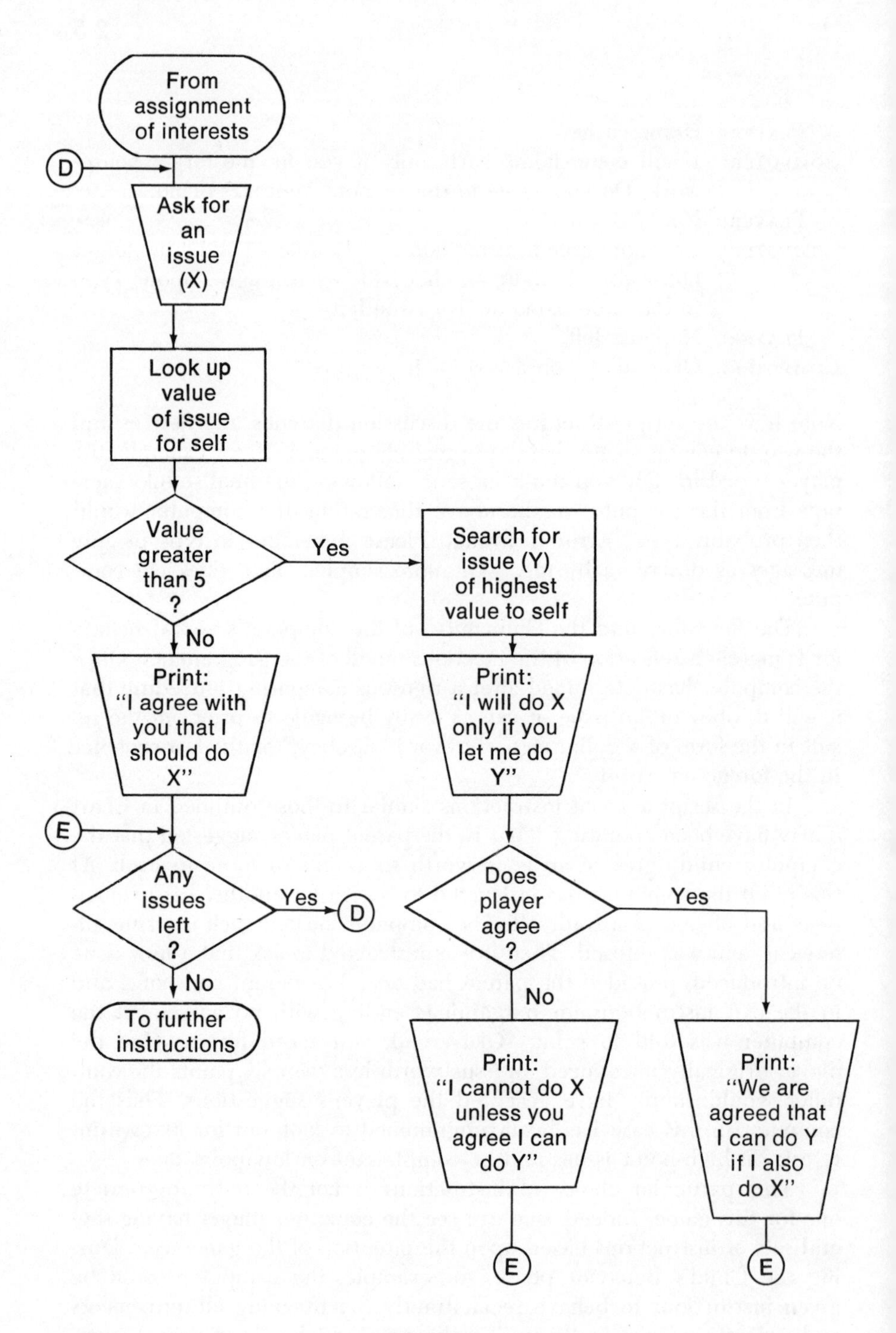
From assignment of interests
D
Ask for an issue (X)
Look up value of issue for self
Value greater than 5 ?
Yes
Search for issue (Y) of highest value to self
No
Print: "I agree with you that I should do X"
Print: "I will do X only if you let me do Y"
E
Any issues left ?
Yes
D
Does player agree ?
Yes
No
No
To further instructions
Print: "I cannot do X unless you agree I can do Y"
Print: "We are agreed that I can do Y if I also do X"
E
E

Chart 3

behaving randomly). The player would play four versions of the basic game, with the computer responding as a different type of child in each case.

Computer gaming requires the skills for both game and computer design and thus multiplies the potential problems in completing the project. Not only must the program go through the debugging process, but also the game with the players must be interesting and manageable. Computer games are typically developed when the environmental response rules are complex. The fast and complex bookkeeping of which the computer is capable makes it ideal for such cases. (See, for instance, Leonard's paper in this volume.)

COMPARING THE MODES

The similarity among the three versions of the parent-child simulation expresses the underlying identity of the simulation as a method. Because of the extreme precision required for programming a process, only certain problems tend to be computer-simulated. Yet this does not make them any different in principle from those embedded in man simulation. For the parent-child process many—probably too many—assumptions have to be made about the decision-makers (the parent and the child). The practical value of the pure machine simulation is therefore highly questionable, and the likelihood of its ever being executed is very small indeed. But the fact remains that whether one decides to simulate with human actors, a computer, or some combination of both is above all a matter of convenience, not of topic or discipline.

Two general considerations usually guide one's choice of mode of simulation. One has to do with how much we know about the process; the other, with what we want to do with the simulation. As a rule of thumb, the more we know about a process, the more useful it is to computerize it.[8] The reason is that we can observe the outcomes and the implications of the various and well-understood components of the process when they interact under different sets of conditions. On the other hand, the more one intends the simulation to be used for teaching rather than for research purposes, the more it should take on the form of a man (or man-machine) simulation so that the players have a chance to learn about the process. As a matter of fact, it turns out that most computer simulations are about fairly well understood complex processes which are further researched (e.g., economics, demography, voting behavior);

[8] It should be pointed out that designing a simulation (of either mode) is in itself one of the best ways to learn about a process. The contributions to this volume present the best evidence for this.

similarly man-machine simulations are usually about the same complex processes but for teaching purposes (e.g., business and management games); finally, most man simulations are pedagogical in intent and are about processes where only general knowledge is available.[9]

FORMAL KINS OF SIMULATION

Throughout the preceding sections we noted that core aspects of the Parent-Child simulation remained unchanged across the three modes of design. Each of the versions was a different reproduction of essentially one basic structure. In other words, the *model* was the same in each case. The concepts of model and theory are formal kins of simulation and are basic to understanding it as a methodology. Because these terms are used in a variety of ways, we must define precisely the manner in which we are using them in our discussions.

Models

In the case studies appearing in this volume the term "model" is often used to refer to anything which influenced, shaped, or inspired a

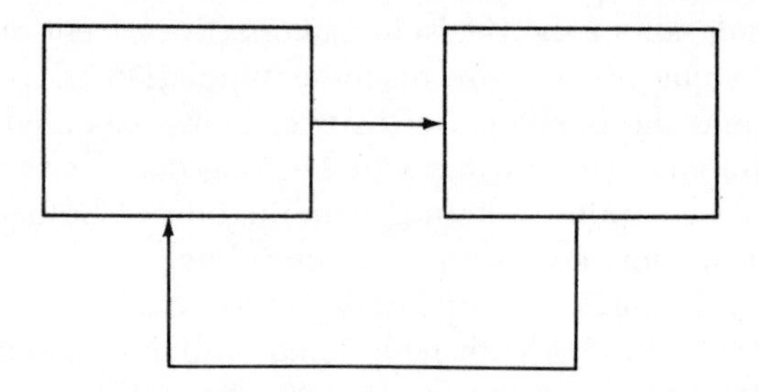

Figure 1: Feedback model

simulation. For the present discussion we find it useful to conceptualize the term more specifically. Namely, *we define a model as referring to a set of relationships among units, where both the relationships and the units are stated in abstract or highly general terms.* Thus by this definition very different processes can be represented by the same model. Consider the situation of a school teacher attempting to enforce discipline in a classroom. If the teacher becomes too lenient, the class will become disobedient. The teacher will then become more strict, and the

[9] These "rules of thumb" are based on historical trends in the use of simulation. In fact, as we discuss in Chapter 16, they are very crude, and there is much more to consider.

class will respond by being more obedient. The teacher may then feel she can afford to be more lenient—and the cycle is repeated. This process can be represented by the classic feedback model, represented in Figure 1.

Precisely the same model can be used to represent the control of the temperature in a refrigerator by a thermostat. When the refrigerator becomes too warm, the thermostat turns on the motor. The motor causes the refrigerator to become colder, and the thermostat turns off the motor. With the motor off, the refrigerator warms up, and the cycle is repeated.

Again, the same model can also represent the relationship between the rabbit and lynx populations in certain sections of Canada. The rabbits are the lynxes' principal food. When rabbits become scarce, lynxes starve. With fewer lynxes in the area, rabbits are free to grow and multiply, providing food for the lynxes. As the lynx population grows, rabbits again become scarce, and the cycle is repeated. The point of these examples is that the three processes—a social process, a physical process, and a biological process—can all be represented by the same general model.

Not all models are graphically representable. For instance, one can simulate a social situation using a competitive model rather than a cooperative one. In this example the units constituting the system are assumed to have a relationship whereby the more one unit gets, the less is available for other units to get. Obviously, this is a model, although it is not easily illustrated pictorally.

Models and theories are intimately related. Indeed the relationship is largely one of degree of elaboration. A model is always at a higher level of generality than a theory, and thus is always simpler. *A model is elaborated into a theory once the qualitative and quantitative nature of both the units as well as of their input-output relationships has been specified.*

For instance, if one takes the model represented in Figure 1, identifies the units as human decision-makers and the inputs and outputs as speech, then one has started to transform the model into a theory of social interaction. Had one identified the units as a heat outlet and a thermostat the eventual theory would be quite different. The theories would have in common the fact that they rest on a feedback process. To complete the transformation of the model into a theory it is necessary also to specify the *conditions* under which qualitative or quantitative differences in the input-output relationships will occur. Once this is done, a theory can be analyzed into a standard set of elements.

A. Simulation for theoretical exploration

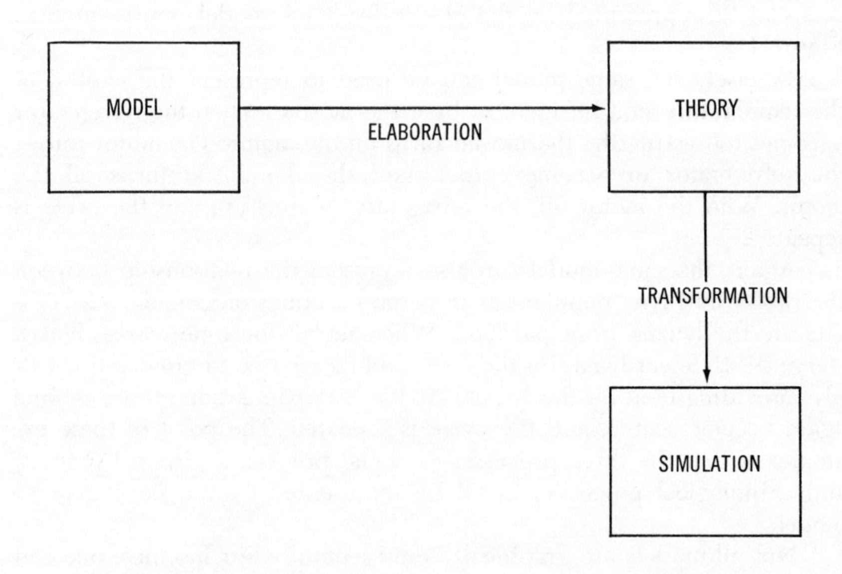

B. Simulation for theory development

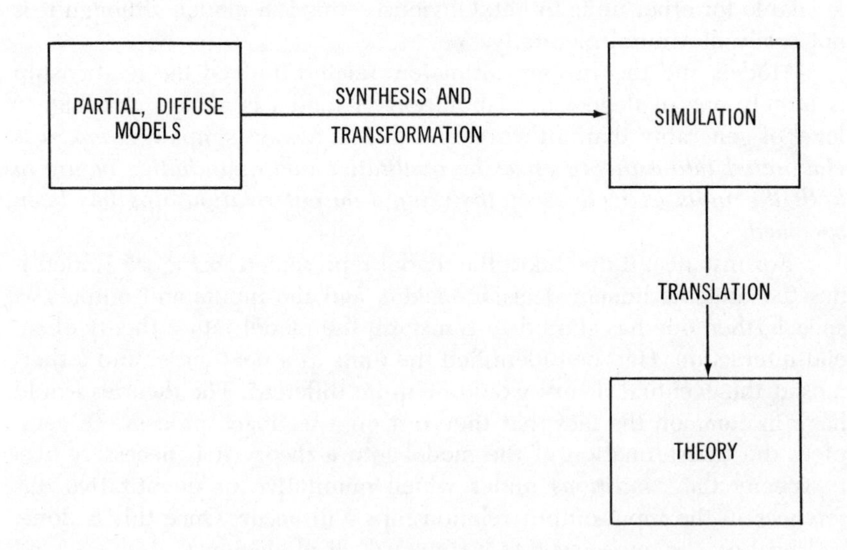

Figure 2: Models of simulation design

The Anatomy of a Theory

The elements of a theory are components, variables, and relations.

Components are the units, often in the social sciences, the actors, be they individuals, groups, organizations, societies, or some interlinking combination of them.

Variables take several forms. *Status variables* describe the condition of the components at the beginning of a time period. Individuals may be identified by sex, attitudes, hair color, or whatever is salient for the theory at hand.

Exogenous or *input variables* are assumed to have been predetermined and given independently of the system being considered. Input variables arise outside of the component and act upon it. Individuals are influenced by the laws of man and nature. Industrial firms are affected by the external economy, government regulations, and the weather.

Endogenous or *output variables* are the dependent variables of the system and are generated from the interaction of the system's exogenous and status variables according to the system's operating characteristics. Outputs for an individual could be anything from having children, to casting a Republican vote, to breaking rules in Army camp. Outputs for industrial firms might include total sales, change in labor force, or bankruptcy.

Operating characteristics state the relationships of the endogenous and status variables to the exogenous variables. They are akin to propositions. For example, in a study of friendship formation, part of the theory might deal with the consequences of interaction among individuals. In a way models express the essence of the operating characteristics of a system.

Parameters are values which specify the strength or degree of relationships between variables in the system. These values are fixed or constant for the situation at hand. Often the exact value chosen is arbitrary and a matter of convenience. For instance, in the Parent-Child simulation the values 10, 8, 6, 4 and 2 for the issues are parameters. Similarly, in many simulations the probabilities which determine the likelihood of certain events are parameters. Take for example, Homans' proposition about interaction and liking. If two individuals interact daily and are assigned a higher probability of liking one another than a pair of individuals who interact less frequently, the values of the probabilities are parameters.

Hence, a theory is a set of statements about the way empirical units affect each other under specified conditions. For example, given a theory of classroom learning one could predict the amount of learning (endogenous variable) occurring under a schedule (parameter) of reinforcement (exogenous variable) upon students (components) with known I.Q. characteristics (status variable). (For an expanded discussion of this issue, see Stoll, 1972.)

Simulations

If theories are elaborated forms of models, then simulations are a special form of theories. In essence, when a theory has an autonomous source of energy, whether a computer or human decision-makers, it becomes a simulation. Indeed, formally speaking a simulation is merely an automated theory, having physical form and characteristics.[10]

Practically speaking, however, it is not always the case that a statement of theory precedes the development of simulation. More often, simulation is used as a device for elaborating a model into a theory. In the process of simulation design, the investigator is in fact developing a theory, though he may not acknowledge the result as such. It should be possible, after the fact, to translate any simulation into an explicit verbal, mathematical, or symbolic statement of theory. Figure 2 schematizes the logic of these two approaches to simulation design.

Type A illustrates how a simulation is built from a theory for purposes of further experimentation or analysis. Type B simulations begin with a more diffuse base—partial models based on hunches, data, etc. —and serve as a heuristic and *synthetic* technique. In either case the end product is adapted to a physical framework. This conceptualization points to a major potential problem in simulation design, namely unanticipated distortions due to material constraints.

The implication of the foregoing discussion is that the fact of using an energy source—computers or humans—is likely to introduce insidious changes in one's intentions. For example, a theory about international relations which is translated into a game will be affected by some of the micro-sociological processes found in small groups. These effects

[10] This perspective on simulation, model, and theory is quite different from the view typically presented in the simulation literature. More generally, simulation advocates define simulations to be models of theories. Model, in this sense, refers to a representation of something, and not, as we use the term, an idea for building something. They then point out that simulations are likely to have distortions of the theories, as a result of the modelling process. We find this point of view curious because it assumes that somehow a verbal or mathematical statement of a theory is "pure" while a computerized or physical statement is not. We contend that any statement of a theory may have distortions or deficiencies with regard to the theorist's "real intentions"—if one in fact can speak of such a thing. Hence we propose that simulations have the same ontological status as the other modes of theory presentation, verbal, mathematical, or any other symbolic form. For an elegant statement of the opposing view, see Cherryholmes and Shapiro (1969; especially Chapter 1).

may be detrimental to analysis and elaboration of the theory. Similarly, computers may require an experimenter to assign specific numerical ranges to represent measures of variables he perceives in a more diffuse way. Or, the limits of computer memory may require a theorist to ignore a variable he may actually consider to be quite important.

These problems raise an obvious question, namely, to what extent are the simulations faithful to the designer's intentions? In other words, how has the process of computerization or gaming affected the isomorphism between the elements in the designer's basic reference and the elements as they are expressed in the simulation? This issue is obviously one of validity, a much-debated problem in the area of simulation. We shall consider its features at greater length in Chapter 18.

REFERENCES

Blau, Peter
1967 *Exchange and Power in Social Life.* New York: Wiley.

Cherryholmes, Cleo and Michael J. Shapiro
1969 *Representatives and Roll Calls.* Indianapolis: Bobbs-Merrill.

Green, Bert F.
1963 *Digital Computers in Research.* New York: McGraw-Hill.

Gordon, Geoffrey
1969 *System Simulation.* Englewood Cliffs, N. J.: Prentice-Hall.

Homans, George
1950 *The Human Group.* New York: Harcourt, Brace and World.

Naylor, Thomas H., Joseph L. Balintfy,
Donald S. Burdick, and Kong Chu
1968 *Computer Simulation Techniques.* New York: Wiley.

Schild, Erling O. and Sarane S. Boocock
1969 *Generation Gap.* New York: Western. (Also published as *Parent-Child.* Baltimore: Academic Games Associates, Inc., 1967).

Stoll, Clarice S.
1972 "Simulated Environments" in Robert B. Smith, *Social Science Methods.* New York: Free Press.

Chapter **3**

The Origins of Simulation

The Origins of Simulation

It is impossible to establish precisely the historical origin of simulations. For centuries the game of chess has been treated as a symbolic representation of warfare. Carnivals, especially in the ancient world, have been interpreted as institutionalized simulations of social revolutions. The young and the elderly, the beautiful and the ugly, the master and the slave would exchange roles for the duration of the festivities (Baroja, 1965).

The first use of simulations is equally hard to identify. In the middle ages hunting was often seen as a training ground for potential warriors; the participants learned the terrain they might have to defend, horsemanship, endurance, and so forth. Similarly, generations of knights learned and practiced the handling of weapons while preparing for the tournaments' colorful simulated fights.

Perhaps the first use of simulation for research was in the seventeenth century. By analyzing a dice gambling problem Pascal and Fermat laid the foundations of probability theory. They examined the rationale for various odds by approaching dice throws as simulations of independent random events. They proceeded to compute the probability of occurrence of a small number of events (e.g., a six coming up, two ones in a row, etc.). Their results and their conceptualization are still valid today. More particularly, throws of dice (or coins) have become a standard way to illustrate problems involving probability. (Marks, 1964:3–24)

But if one were willing to play the game of analogies further, it would not be difficult to show that the seeds of modern simulations were sown much earlier in history. From Plato onward, philosophers of education have indicated to some extent the value of simulated situations in the form of various drills and training exercises. This viewpoint is most explicit in Rousseau's *L'Emile*, where an educational program is proposed which includes games and exposure to artificially-created situations. As one might expect, Rousseau's rationale is very similar to the modern pedagogical philosophy on which educational gaming rests. (See Chapter 16 in this volume.)

Notwithstanding such historical antecedents, it is generally agreed that systematic simulations, in the sense of those described in Chapter 1, formally appeared at the end of the eighteenth century in the form of war games. The *Neue Kriegspiel*, probably inspired by chess, was introduced at Schleswig in 1798. It was a board game using a map divided into 3,600 squares on which token troops were moved according to rules which took into account the topographical features of the ground. War games underwent various developments during the nineteenth century. In particular they branched out into two main directions, a "rigid" game and a "free" game. The former variety made increasing use of formal rules to mirror reality and to determine the outcomes. For instance, numerous charts and tables were used to compute as accurately as possible the extent of troop movements, the effects of fire, and so forth. Free-form games became more like role-playing settings. The participants were given more freedom in interpreting their roles and the demands of the situation. The outcomes were determined by expert referees. By the early twentieth century both varieties of simulations had spread from Prussia to most modern countries, although up to World War II Germany and Japan made the most extensive use of the technique. In fact, in 1941 Japan simulated a two-year period of time to study the implications of an eventual attack against the United States upon their own economic, political, educational, financial, psychological, and military life (Jackson, 1959; Specht, 1957:7–10).

At about the same time that war gaming was reaching its peak, several intellectual developments provided additional roots to the modern conception of simulation. One anchorage was the concept of a system as originated in electrical engineering in the 1930's. Throughout the study of simple electrical circuits, engineers formulated, defined, and introduced such ideas as feedback, control theory, stability, and synthesis. These concepts, clearly defined in a system context, have diffused outward to become applicable in a less precise way to theoretical ideas in the social sciences (Huggins, 1969).[1] What the "systems approach" provided was a way for conceptualizing a problem that was particularly amenable for the adoption of simulations, because simulations are themselves systems.

Another intellectual root was the new era of laboratory experimentation in social psychology started by Lewin and Sherif in the late thirties. The laboratory became the setting where human behavior was studied in situations which were contrived so as to reproduce some significant features of real life. Although many of these experiments were highly contrived in appearance and were criticized as being too artificial, others were more realistic. Notable here are Strodtbeck and Mann's (1956) studies of simulated jury sessions, Allport and Postman's (1945) research on rumor diffusion, or Lippitt and White's (1958) investigation of styles of leadership. These studies did not however discuss the simulation-like features of their research designs. Rather, they were instrumental in predisposing to receive favorably the extension of laboratory techniques to the investigation of macro-level topics.

Another important intellectual development was the appearance of

[1] The input-output model and its variations discussed in Chapter 2 exemplifies this diffusion.

von Neumann and Morgenstern's (1944) work on game theory. Though the theory is essentially mathematical, it contributed important concepts and a seminal framework of analysis for the study of competitive and cooperative behavior. Conflict became differentiated into "zero sum" and "non-zero sum" types.[2] The notions of threat, credibility, bargaining, and coalition formation became foci of research. Perhaps even more important for the development of simulations was the enormous interest that game theory stimulated in game-like simulations, partly because of the glamour provided by the mathematical basis of the theory.

Von Neumann contributed to simulation in another way. The first automatic computer based on electronic technology appeared on the scene in 1945.[3] ENIAC, as it was named, was somewhat of a monstrosity, consisting of 18,000 vacuum tubes, each one subject to failure. More seriously, every job required new rewiring of plugboards. Von Neumann then made a critical contribution, by conceiving of the stored program as a means of overcoming the rewiring problem.

By the early fifties, then, the conditions had independently matured for the emergence of simulation in its modern form. Both the technology and the proper intellectual roots were present.

Actually, the first simulations in social science did not utilize digital or symbol-manipulating computers. Rather, they were run on analog computers. Analog techniques represent numbers by physical aspects of some system. (The plotting of points within two axes to uncover the pattern of a relationship is an analog procedure.) In 1950 Phillips used a hydraulic system as an analog computer to simulate the Keynsian mechanism of income determination. His device consisted of transparent plastic tanks and tubes through which it was possible to examine the flow of variously-colored water. Other early economic simulations utilized electrical analogues (Strotz, *et al.*, 1953).[4]

Analog techniques proved to be of little value in the social sciences because of their physical limitations; the results of the simulation were distorted by the physical characteristics of the model. For example,

[2] In a zero sum game, there can be no outcome which is preferred by both of two opponents to another outcome. Thus no negotiated agreement can simultaneously benefit both parties to complete satisfaction. (See Chapter 17.)

[3] The idea for a modern form of computer was developed by Charles Babbage in the 1820's. Lord Byron's daughter, Lady Lovelace, encouraged and supported Babbage's attempts to construct the machine. Technology unfortunately was inadequate for its needs. In 1890 the first ancestor of the modern card-reading machine, the Hollerith tabulator, was built. A telephone relay computer was constructed in the late 1930's, pointing to the value of on-off switches for symbolic manipulations. (Engineering Concepts Curriculum Project, 1968.)

[4] Analog simulations in engineering really go back to the late 19th century. For an introduction to the technique, see Karplus and Soroka (1959).

while friction affected the flow of the hydraulic model, there was no analogue to friction in economic theory. Soon, too, the digital computer proved much faster than analog techniques. It is not surprising, then, that these first simulations did not play a major role in alerting social scientists to simulation techniques. As it turned out, it was the business world which provided the first widely-publicized use of simulation.

In 1956 the American Management Association was spurred by the following exhortation to sponsor a business simulation game:

> In the war games conducted by the Armed Forces, command officers of the Army, Navy, and Air Force have an opportunity to practice decision-making creatively in a myriad of hypothetical yet true-to-life competitive situations. Moreover, they are forced to make decisions in areas outside their own speciality; a naval communications officer, for example, may play the role of a task force commander.
> ——Why then shouldn't businessmen have the same opportunity? . . . Why not a business "war game" in which teams of executives would make basic decisions of the kind that face every top management—and would see the results immediately? (Ricciardi, 1957: 59).

The resulting game, the AMA Top Management Decision Simulation was a relatively simple game in which teams representing companies competed in a common market. Players were to make basic decisions common to any company officer's experience, such as budgeting, expansion, planning, and market research. Furthermore, only marginal changes were allowed, a limit on decision-making typical for industrial executives. Simplified as the game was, it required a computer for speedy end-of-round calculations to feed back the consequences of decisions to the players.

The response by participating executives and educators was so enthusiastic that a proliferation of games appeared very quickly. Only four years later review articles (Cohen and Rhenman, 1961; Kibbee *et al.*, 1961; Greenlaw *et al.*, 1962) on management games listed over 85 games in use in the United States and referred to sources of information on comparable games in Europe. Two-thirds of the graduate schools of business soon adopted the games or developed their own as part of the standard curriculum (Dale and Klasson, 1964).

In short, the digital computer served as a catalyst for the large-scale adoption of simulations in the social sciences. However, the very same conditions which made the catalysis possible, that is, the general readiness of the disciplines, led almost simultaneously to the development of the whole gamut of simulations, including the purely man simulations, once the process was sparked.

The Origins of Simulation

To highlight the trends in the use of simulation since the appearance of the first contemporary ones in the mid-fifties, examples of man, man-machine, and machine simulations are presented below. The reader should keep in mind that nothing but an illustrative task is attempted. Recent bibliographies list hundreds of simulations in the area of social science alone (Werner and Werner, 1969). Thus a reader should not assume that there has been no simulation in his particular subfield or specialty simply because it has not been mentioned here.

COMPUTER SIMULATIONS

Chart 1 presents some of the best-known computer simulations grouped by major substantive subdivisions.

It can be seen that the economists were early utilizers of the technique. More than the other social sciences, they had been amassing the kind of statistical data amenable to the needs of computer simulations. Furthermore, economic theorists had developed mathematical models, which were readily available for study by means of simulation techniques. Thus, they could use simulations both to observe the implications of complex models under varying conditions and to see how closely they could reproduce the distribution of empirical data using various models. Not surprisingly, this led to a wide range of simulations, from micro- to macro-economics.

The effect of the type of data and level of theoretical development on computer simulation is no less clear in the case of political or sociological simulations. The political simulations have generally focused upon the voting process, an area rich in data collection. Sociologists, being poor in what is known as "hard data," were slow in turning to computer simulation. Yet a wide variety of processes have been formalized in the late sixties, leading to such diverse simulations as friendship formation, military authority, and innovation diffusion. Another reason for the slow adoption of the technique by some sectors in the social sciences lies in the less mathematical character of their theories. Their qualitative features are more difficult to treat, and programming methodology and procedures are still in development.

The psychological processes described in the chart might have appeared much later were it not for a programming language innovation. Most of these theories involve a conception of the individual as an information processer, requiring the computer to store lists of symbols continuously changing in length and content. The algebraic languages first available for the computer did not feasibly handle this type of model. The development of a new type of program language, the list processing

Chart 1 Survey of Selected Computer Simulations by Discipline

A. Economic Processes	
Adelman and Adelman (1959)	**The Klein-Goldberger model**
Cyert *et al.* (1959)	**Duopoly and the tin can industry**
Duesenberry *et al.* (1960)	**Macroeconomics of the U. S.**
Cohen (1960)	**Economics of the shoe, leather hide industry**
Orcutt (1961)	**Demographic features of households in the U. S., 1950–60**
Balderston and Hoggatt (1962)	**Market processes of the West Coast lumber industry**
Bonini (1963)	**A hypothetical firm**
Holland and Gillespie (1963)	**A stylized underdeveloped economy**
Amstutz (1967)	**Competitive markets**
B. Political Processes	
Raytheon (see Clemens, 1968)	**Cold war conflict**
Benson (1961)	**International relations**
McPhee (1961)	**Voting Behavior**
Abelson (1963)	**Community fluoridation referenda**
Pool *et al.* (1964)	**1960 presidential election**
Crecine (1968)	**Municipal budgeting**
Cherryholmes and Shapiro (1969)	**Roll calls in the House of Representatives**
C. Sociological-Social Psychological Processes	
Hare (1961)	**Small group decision-making**
Gullahorn and Gullahorn (1962) *	**Elementary social behavior**
Coleman (1962)	**(1) reference group behavior; (2) interactions in triads**
Ranio (1966)	**Friendship formation**
Gilbert and Hammel (1966)	**Kinship structures**
Hanneman *et al.* (1969)	**Innovation diffusion in a peasant village**
Smith (1969) *	**Models of residential mobility, military authority, prison riots, collective disturbances**
Freeman (1969)	**Residential segregation**
Findler and McKinzie (1969)	**Kinship structures**
D. Psychological Processes	
Newell and Simon (1963)	**Problem-solving**
Feigenbaum (1963)	**Verbal role memorization**
Clarkson (1963)	**Decision-making by investment counselors**
Colby (1964)	**Therapeutic manipulation of patients**
Coe (1964)	**Conflict and emotion**
Reitman (1964)	**A Hebbian model of thinking**

NOTE: For complete references to this chart, see Appendix A. The dates in parentheses are those of published reports on the simulation; the simulations themselves are always older, sometimes by as much as several years. The rank-order of dates in this and the following charts should only be taken as an approximation of the actual order of origin of the simulations. Asterisked entries are the subject of a case study in this volume.

language, facilitated simulations of psychological process. With such a language[5] the computer could easily be programmed to store various

[5] The first widely used list processing language was IPL-V (Information Processing Language Five), the fifth version of a family of information processing languages designed by Newell, Shaw, Simon, and their collaborators. Other list languages are LISP and FLPL, a list processing language within the Fortran system (Green, 1963: 96).

kinds of lists or hierarchies of lists, which could expand or contract, during a run. The result was a large number of attempts at psychological simulation, including bridge and chess players, with the entries in Chart 1 giving an idea of the scope though not the extent of the work.

MAN SIMULATION

While computer simulations have been developed for research and experimentation, man simulations have been developed predominately for teaching. Chart 2 presents a selected list of all-man simulations.

Historically, Inter-Nation Simulations (INS) was probably the first serious social simulation game. Influenced by his acquaintance with war

Chart 2 Selected List of Man Simulations

A. Economic Processes	
1966 Consumer (Zaltman) *	Teaches consumer economics (high school and above)
1967 Economic System (Coleman, Harris)	Teaches principles of economics (high school)
1967 Economics Decision Games (Rausch)	Eight games of basic economics (high school)
1968 Trade and Develop (Livingston)	Internation trade (junior high school)
1969 Market	Simple economics (grade school)
B. Political Processes	
1959 Inter-Nation Simulation (Guetzkow et al.) *	Research and teaching game of international relations
1961 Diplomacy	Origins of World War I
1962 Legislature (Coleman)	Teaches legislative process (high school)
1965 PLANS (Boguslaw et al.)	Research on pressure group dynamics
1968 American Government Simulations (Stitelman and Coplin)	Teaches political processes such as budgetary politics, campaigning, etc.
C. Sociological Processes	
1963 Life-Career (Boocock) *	Teaches career decision-making
1964 SIMSOC (Gamson) *	Teaches about social order in a society (college)
1965 Disaster (Inbar) *	Teaches dynamics of community response to a disaster
1966 Generation Gap (Boocock and Schild)	Parent-child interaction: a teaching and research game
1967 CLUG (Feldt)	Urban economics, ecology, and development for training and planning
1968 Ghetto (Toll)	Teaches mobility and career problems of ghetto residents
D. Psychological Processes	
1969 Simdream (Breznitz and Lieblich) *	A theoretical model of dream processes

NOTE: References and information are in Appendix B. Dates are approximate of time of completion. Asterisked entries are the subject of case studies in this volume.

games, in the mid-fifties Guetzkow conceived of a gaming technique as a research and teaching tool for the study of international relations (Guetzkow, 1963: 25–6). INS was designed for use at the college level and, without a doubt, has been the focus of more research than any game to date. (See a review of research in Raser, 1969: 93–110; Hermann, 1969: 45–6.)

Gamson's Simsoc is also a college-level game. As he explains in his contribution to this volume, the author was dissatisfied with the usual procedures for teaching an introductory social psychology course. He wanted an activity that would engage and interest the students. The result was a game (which he designed in the early 60's) in which the entire class became participants in a simulated society that lasted over many sessions.

Most of the other games have also been used in colleges, but except for a few of them (like CLUG) which were genuinely designed for college use, their target population is high school or grade school students. Coleman is probably the single most influential figure behind these high school and grade school simulation games. His *Adolescent Society* (1961, Chapter 11) spelled out the rationale for introducing academic games into the curriculum. In addition to producing several games (the most widely known probably being The Legislative Game), he has also led a group of students and colleagues at Hopkins who are responsible for such diverse games as Life-Career, Parent-Child, Disaster, Consumer, Ghetto. Some of these games are now being used in basic research (Stoll and McFarlane, 1969; McFarlane, 1969; Raser, 1969: 93–110).

MAN-MACHINE SIMULATION

Let us move finally and briefly to the computer games. Chart 3 has a selected list of this type of simulation.

Despite the appearance to the contrary (see footnote to Chart 1) it is the case that computers were wed with game players prior to the appearance of pure computer simulations. One reason is that in these early simulations the computer was used primarily as a bookkeeper. The computer represented a portion of the economy; it determined the complex interactions of the players' decisions and fed the information back to the players.

Later computer games have given the computer more sophisticated tasks. In Duke's urban game METRO, there are three major sub-simulation operating in the computer: (1) a voter response process, (2) a macro-economic and growth process, (3) an ecological redistribution process. In addition, there are actually four separate games that any individual player might be involved in.[6]

Although the first computer games were designed for training purposes, more recently they are being approached as research tools. Smoker's Inter-Process Simulation (an outgrowth of Guetzkow's INS) was designed specifically to encourage experimental work on issues in international relations. Similarly, the Romes have examined the effects of computer-simulated organizational structures upon player communications. And Envirometrics is an organization devoted to research on urban processes by means of its man-machine simulations.

Chart 3 *Selected Listing of Man-Machine Simulations*

Carnegie Tech Management Game (Cohen *et al.*, 1964)	**Training for executive decision-making**
Leviathan (Rome and Rome, 1962)	**Research on communication in formal organizations**
Metropolis (Duke, 1964)	**Urban decision-making training**
Surfboards, Toy Store, Sumerian Game, Sierra Leonne (Wing, 1966) *	**Teach economics in elementary school**
Inter-Process Simulation (Smoker, 1969)	**Research on international relations**
METRO (Ray and Duke, 1969)	**Urban decision-making for training and research**
City I, II (Envirometrics, 1969) *	**Urban models for research, training, planning**

NOTE: References appear in Appendix A. Asterisked entries are the subject of case studies in this volume. For references to management games not listed here, see Cohen and Rhenman (1961).

CASE STUDIES

The case studies comprising the next part of this volume include two computer games, two computer simulations, and eight games. This distribution may strike the reader as having a strange imbalance. More than the personal biases of the editors explains the emphasis on games.

Prerequisites for computer games and computer simulations are facility with programming, and often, with mathematical manipulation. Publications on computer technology, programming skills, and mathematical models as applied to simulation are readily available.[7] One of the purposes of this book is to help the reader decide whether he needs to acquire these skills for his purposes.

[6] These man-machine games have been sponsored and developed in settings rich with facilities and resources. Except for the simple teaching games, such simulations seem to require team-work for their efficient development and testing.

[7] See Naylor (1966), Mize and Cox (1968), Green (1963), Meier *et al.*, (1969) on computer technology and programming; Simon (1957), Bartos (1967), Coleman (1964) on mathematical models.

On the other hand the prospective game designer *per se* has no source of information to which he can turn to get started. The inclusion of a large number of games studies was intended to provide the beginning of such a reference. The reader who is undecided as to whether or not he should use a computer simulation will have enough examples to discern the main differences implied by his choice. More importantly, the range of substantive topics, as well as the variety of uses covered, should make the reader aware of the commonality in all simulation work, and enable him to decide whether simulation might be worthwhile in his own work. At the very least, he should have acquired the vocabulary and acumen to read simulation literature with a knowledgeable, critical eye.

REFERENCES

ALLPORT, GORDON W. AND LEO J. POSTMAN
1945 "The basic psychology of rumor." *Transactions of the New York Academy of Sciences*, Series II, 8, 61–81.

BAROJA, JULIO CARO
1965 *El Carnaval*. Madrid: Spain.

BARTOS, OTTOMAN J.
1967 *Simple Models of Group Behavior*. New York: Columbia.

COHEN, KALMAN J. AND ERIC RHENMAN
1961 "The role of management games in education and research." *Management Science*, 7, 131–66.

COLEMAN, JAMES S.
1961 *The Adolescent Society*. New York: Free Press.
1964 *Introduction to Mathematical Sociology*. New York: Free Press.

DALE, ALFRED G. AND CHARLES R. KLASSON
1964 *Business Gaming: A Survey of American Collegiate Schools of Business*. Austin: Bureau of Business Research, The University of Texas.

ENGINEERING CONCEPTS CURRICULUM PROJECT
1968 *The Man Made World*. New York: McGraw-Hill.

GREEN, BERT F.
1963 *Digital Computers in Research*. New York: McGraw-Hill.

GREENLAW, PAUL S., LOWELL W. HERSON, AND RICHARD H. RAWDON
1962 *Business Simulations in Industrial and University Education*. Englewood Cliffs, N. J.: Prentice-Hall.

GUETZKOW, HAROLD
1963 *Simulation in International Relations*. Englewood Cliffs, N. J.: Prentice-Hall, 1963.

HERMANN, CHARLES F.
1969 *Crises in Foreign Policy*. Indianapolis: Bobbs-Merrill.

PART I. ANATOMY OF SIMULATION

The Origins of Simulation

HUGGINS, WILLIAM
1969 "On the importance of becoming a bottleneck." Baltimore: Johns Hopkins, Department of Electrical Engineering. Mimeo.

JACKSON, JAMES R.
1959 "Learning from experience in business decision games." *California Management Review*, 1, 92–107.

KARPLUS, WALTER J. AND WALTER W. SOROKA
1959 *Analog Methods: Computation and Simulation*. New York: McGraw-Hill.

KIBBER, JOEL M., CLIFFORD J. CRAFT, AND BURT NANUS
1961 *Management Games*. New York: Rhinehold.

LIPPITT, R. AND R. K. WHITE
1958 "An experimental study of leadership and group life." In Eleanor E. Maccoby et al. (editors), *Readings in Social Psychology*. New York: Holt.

MCFARLANE, PAUL T.
1969 *Pilot Studies of Role Behaviors in a Parent-Child Simulation Game*. Baltimore: Center for Study of Social Organization of Schools, Johns Hopkins University.

MARKS, R. W.
1964 *Space, Time, and the New Mathematics*. New York: Bantam.

MEIER, ROBERT C., WILLIAM T. NEWELL, AND HAROLD L. PAZA
1969 *Simulation in Business and Economics*. Englewood Cliffs: Prentice-Hall.

MIZE, JOE H. AND J. GRADY COX
1968 *Essentials of Simulation*. Englewood Cliffs, N. J.: Prentice-Hall.

NAYLOR, THOMAS H., JOSEPH L. BALINTFY, DONALD S. BURDICK, AND KONG CHU
1966 *Computer Simulation Techniques*. New York: Wiley.

PHILLIPS, A. W.
1950 "Mechanical models in economic dynamics." *Economica* (New Series), 17, 283–305.

RASER, JOHN
1969 *Simulation and Society*. Boston: Allyn and Bacon.

RICCIARDI, FRANC M.
1957 *Top Management Decision Simulation: The AMA Approach*. New York: American Management Association.

SIMON, HERBERT A.
1957 *Models of Man*. New York: Wiley.

SPECHT, ROBERT D.
1957 "War Games." P-1041. Santa Monica: RAND.

STOLL, CLARICE S. AND PAUL T. MCFARLANE
1969 "Player characteristics and interaction in a Parent-Child simulation game." *Sociometry*, 32, 259–272.

STRODTBECK, FRED L. AND RICHARD D. MANN
1956 "Sex role differentiation in jury deliberations." *Sociometry*, 19, 3–11.

STROTZ, R. H., J. C. MCANULTY, AND J. B. NAINES, JR.
1953 "Goodwin's nonlinear theory of the business cycle: an electro-analog solution." *Econometrica*, 21, 390–411.

VON NEUMANN, NEUMANN AND OSKAR MORGENSTERN
1944 *Theory of Games and Economic Behavior*.

WERNER, ROLAND AND JOAN T. WERNER
1969 *Bibliography of Simulations: Social Systems and Education*. La Jolla, Calif.: Western Behavioral Sciences Institute.

Part II

CASE STUDIES

"The pitcher got through the inning without further difficulty. After the last out he came walking in toward the third-base dugout. . . . . . I envied him—even his difficulty with Mantle. I leaned far out of my seat trying to hear—hoping to get some indication of what it was really like out there, what it was like to face Mantle from the pitcher's mound, to see him begin to uncoil his swing at a pitch, and yet I knew that no matter how articulate the pitcher, still it wouldn't be enough. It was something you had to experience yourself to know truly."

—George Plimpton
Out of My League

Section **A** MAN SIMULATION

WILLIAM A. GAMSON

Chapter **4**

Simsoc: Establishing Social Order in a Simulated Society

Simsoc, which is now widely used in introductory sociology courses, originated with Gamson's dissatisfactions with orthodox college teaching. In the course of designing an active participation environment, he encountered a variety of problems. One was to create a workable game which at the same time would be a reasonable reproduction of social order. Another was to maintain student interest over time and over lull periods. He also had to confront such academic issues as grades and attendance. The outcome here is a lively, candid report on the emergence of his game, which accommodates up to sixty players for up to ten sessions of play.

—EDITORS

Simsoc: Establishing Social Order in a Simulated Society

Developmental processes frequently seem more orderly and logical in retrospect than at the time. It is easy to forget, after the fact, that many decisions were made for poorly articulated and ephemeral reasons. Good sense can be made of many choices which are better attributed to good fortune. I mention this because I am aware that the account I am about to give of the development of a simulated society (Simsoc) will inevitably exaggerate the self-conscious planning involved in the evolution of this game.

This paper will be divided into three sections. First, I wish to describe the initial stimulus to the development of Simsoc and my objectives at the beginning. Then, I will describe my troubles and triumphs in actually running the game in various versions over a period of about four years. Finally, I will make some general observations about developing game simulations, based on my own experience with Simsoc.

GETTING STARTED

Two general predisposing factors combined with two more immediate events in directing my energy toward developing a game simulation. The first predisposing factor was simply an attraction for games. I enjoy playing games, and perhaps more important, I have always manipulated rules of existing games in efforts to remove defects or to make the games more exciting. Second, I have been concerned for some time about making the learning process less passive. This concern is reflected in an interest in cooperative work-study programs such as the one I experienced as an undergraduate at Antioch College and in courses which have a workshop atmosphere—for example, those in which the class collectively attempts to carry out some research project.

More immediate events played on these predispositions. During the Spring semester of 1964, I was scheduled to teach a large introductory social psychology course. It had previously been taught in the conventional manner of such courses at large state universities—with a large lecture and a division into small discussion sections staffed by graduate-student teaching-fellows. I sought some substitute for the lecture which would involve a less passive experience. My thoughts focused on substituting a lab for the lecture but I was uncertain what form such a lab should take.

At about the same time, I had occasion to review Harold Guetzkow *et al., Simulation in International Relations* (1963) and to discuss the Inter-Nation Simulation with some observers and students who had participated in it. I was impressed at the sense of involvement it produced and at the greater salience certain aspects of international relations seemed to have for these students. Of course, I had no way of knowing if the game produced these animated concerns or if the students had them from the beginning. But the fact remained that they *believed* they had learned something new, and, if this belief was an illusion, it was at least the sort of illusion a student ought to get at college.

If important aspects of the international system could be simulated, surely there were many social psychological concerns that would lend themselves to such treatment. Here was a possibility for an unusual and exciting social psychology lab, if I could think of a game simulation appropriate to the course material. My point of departure contained two premises which have remained constant through several revisions of the basic game.

1. The demands of a game simulation as a learning device and as a useful research device are, to some degree, in conflict. If one is to interpret the outcomes of a game simulation, it is necessary to put some fairly severe restrictions on the interaction of the participants. If everyone is allowed to communicate freely and simultaneously with everyone else, it will be difficult to know and control enough of the conditions of the simulation to be able to attribute the outcomes to any particular parameters. While it may not be necessary to control interaction completely, the demands of research push toward systematic record keeping and well-channeled and observable transactions among participants.

In contrast, the effectiveness of game simulation as a learning device is due in large part to its motivational impact on participants. Its ability to involve them in the learning process is enhanced by spontaneity and the opportunity for improvisation. Heavy demands on recording and controlling interaction, it seemed to me, would interfere with such spontaneity and would slow down the pace of the game for reasons which contributed little to the learning process.

It is possible to overdraw the conflict and one can, I suppose, attempt to strike some balance in restricting interaction. But the balance is likely to produce a different and less appropriate game than one would have developed for either single purpose (learning or research). My own task, I believe, was greatly simplified by a clear commitment to a single purpose. It enabled me to introduce complications and innovations quite readily and to eliminate a great deal of paper work and recording which served no educational purpose. Where the main action of the Inter-Nation Simulation centered around the filling out of some rather elaborate forms, the main action in Simsoc increasingly centered around a series of complicated verbal transactions, and the forms became simpler as the game developed.

2. The second premise concerned the central purpose of the simula-

tion I intended to develop. I wished to center attention on a central problem of collective decision, a problem epitomized by the "mixed-motive" or bargaining game (cf. Schelling, 1960). Such games are characterized by a mixture of mutual dependence and conflict, of partnership and competition among the players.

I wished students to confront this problem collectively and as an organizational problem. Given the advantages to each individual of improving his relative position, how could he manage collectively to deal with his common interest? The dilemma is well illustrated by the "free rider" problem (cf. Coleman, 1966). It is to everyone's advantage to see to it that certain collective goods and services are produced. But it is even more to the advantage of any individual *not* to participate in the cost if all others do, since he will get the benefits anyway. In confronting this fundamental problem of collective decision, I expected students to confront a number of issues of deviance and social control, of legitimacy and the development of social norms, of leadership and role differentiation. These issues were central to the content of the social psychology course for which Simsoc was to serve as a lab.

PROBLEMS OF DEVELOPMENT

It should be obvious that the points of departure described above offered only the mildest sort of constraint on the form and content of Simsoc. In developing a playable game from such considerations, a great many features had to be specified, and many of these decisions were made casually or on the basis of practical considerations. Some of these vaguely considered details turned out to have important consequences for the effectiveness of the game. It seems useful to me to describe the evolution of the game, identifying features which were omitted in later versions and the reasons for eliminating them. I will also describe features which were added and the effects of these additions. But before proceeding, some basic description of Simsoc seems in order.

The game attempts to provide a rich environment for sustained exploration and learning, rather than to illustrate the impact of environmental constraints on the participants. As in the Inter-Nation Simulation (INS), the goals of the players are not sharply defined; rather, they are given certain resources, opportunities, constraints, and general objectives and are then put on their own (cf. Raser's description of the INS, 1969).

The game is designed to be played for a period of from five to ten sessions, allowing from 1½ to 2 hours per session. Groups ranging in size from 20 to 60 can play it in any setting in which there are four or more rooms in reasonably close proximity. Players are dependent on others for survival and for achievement of their goals. Some of their goals conflict with those of other players, and all players are competing over the allocation of rather scarce resources which they need to continue functioning.

The society has certain basic groups—economic, political, mass media, and others—but it has no government. The game starts with a collection of diverse interests and it is up to the players to create institutions (especially governmental ones) and a normative order as the need arises. To do this, they meet with other individuals of like interest, bargain with individuals who have different interests, travel about to influence players in other regions, threaten others with arrest and confiscation of their resources, and generally "wheel and deal." Inevitably some stay strictly in their own region and don't initiate much interaction. At the end of each session, there is an occasion for investing resources in a manner which affects the "National Indicators" of Food and Energy Supply, Standard of Living, Social Cohesion, and Public Commitment. Everyone is affected by what happens to these indicators, which are altered not only by direct investment, but by various other actions of the members of the society (including absenteeism, arrests, unemployment, and death).

The action of the game typically centers around the ability of collectively-oriented leaders to win legitimacy and the compliance and cooperation of others. Any group or individual with sufficient resources can create a police force, and a major axis of conflict has frequently been between relatively popular leaders without a force and a small group with little legitimacy which possesses a force and is challenging the leaders. There are many variations on the basic theme and some Simsocs have borne little resemblance to it. Peaceful Simsocs have generally been dull, and, as the discussion below will indicate, much of the tampering with the rules in different versions has aimed at strengthening private and sub-group interests and weakening the emphasis on the common interest. Fortunately, only a small number of deviants are necessary to keep things interesting and there are usually a few individuals who—perhaps out of mischief or boredom—try to make trouble for any established leadership group.

Early Versions

The brief description above is intended to convey something of the type and flavor of the game. The full rules are too detailed to review here and run over 20 single-spaced pages in length. They have changed dramatically over the years, and it is an instructive exercise to examine some of the differences between the current version and various early versions of the game.

The original version of Simsoc was designed to be played one hour per week over a six-to-eight-week period among the 25 students in an honors section of an introductory social psychology course. It was played in one ordinary class room in which players were allowed to meet in buzz groups but could, by petition, call a meeting of the whole class. Each player had a private interest group to which he belonged. His points were determined by the value of his private interest group and by the state of the National Indicators mentioned above. Grades were attached to these points. The state of the National Indicators determined the average grade for the class as a whole, in a range from C− to B+; an individual's private group score determined whether he would get above or below this average. (In addition, of course, the lab grade was based on written work analysing Simsoc and relating it to other course material.)

The private interest groups (six in all) had a series of complicated effects on each other and on the National Indicators. An increase in the score of any given group raised the scores of some other groups and lowered the scores of still others. Increases in score for most private groups tended to lower the National Indicators, with the exception of one or two private groups whose interests were complementary with the National Indicators but competitive with most of the other private groups. Players were given a complicated matrix describing these effects. The mechanism for raising the private group scores or National Indicators was resource units which players were given in fixed amounts each session to invest at the end of the session. Players could also increase their "annual" income of resources by personally investing them, rather than putting them in their private interests or National Indicators.

This first version of Simsoc had an interesting history. First of all, the problem of social order was apparently solved quite rapidly and effectively. After about the second session, the group met entirely as a whole and strongly discouraged any private meetings or communications. A set of three leaders developed, covering a diverse and conflicting set of private interests. They proposed and won acceptance of a plan in which all members of the society would turn over all resources to them and they would invest all of them in the National Indicators with the exception of a small amount needed to keep the private groups all at an equal level. This plan had some technical difficulties which kept the leaders busy a good part of the time.

However, two events occurred which prevented the full achievement of the collectively-oriented, smooth society envisioned. First, one individual and later a few others refused to turn their resources over to the leadership. They were subjected to strong social pressure and vilification from other class members although the leaders treated them rather gently. However, most of these holdouts *actually invested their resources according to the leadership's plan.* In short, they insisted on the right to do themselves what the developing norms dictated that they do, an interesting and subtle form of control within a context of apparent deviance. Furthermore, the exclusion of their resources from the general pool enabled the leadership to excuse a continued imbalance among the private groups, stemming from the technical difficulties of keeping them equal. They were able to blame the inequalities on the deviant societal members and thus divert criticism directed against their leadership.

A second event came near the end and took a dramatic form. One of the three leaders who was charged with carrying out the investment of the pool of resources departed from the general plan and invested the entire pool in his own private group. The hostility directed toward him became so intense that he stopped coming to the lab sessions. I personally was rather delighted because this action reopened for the class the dilemma of social order that they had apparently so successfully solved, and in the remaining couple of weeks they began to wrestle again with the problem that had seemed quite simple to solve earlier.

I considered this initial version of Simsoc a qualified success, but there were many serious problems that emerged. Now, six versions later, with approximately 30 independent trials, I can not claim that all problems have been eliminated. There are two classes of problems: (a) those that were relatively superficial and even mechanical and proved not too difficult to eliminate, and (b) those that are related to the fundamental design of Simsoc and have proved exceedingly stubborn. There are two problems in this latter category, and they remain only partially solved: (1) unequal participation, with some students extremely busy and others doing almost nothing, and (2) a need for meaningful private goals for the players to compete with the raising of the National Indicators as a goal. Before discussing the only partly successful attempts to deal with the stubborn problems, I will describe the removal of several minor bugs that infested early versions of Simsoc.

Minor and Soluble Problems

1. Consensus formation. If the members of a real society could gather in a single room, communicate about their problems, and put pressure on deviants, the difficulty of achieving consensus would be greatly simplified. If Simsoc was to be a simulated society rather than a small group, its citizens should face the problem of achieving consensus *without the possibility of face-to-face communication among all members.* Consequently, in all subsequent versions of Simsoc, including the present one, members are divided into four regions with provisions for travel between regions but with the restriction that there can never be more than 50 percent of the members of the society in any given region at any time.

2. Focus on technical aspects. An inordinate amount of time in early Simsocs was spent working out the implications of the highly complicated matrix of interdependencies for investment policy. The major question for the class concerned "How do we best achieve our agreed-upon collective goal?" rather than "How do we achieve collective goals in the face of substantial conflict of interest?" The focus on technical aspects helped to transform the game from a mixed-motive situation to a pure coordination game. Furthermore, the focus on technical issues tended to be dominated by a few experts, leaving most societal members with very little to do. Through several revisions, the devices for building in significant elements of conflict and private interest have become less and less technical.

Nevertheless, even in the current version, some subjects report that Simsoc has "an overemphasis upon the economic aspects of society." Since there is no serious effort to simulate the economy and economic complexity is now minimal, this reaction requires some interpretation. It arises, I believe, from the fact that competition over scarce resources inevitably becomes the focus of much of the action. The remark that economic aspects are overemphasized can be interpreted to mean that the game produces a society that is "too materialistic" for the taste of many players. This, it should be recognized, is a comment about the "quality of life" in their Simsoc and not a comment about its value as a learning experience.

Another reaction, in a similar vein, suggests that Simsoc imposes an individualistic and capitalistic order. There is a partial truth in this since, initially, resources are controlled privately. However, there is nothing to prevent or discourage collective control of one sort or another and this is, in fact, a frequent outcome. One Simsoc user in a business school reported with some surprise that his students created a "full-fledged socialist state." Private control, then, is simply an initial condition that may or may not be maintained in the course of play as participants erect their own institutional order around the bare bones given them in the Participant's Manual.

3. Instructor as participant. I had intended to limit my role to observer once the initial rules had been explained and the society was in process. This proved to be impossible in the early versions because the rules were ambiguous on a number of points. I was continually being called upon to interpret rules and to adjudicate conflicts about interpretation. Since such adjudication invariably favored some individuals at the expense of others, it became more and more important to members of the society to control this source of power. Allowing myself to become involved as an important and influential member of the society seemed to be subversive of the basic purpose of the game.

It took me several revisions and trial runs to solve this problem, but it has now been solved by a simple and effective device. The interpretation of the rules was turned over to a group within the society. The rules grant them the right to resolve whatever ambiguities arise. This has the double advantage of removing the instructor from the society and presenting the members with an important additional problem of controlling a powerful group in the society with great potential for arbitrary and self-interested employment of its authority.

4. Intervention in ongoing processes. In the early trial runs of Simsoc, I attempted several times to add new rules while the game was in progress, each time with very poor results. These interventions tended to change the focus of the game from dealing with conflict among participants to dealing with conflict *between* class and instructor. They were received as unwanted intrusions whose purpose it was to disrupt the social order and as a kind of "cheating" by the instructor to overcome the fact that the players had "beaten" the game. They also produced a kind of anomie in which players felt paralyzed to act, for fear that the ground rules for action would suddenly be changed. I resolved, finally, to refrain from changing any rules once the society was in process and to reserve changes for future iterations of the game.

The latest version, however, contains a provision for the introduction of certain "events." These events take the form of crises with which members of the society must deal (e.g., epidemics and natural disasters). Players are warned in advance that such events will occur as a normal part of the game although they are not told of their nature or when they will happen. The forewarning on these events and their inclusion in the written rules serves to remove them from the category of the instructor's arbitrary intervention and allows them to be perceived and accepted as a normal part of the game.

5. Lack of structure and purpose. I wished to avoid a highly structured, role-imitation situation in favor of one which created a rich context for continued exploration and learning. This lack of specification about what was expected from the players was a source of anxiety for many of them and, because of their pressures for greater direction, a source of anxiety for me as well. I have responded to this problem in three ways. First, I began to recognize that the uncertainty and confusion tends to disappear by the third session. The knowledge that this is true gives me more courage in being able to reject requests for specification. Second, I have made a point of calling attention to the lack of structure and to the confusion at the beginning about what is expected as a normal and desirable feature of the game. I hope it makes people feel less anxious to be told that it is normal and proper for them to feel anxious at this particular point in time. Third, I have made a number of concessions to structure, perhaps too many. These changes and concessions are only partly directed at relieving anxiety in the early stages; they have an additional purpose of relieving boredom and alienation which may develop in the late stages.

The major effect of the changes on the early sessions is to provide a fairly clear-cut task for the opening session. This seems desirable on two accounts: (1) It helps students over the initial shock which occurs when the explanation of the rules is completed and they are told, "All right, the society is in session." In the early versions, a considerable period of staring at each other and rereading rules took place at the outset. (2) Perhaps more important, it helps to prevent premature closure and the rapid acceptance of any suggestion for action which helps to resolve the ambiguity about what constitutes appropriate behavior. Under the current rules, some basis of sub-group orientation has an opportunity to occur before an elite can mobilize a mass of unintegrated individuals for collective action. The preliminary organization which takes place in the opening session makes the citizenry less accessible to rapid mobilization and reinforces some sense of private or sub-group interest below the level of the society as a whole (cf. Kornhauser, 1959). This serves to keep the central problem of collective decision a more difficult one to solve.

6. Ambiguity about obedience to rules. Once the interpretation of the rules was vested in a group of participants in Simsoc, a new problem arose. The instructors made it clear that it was up to the society to enforce the rules. The players were told that this was an important problem with which they would have to deal. However, some players violated the rules with impunity, even doing such things as simply removing resources from other players' folders. Young ladies were known to seek refuge in the ladies' room to protect their resources—a modern sanctuary equivalent to the churches of olden days.

Much of the problem was created by confusion on the part of the instructors, including myself, about the difference between two kinds of rules. The difference may be thought of as that between natural constraints and man-made laws. We failed to distinguish the basic constraints which made the game possible from those which the players imposed to run their society successfully.

The current version of Simsoc makes this distinction very sharply. The players are asked tc accept the rules which the manual supplies as equivalent to natural constraints. The rule, for example, that one may not travel while under arrest should be taken as the equivalent of the physical prison which makes this impossible. For the simulation to have any meaning, it is necessary to accept such constraints.

In contrast, the members of the society may decide, through an elected legislative body, for example, to introduce certain regulations on travel. Here we emphasize the rules of the game *do not require* obedience to man-made regulations. It is up to the society to enforce such laws or norms or to tolerate deviance as its members see fit. This is not, we emphasize, a distinction between a constitution and the laws of a particular administration. Both of these are man-made laws and can be changed by common agreement, but the rules of the manual are not subject to change by the members of the society any more than we can change the law of gravity by common consent. Nevertheless, interpretation may be required about whether some action or agreement is possible or impossible under the meaning of some given constraint, and a group within the society is charged with this decision. This leaves some remaining tension about what is deviance within Simsoc and what is simply cheating (or not playing the game), but the problem has occurred with much less frequency since the distinction has been made explicit in the rules.

7. Mechanical difficulties. In the earliest version of the game, time pressure was omnipresent. It operated as a distorting factor because discussions were continually being cut short and acquiescence obtained on the grounds that time was running out and some action had to be taken. This fault was corrected in a shift to two hour sessions, and experiments with 1½ hour sessions also appeared reasonably free of undue time pressure, especially when some flexibility about running over the limit existed.

Reinvolvement in the world of Simsoc after a one-week layoff has generally presented some problem. Much of the involvement which was present at the end of the previous session is now dissipated and is not always easy to recapture. Situations in which I have run Simsoc continually over a two-day period have generally been more effective. This procedure has involved three 1½–2 hour sessions per day, with half-hour breaks in between.

Players are not informed which session is the final one, in order to avoid end-game effects. Typically, the game has ended amidst groans and protests when the players have assembled for a session. There is generally some frustration over termination at a point when many people feel they are about to execute some long-planned program of action or *coup d'etat.* However, ending the society while action is at its peak has certain educational advantages, although it takes longer for the players to adjust from their role in Simsoc to their role as social analyst in the course. In this latter role, they frequently generate an excellent discussion about what would have happened in the next few sessions and why.

8. Feckless rules. A number of provisions were included in the original version, some of them for poorly articulated reasons, which proved quite worthless although they did little harm. For example, the first version allowed death and reentry into the society as a new person. I believe I wished to include certain aspects of socialization, but it is difficult to recall at this late date the specific reason for the rule. In any event, the attempt was a double failure. Not only did it fail to capture any significant aspects of the process of socialization, but it produced a series of self-interested "suicides" which had absolutely nothing to do with actual suicide. Players who were unhappy with their position found this a convenient way to liquidate and begin afresh. Furthermore, those whose private interests conflicted with the national indicators were advised by their fellow citizens to drop out in the interest of the society. Many players were happy to oblige with such altruistic "suicide." This aspect of the simulation hardly seemed integral to the central purposes and was simply abandoned in later versions.

A number of other features of early versions were dropped in subsequent revisions. There is no point in describing these in detail, for they contain no general lesson other than underlining the following observation: Mistakes with little or no effect are not as disturbing as those which produce unintended side effects, since they do not interfere with the processes being simulated or create new problems.

Stubborn Problems and Attempted Solutions

1. Alienation and apathy. A major problem in the early versions of Simsoc was the tendency for the society to become dominated by a collectively-oriented elite which served the society well. This, of course, was no problem from the standpoint of Simsoc members. They had engaged in a classic interchange of support for effective leadership. In a real society, they could then turn to private pursuits such as love and leisure. However, in Simsoc, the educational objectives required that they participate in some active way in a societal role; neither they nor the instructors could see the point of them coming to class for two hours in the evening simply to write letters to friends or to study for examinations in another course.

I sought a solution to this problem which would provide enough structure so that every individual had to hold a job to live but, at the same time, would leave room for a great deal of innovation and ingenuity in achieving goals. The problem still remains only partly solved. Involvement remains unequal, but the inequality now seems more a product of choice and lack of interpersonal skill than of something intrinsic to the rules.

2. Tying grades to performance. My intention in attaching grades to performance in the game was to make the conflict and the stakes more real and vivid. Far from increasing conflict, the introduction of this stake had the effect of all but eliminating conflict among the class members. Powerful norms developed against pursuing private interests, and as in the case of the instructor's intervention, the meta-game was between class and instructor. The class believed that the instructors (myself or, later, several teaching fellows) wished to create conflict among them and their problem centered on how to prevent this from happening. The fear of untrammeled conflict was frequently expressed in Hobbesian terms by the participants: "Unless we stick together this whole thing is going to degenerate into a situation in which everyone is going to be cutting everyone else's throat." Those who deviated did so, in my judgment, for reasons which had little to do with grades. Motivations such as curiosity and rebelliousness against the authority of societal leaders were much more often dominant.

Now, it might be argued that the condition described above is realistic and should be welcomed in the simulation. The fear of a short, nasty, and brutish existence if the fragile web of order is destroyed may be a genuine and important presence in society. The problem came not from a lack of correspondence between the simulation and the world but in the breakdown of the boundaries between the two and the transformation of the simulation. The "real" game became the familiar one the students were accustomed to playing—the college game. Furthermore, they had available to them a powerful set of controls over their fellows that is not usually present. Each student could very clearly see who would be effected adversely by any self-serving actions he might take, and those who were affected would know and be able to hold him accountable. Far from making the dilemma of social order more intense, the introduction of grades created such powerful forces for coordination and order that the dilemma was largely removed. Several societies very quickly became smoothly functioning welfare states with few or no challenges and little or no occupation for the mass of participants.

I became convinced that it was desirable to separate the student role from the role of citizen of Simsoc if the educational purposes were not to be subverted. This involved basing all grades on the written work in connection with Simsoc, a task which emphasized skill as an observer and analyst of events, rather than skill as a participant. Rewards for skill in the society became purely symbolic, but this change did not lead to any lessening of involvement. On the contrary, the students appeared able to play the game more freely and creatively and with more enjoyment as conflict became less threatening. This change produced a more realistic simulation of the *balance* between the forces for order and the forces for conflict. It was this balance, and the dilemmas arising out of it, which I wished to simulate and would lose by making either set of forces predominate. Achieving this balance has been the most difficult problem of Simsoc, with imbalance invariably coming from having too little conflict. Ironically, the removal of grades contingent on performance greatly increased self-interested behavior and thus made the basic dilemma of the game more realistic.

3. Lack of force. An important omission in the early versions of Simsoc was the absence of any functional equivalent of force. This exclusion turned out to be important for unexpected reasons. There has never been much need in Simsoc for force as a facility to be used on behalf of the society as a whole. Social pressures are so strong when backed by a leadership with high legitimacy that few individuals have been able to muster the will or the resources to resist. The importance of force is that it offers some possibility for competing against legitimate power. The most important innovation added to Simsoc was the provision for a police force or army that could be created by any individual or group of individuals with sufficient resources to do so. This police force, once created, can restrict the travel and confiscate the resources of any member of the society on any grounds it deems appropriate. One can, of course, also be created on behalf of a central government or leadership group, but the essential point is that access is not limited to such a group.

The use of the police force option has varied greatly in different runs of Simsoc. Some societies had no police forces; some had only a highly legitimate one; some had a private or guerrilla force; and some had two or more forces engaging in what amounted to a civil war. But even in those societies in which no police forces were created, the possibility of resort to such a force by a regime or its opponents remained an important and fundamental constraint.

4. Scarcity. A major difficulty in creating meaningful private interests has been the lack of anything to do with one's money (Simbucks) other than using it to raise the National Indicators. In early versions, players learned after a few sessions that they really didn't need Simbucks and couldn't do much with them, especially when the leaders were providing for all members those few things on which money could be spent. They couldn't buy cigarettes, vacations, or grades with such Simbucks, so why seek them or try to hold onto them?

I have attempted to deal with this problem by creating a combination of scarcity and personal need. In the current version, travel tickets are severely limited in number so that they have real value as a social object on which to spend Simbucks. Furthermore, all members must provide for their subsistence through the purchase of subsistence tickets and the failure to do so on successive weeks eliminates them permanently from the society. These subsistence tickets are also in scarce supply. In addition, certain events will occur which will require Simbucks for personal protection. For example, when an epidemic occurs, members will have to purchase immunity or run the risk of being eliminated from Simsoc through contracting the disease. Other minor privileges may also be purchased. Hopefully, these provisions will make the acquisition and holding of Simbucks a more meaningful action than it has been in the past and will complicate the problem of providing sufficient money for keeping the National Indicators high.

5. Inequalities. Early versions of Simsoc had a strong bias toward equal opportunity. This bias was introduced partly for "fairness" when grades were attached to performance and partly without thought because such initial equality is so typically a part of games. The players bring a strong egalitarian norm into the game as well.

The most recent version of the game seriously departs from the equal-opportunity bias. Heads of seven basic groups are designated at the beginning and these seven individuals have complete control over the Simbucks assigned to those groups. The others have no money and must acquire it by getting one or more jobs with the basic groups. There are opportunities to depose the head of a group but no way of guaranteeing control over the new head.

In addition, a limited number of people in the society own Travel Agencies and Subsistence Agencies. These Agencies allow the owner to dispense a limited number of travel tickets or subsistence tickets each session. The instructor has the option of making the inequality cumulative by assigning these agencies to the seven group heads or of diffusing power somewhat by assigning them to other individuals. In either event, the current Simsoc will contain "have" and "have-not" members from the beginning, as well as conflicts and differences among the basic groups. It remains to be seen how successful these built-in inequalities will be against the strong egalitarian norms which players bring to the game.

6. Collectively oriented groups. I made the mistake of introducing into Simsoc a procedure for electing a Council. Having such a procedure as an explicit part of the rules moves a long way toward solving at the outset the problems which the players are being asked to solve. The council has overwhelming legitimacy immediately and is difficult for any group to challenge except by the use of force. An important problem for the players is to go through the process of establishing governmental institutions which have the allegiance of members of the society. But the emergence of a State loses much of its interest and difficulty when it is virtually established by the rules of the game from the beginning. The current rules of the game eliminate any government, leaving the players free to create whatever institutions seem appropriate to them as the need arises.

Certain of the basic groups in earlier versions had essentially collective goals—for example, to advise the society on proper investment policy and to reward various kinds of socially useful contributions. These groups served to reinforce the already strong collective-orientation of the members and have been eliminated in the current version in favor of groups with private goals which conflict with or at least are independent of collective goals.

Thus, my private war against *e pluribus unum* continues.

SOME GENERAL OBSERVATIONS

I have found the process of continual modification of Simsoc a peculiarly absorbing and rewarding intellectual experience. It has a concreteness and immediacy which is lacking in much of the intellectual work I do. If I am trying to understand why, for example, a particular social movement developed at one time and not another, I will usually struggle through a sequence of questions until I achieve some vague sense of closure. This suffices until enough questions have been raised about my explanation to give me again a vague sense of uneasiness.

The process is somewhat different with the development of a simulation. It is as if I have a complicated Rube Goldberg device in front of me that will produce certain processes and outcomes. I want it to operate differently in one way or another but it is difficult to know where and how to intervene to achieve this purpose because the apparatus is delicate and highly interconnected. So I walk around it, eyeing it from different angles, and imagine adding a nut here or a bolt there or shutting it off and replacing some more complicated parts.

Each of these interventions must take the extremely specific form of a rule. To intervene, one must play a mental game in which the introduction of every specific change must be weighed in terms of how the whole contraption will operate. Such mental games force one to develop a clear picture of what the apparatus looks like and why it operates as it does. Each hypothetical alternative must be put in place and imagined in operation. Finally, an explicit choice has to be made and the game actually run under the altered rules, and one has a chance to discover whether he really understands the contraption or not. When a rule-change has the effect it is supposed to have, the experience can be very exciting—as exciting as predicting a non-obvious outcome in any social situation and having it turn out correctly.

Playing a game may be a more active experience than listening to a lecture, but developing a game is more active still. In fact, one begins to wonder if students learn anything from actually playing a game like Simsoc. Involvement is, after all, a mixed blessing in the learning process. Some students become so involved in the game as an end in itself that they have difficulty analyzing its events in a detached fashion. In the discussions which follow the playing of Simsoc it is sometimes difficult to get players past self-justifying descriptions of their actions and motivations. I have seen students who have *continued* to maintain a deception which they had practiced in a completed game to a point where it obscures their own and others' understanding of what happened.

Other students, at least in an introductory course with a partly captive audience, just don't like games. Games require an active, instrumental, and controlling posture toward the environment. Those who are shy or passive, or who simply like to let things happen and take their enjoyment from whatever occurs, may not enjoy the whole experience.

However, it is not necessary to enjoy a game or to do well in the playing of it to learn from it. I would hypothesize that whatever learning takes place happens not at the time of playing, but afterward, and only if some conscious effort is made to convert the experience into some knowledge or insight. In Simsoc, if students learn anything, it is because their participation produces a rich array of stimulus material centered around questions of social control and social order. Then, having played the game, they analyze and think about what happened in a manageably complex setting in which they were intimately involved. Students begin to construct their own picture of the Rube Goldberg device and to understand why obtaining compliance was so easy in one instance and so difficult in another. Once they have reached that point, it is not difficult to get them to consider the same questions about their own society or others which they have observed or read about.

One learns, then, not only from playing but also from discussing the experience and thinking about it afterward. The use of games for teaching seems to me to be most successful when the students are asked to make the jump from player to simulator. As players they accept certain constraints which are given in the rules and use resources to achieve certain objectives specified or suggested by the rules. When the students become simulators, the *rules themselves* become the resources and they can manipulate these resources—hypothetically or actually—to see whether the resulting process will take the form which they believe it will. Developing simulations is too enjoyable and valuable a learning experience to be hoarded by professors.

REFERENCES

COLEMAN, JAMES S.
1966 "Foundation for a theory of collective decisions." *American Journal of Sociology*, 71 (May), 615–627.

GAMSON, WILLIAM A.
1969a *Simsoc: A Participant's Manual and Related Readings*. New York: The Free Press.
1969b *Simsoc: An Instructor's Manual*. New York: The Free Press.

GUETZKOW, HAROLD, CHADWICK F. ALGER, RICHARD A. BRODY, ROBERT C. NOEL, AND RICHARD C. SNYDER
1963 *Simulation in International Relations: Developments for Research and Teaching*. Englewood Cliffs, N. J.: Prentice-Hall.

KORNHAUSER, WILLIAM
1959 *The Politics of Mass Society*. New York: The Free Press.

RASER, JOHN R.
1969 *Simulation and Society*. Boston: Allyn and Bacon.

SCHELLING, THOMAS C.
1960 *The Strategy of Conflict*. Cambridge, Mass.: Harvard University Press.

SHLOMO BREZNITZ
and
AMIA LIEBLICH

Chapter 5

How to Simulate If You Must:

Simulating the Dream-Work

Simdream, the game playfully discussed in this paper, is an example of a heuristic simulation. The theoretical insights that the authors gained during the design process led them to develop a game far different from the one they had envisioned at the outset. Breznitz and Lieblich describe their endeavor in light of an original conceptual framework for analyzing simulations. It is a most stimulating framework, yet it is also no doubt controversial.

—The Editors

PART II. CASE STUDIES   SECTION A. MAN SIMULATION

How to Simulate If You Must: Simulating the Dream-Work

THE LESSON

Let us reverse the chronological order and begin with lesson. In a nutshell it reads that *one should never believe a single word about simulation construction.* This does not imply that students of simulation construction are deliberately misleading the rest of us; the problem is that they just happen to be wrong. It is doubtful whether the surprise value of this discovery justifies our investment in time and effort, since a colleague with a clearer vision claims that he could have made the revelation long ago. The scientific basis for his intuition is, however, still lacking and the purpose of this paper is to furnish the proof.

The task of telling the story of a simulation from birth to maturity is extremely difficult. Try to ask the artist how he went about his painting, what sorts of arguments guided his hand, how his hand corrected his arguments, and whether it was the original idea of the picture that finally emerged from all his labors, or a completely distorted, different one. He is not in the position to answer these queries properly; neither is the writer or the poet able to do better. Consider the case of E. A. Poe's description of his deductive reasoning which produced "The Raven." All his arguments come to explain the final product rather than its origins:

> No one point in its composition is referable either to accident or intuition—that the work proceeded, step by step, to its completion with the precision and rigid consequences of a mathematical problem. (Poe, 1951, pp. 551.)

To put it mildly, this touches the absurd. But what about the scientist who is trained by competition and experience to keep records of his thoughts and observations? Is he in the position to describe the evolution of a particular idea? We contend that even he is unaware of most of it. Whatever our theory of creativity, unconscious inference must receive a major credit (Koestler, 1964).

There is another difficulty to be overcome. The polished final product is kept with care; its crude fragmented forerunners are readily disposed. Who will forfeit the pleasure of throwing these drafts into the waste basket? The temptation is too great, and the alternatives look too much like bookkeeping.

It follows that as there is no substantial difference in this matter between the artist and the scientist; the question as to where the simulation constructor belongs becomes secondary. A safe statement would be that some developers are more scientific than others. On the whole, however, we view the non-scientific, artistic aspects as particularly important. Since there is not yet any theory of simulation games available, everyone is very much on his own. Yet, a set of commonly-accepted generalities seems to be in circulation.

Which are the accepted "truths" that by consensus became unchallengable? We would like to deal with four statements that are commonly accepted by the expanding family of simulation designers (as we know them).

I. *Before constructing a simulation, one should learn as much as possible about the phenomenon to be simulated.*

The advantage of knowledge is self-evident, and to be against it is to be for sin. Learning at the start saves trouble later, so the scientist must do his homework properly. Because some areas of research require more study than others, there is a corollary to this maxim that reads:

Ia. *The more abundant the available information about a phenomenon, the better it is suited for simulation.*

The prerequisite for maximal knowledge implies, therefore, which among several possible ventures a simulation designer should choose, in addition to how he should prepare for the venture. In brief; out of ignorance only ignorance can come, and woe to the amateur. You have been warned!

The second truism claims that:

II. *The more one knows about other simulations, the better he is equipped to build his own.*

This too seems self-evident to the point of triviality. After all, why should one replicate one's fellows' mistakes? By studying their finished products a designer may learn a lot and occasionally even get an original idea applicable to his own problems. This implies that all simulations have some things in common, and that these are worth study. Thus the third truth:

III. *Verisimilitude is a virtue "devoutly to be wished."*

The external resemblance between the simulated phenomenon and the roles and laws of the game reduces the chances of some alien factor entering into the system and spoiling the works. The concern over verisimilitude is so great that it almost serves as an encompassing criterion of success in simulation construction, a measure of validity. If the simulation cannot be proved valid, it should at least look so.

And last but not least:

IV. *A game simulation is just a means for studying a phenomenon and not a goal in its own right.*

This obvious, since we claim to use games for the purpose of advancing our knowledge in respectful legitimate areas of study. A model is just a model to be discarded the moment it is proved wrong, and the sooner the better. Hence, simulation games are nothing but a method of investigation that should be judged strictly upon their merits in relation to the real phenomenon they simulate. To have any vested interests in the product is not only beside the point; it is wrong.

Thus ends our short list of some of the generalities which are often accepted without question. And because at present there is no theory of game simulation available, the arguments for and against any relevant statement about the topic are just a set of logically disconnected ideas. In order to make the task before us easier, we will now propose a preliminary framework of analysis. Although it is not a complete and formal theory of simulation, it may make some of the central issues clearer and better suited for systematic analysis and reevaluation.

A PRELIMINARY FRAMEWORK FOR THE ANALYSIS OF SIMULATION

When we deal with simulation the three things which are in the focus of our interest are (1) that which is being simulated, (2) that which simulates it, and (3) the relationship between the two. Let us, therefore, right at the start, attempt to conceptualize and illustrate some of the properties of these problem areas.

The Simulandum

The simulandum is the phenomenon of interest to the scientist that has already been partially explored. At the same time, for various reasons such as its complexity, rarity, or cost, it does not lend itself to thorough investigation. Some of its elements, part of its structure, or some of the relevant facts about it are still unknown. This is the situation concerning the phenomenon under study at the stage when the behavioral scientist decides that simulation may be of help. It then becomes the object of simulation, or the *simulandum.*

The Simulans

The number of ways to simulate any sufficiently complex phenomenon is practically unlimited. The very nature of a simulation implies that there is no logically necessary correspondence between a simulandum and a particular system that is devised to simulate it. Such a system, or *simulans,* is but a sample from a large population of possible solutions to the same problem. A simulans, however, is a coherent system in its own right, and is at least partially independent of the simulandum.

Unit of Analysis

The unit of analysis is an element of the system. Such an element is a molar statement about the structure, appearance, or function of a system. Take as an example the system of nuclear family. Some of its elements would be the role of a parent, the role of a child, sex division, age division, the fact that parents provide for children, etc. In other words, any characteristic of the nuclear family that is relevant to the way the system operates would be regarded as an element of the system.

The various elements are by no means on the same level of abstraction. Indeed, some may partially overlap with others and constitute a hierarchical arrangement. Some elements are descriptions of structure; others describe roles, people, or empirical evidence. Because these analytical elements are molar statements, one can never be sure that they are actually elementary. It is possible that they might be subdivided into more elementary statements about the system. It follows that the unit of analysis is to a large degree arbitrary and depends upon the particular approach a given scientist has to the problem. Granted that the unit of analysis is relative to its user, the only prerequisite is that it should be spelled out, and that it should be consistent over the simulandum and the simulans.

Correspondence

What is the relationship or *correspondence* between the simulandum and the simulans? In what respect should they correspond? Are there any general features or rules of correspondence that have to be universally observed? *Correspondence can be defined as the existence of common elements in the two systems.* The larger the overlap between the elements, the stronger the correspondence.[1] The basic analytical framework presented here appears schematically in Figure 1.

The elements which are common to both systems form the *area of correspondence.* Relating this area to the total area of both systems defines the *ratio of correspondence.* Let the area of what is being simulated, the simulandum, be (A), the area of the simulation itself, the simulans, be (B), and the area of correspondence be (AB); we then have that:

$$\text{Ratio of Correspondence} = \frac{k(AB)}{(A)+(B)}$$

Where k is a constant of proportionality between the sizes of A and B; if A=B, then k=2. The ratio of correspondence varies from zero to one, and can serve as the index of the resemblance between the simulandum and the simulans. Since the area of elements is an analytical abstraction which is very difficult to translate into operational terms, the index is

[1] This statement needs to be qualified to include a weighting mechanism, since the elements are not of the same importance.

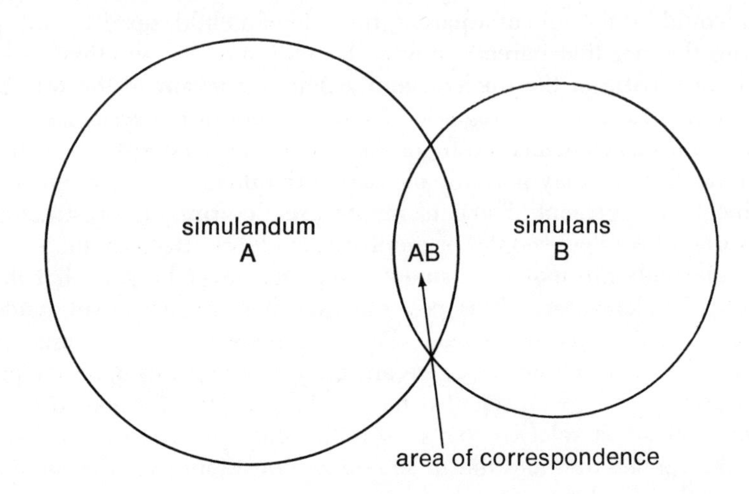

Figure 1: Schematic representation of the analytical framework

unlikely to have practical use. Theoretically, however, *the ratio of correspondence is the definition of the validity of the simulation.* The higher that ratio is, the greater the validity of the simulation. Thus the best simulation is no simulation at all: simulandum equals simulans, and the ratio of correspondence is one. It further follows that *simulation is in principle an invalid operation.*

For a simulation to be of any substantial value, the advantage of simplification must outweigh the cost of diminishing validity. For whatever be the particular aim of simulation, a central feature of the attempt must be the simplification of the simulandum. The aspects in which the simplification occurs can be different and many, but the principle must be observed if the simulation is to serve any purpose at all. It follows that the area of the simulans should be always smaller than that of what is being simulated. The formula (1-B/A) defines the *ratio of simplification.* This ratio varies between zero and one and can serve as the index of the practical advantage of the simulation.

Types of Elements

We must distinguish four types of elements:

(1) Corresponding elements (AB). These are the elements which are deliberately simulated and exist in both systems.

(2) Simulandum-specific elements (A-AB). These are the unsimu-

lated elements of the referent system being simulated. They should be unimportant.[2]

(3) Simulans-specific elements (B-AB). All the elements which do not exist in the referent system being simulated and do exist in the simulation are of this category. These elements pose a great danger to the validity in the simulation, since they may change the context of the corresponding elements. In some cases, such as game simulations, the simulation-specific elements are more specifically defined and include the game properties. The game characteristics of a simulation are always in this category of elements (unless the simulandum itself is a game).

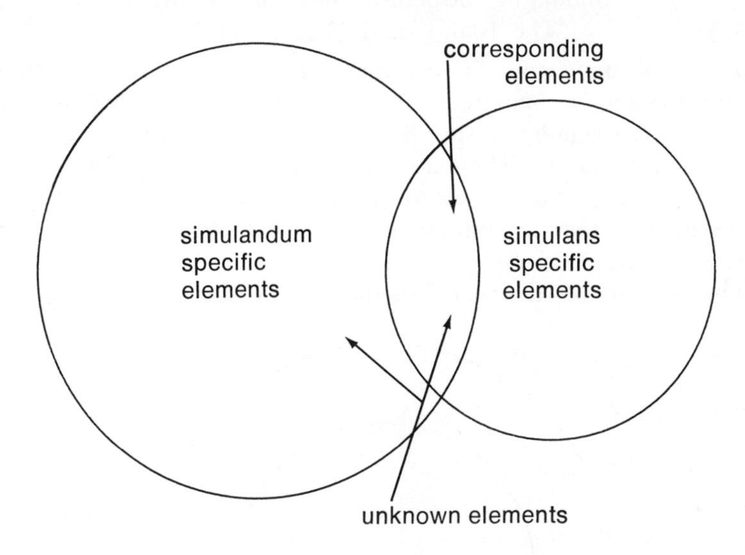

Figure 2: Types of elements

(4) Unknown elements (A_x). There are elements in the referent system which are still unknown to the behavioral scientist. Their existence may actually be the main reason for constructing the simulation. If (A_x) are important features of a system, they can be the source of the complexity and the difficulties with its analysis. This brings us to the most basic problem of many simulations: If the purpose of a simulation is to help us understand a hitherto unknown element of a system, we must

[2] In some instances one may use game simulation as a test of the importance and relevance of these elements: "A game typically will include only some of the variables considered in theory. If, nevertheless, the development of play corresponds with known real life patterns, the importance of the additional variable becomes questionable." (Schild, 1968, p. 152).

make sure that such an element has its corresponding counterpart in the simulation, i.e., that it lies in the area of corresponding elements (AB). But "there's the rub," for *how can one simulate an unknown element?* In order to be able to do so we must have at least some partial knowledge about the nature of the unknown elements, and their probable whereabouts in the system. As we shall see at a later stage, this prerequisite delineates the range of problems that are best suited for simulation.

The different types of elements are schematically presented in Figure 2.

Simulating Structures and Outputs or: "The Island" and "The Bridge"

There is one way to minimize the simulans-specific (B-AB) elements. Computer simulations are the extreme case of this effort, and they reduce the simulation-specific elements to zero. Figure 3 presents this case which may be labelled as the case of "the island." In this case (AB)=(B), the ratio of correspondence k(AB)/(A+B) becomes kB/(A+B), and the ratio of simplification 1-(B/A) equals the ratio of simulandum-specific elements to total elements.[3]

The opposite of "the island" is the case of "the bridge." (Figure 4.)

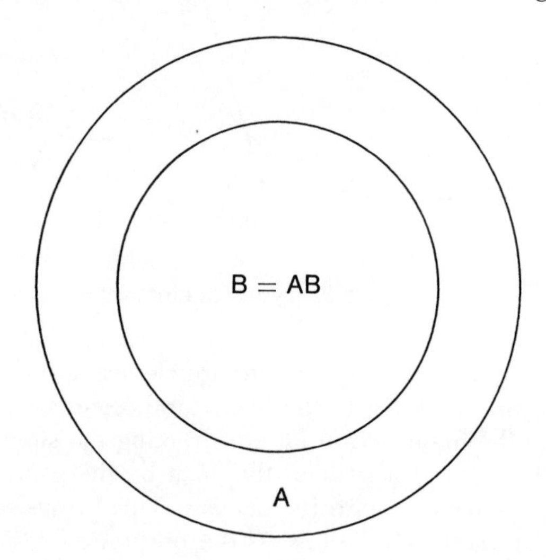

Figure 3: The case of "The Island"

[3] Important work has been done with this type of simulation (e.g., Colby, 1963; Uhr, 1960). Since our special interest lies in the domain of game simulation, the case of "the island" is not representative because of the simulation-specific elements of games.

Here we have a simulandum and a simulation with no direct correspondence of structural elements at all. The correspondence is indirect, being mediated by the *outputs* of both systems. The empirical outputs are the same, and they serve as a bridge between the two. Whereas "the island" is the ideal-type of a simulation of structure, "the bridge" is an ideal-type of a simulation of outputs. Theoretically, the ratio of correspondence, and hence the validity of the simulation, is zero.

However, we should remember that this is only an ideal abstraction. In any concrete instance in which the outputs of two systems resemble each other there is probably some hidden structural correspondence of which we are unaware at the moment. In other words, *two things that look alike are probably more alike than they look.*

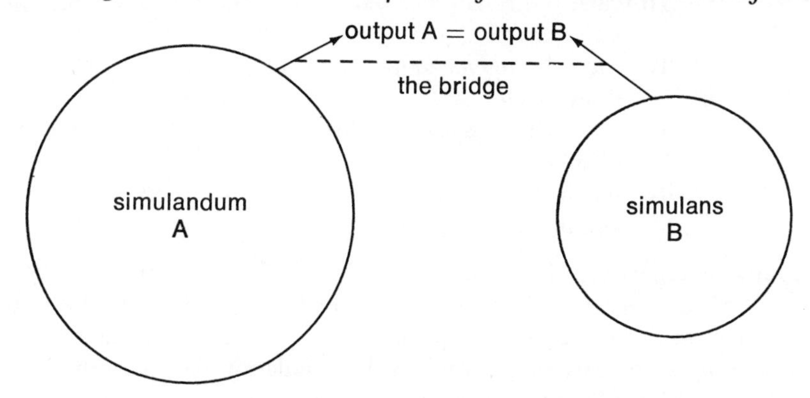

Figure 4: The case of "The Bridge"

For example, if a product of a machine resembles a hand-made product, one may speculate that the structure of the machine or its plan of operation (Miller, Galanter, Fribram, 1960) resembles those of the human producer. Of course, in many instances the structural similarities are apparent already before the machine is developed, and may be the basis for its construction.

Given the two ideal-types, any simulation can be placed somewhere in between. A simulation can be based on both the structural and the output resemblance to different degrees.

The Aims of Simulation and Their Implications

Much has been written on the various purposes for which a simulation is constructed (e.g., Guetzkow, 1962; Kibbee, Craft and Nanus, 1961; Boocock and Schild, 1968). It is our claim that the particular aim of a simulation is one of the major factors that determine the way it should be built. To put this even in stronger terms, at all stages of analysis the aim of a simulation should be taken into serious consideration. The various aims are, therefore, defined in a pedantic way. Using Guttman's (1959) *facet analysis,* the aims of a game simulation are defined in a mapping sentence which has two facets with two elements each. The mapping sentence reads:

"An aim of a simulation is to teach the (researcher/player) more about the (theory/empirical facts) of the simulandum."

Let us name the facet of Subject (S), and the facet of Object (O). Four different aims can now be defined:

1. To teach the *researcher* more about the *theory* of the simulandum (S_1O_1)
2. To teach the *player* more about the *theory* of the simulandum (S_1O_1)
3. To teach the *researcher* more *empirical facts* about the simulandum (S_1O_2)
4. To teach the *player* more *empirical facts* about the simulandum (S_2O_2)

A simple comparison of the four reveals that the aims of simulations have varying degrees of similarity. For example, (S_1O_1) is closer to (S_1O_2) than to (S_2O_2). This is of special interest when the specific aim of a simulation is not very clear or when the simulation has more than one aim. It would be difficult to conceive of a simulation which aims at two completely different purposes. This is not to claim that every simulation has only one fixed aim, but that if there are more aims they should be as closely related as possible.

Let us illustrate some of the implications of one of the aims for the actual process of simulations construction. In the case of a simulation for teaching empirical facts (S_2O_2), the problem of generalization becomes of central importance. To what extent will the experience with the simulation transfer into the context of the simulandum? Will familiarity with the Community Response Game (Inbar, 1968) facilitate adaptive behavior if an actual disaster takes place? This is the crucial test of any simulation that aims to teach the player. Its immediate implication is that the number of corresponding elements should be as high as possible. Transfer of training is a direct function of the ratio of correspondence. This may be one of the reasons which make the stress on verisimilitude a frequent feature of these simulations. The different players may be called parents, children, policemen, telephone operators, or congressmen. Such additional correspondence makes for easier generalization.

There are, however, some pitfalls in this practice which will be analyzed at a later stage.

Enlarging the ratio of correspondence for generalization purposes is not without its price. The greater the correspondence, the smaller the ratio of simplification. In other words, the closer the resemblance between the simulans and the simulandum, the smaller the practical gain from the simulation. Then why not teach the simulandum directly? *It is, therefore, between the correspondence and the simplification that the battle for a teaching simulation is fought.*

The need for a high ratio of correspondence reflects itself in the strategy of validation that is adopted by the scientists. There is an interesting dilemma concerning the validation of the simulans. Given the empirical knowledge about the simulandum, should all of it be transferred into the simulation, or should an important part of it be left untouched so that it can serve as a criterion of validation? In simulations to be used for teaching there is a strong argument for the use of all the information that is available, in order to enlarge the ratio of correspondence. When the aim of a simulation is research, the opposite argument prevails.

With this argument, we finish our brief sketch of a framework for the analysis of simulation, which is the serious part of this chapter. In a happier note we are now ready to question the plausibility of the "truths" that have been presented in the opening section.

THE DIALECTICS OF SIMULATION

THESIS I: Before constructing a simulation, one should learn as much as possible about the phenomenon to be simulated.

ANTITHESIS I: Simulation construction is a two-way street.

During the construction of a simulation ideas flow in both directions: from our knowledge of the simulandum to the attempted simulation and vice versa. We see some of the simulandum's latent characteristics, and may come to understand some of its previously unnoticed intricacies. Sometimes things which appeared clear and simple become mixed up, and new problems are formulated. This may lead to another attempt to simulate, and so on. Not only is the process a two-way street, but this sort of learning about the simulandum is of a special nature (and it would be a waste to miss it). The conclusion is simple: Instead of trying to learn everything possible about the simulandum before attempting to simulate it, one can learn best through the attempts themselves. Even if we did decide to do the homework "properly," its limitations would soon become apparent. Thus, there are no simple shortcuts that can be accomplished a priori before trying at least a vicarious simulation.

THESIS IA: The greater the available information about a phenomenon, the better it is suited for simulation.

ANTITHESIS II: In order to be enjoyable a new game should be different from other games.

If the gentle reader forgave us all our previous sins, this may be the point at which his outrage will finally convince him that this chapter is unworthy of his attention. How can one agree with the hints of abuse implicit in the above antithesis? After all, behavioral scientists learn from one another; they never imitate. Yet we have observed that while the phenomena which are simulated are very diverse, their simulations are surprisingly more similar. After playing four or five simulation games, one feels the differences between them blur and gradually vanish.

Some of the reasons for this situation are more obvious than others. For instance, the obsession with quantification turns everything into points: status points, satisfaction points, anxiety points—or, as in our own simulation, censorship points, tension points, and what-not points. Another factor may be the misleading appearance of the final product of a simulation. The study of the development of simulations likely would reveal that at various stages of their labors behavioral scientists demonstrate a richness of ideas and creative originality which is not necessarily visible in the final product. The thesis should, therefore, read as follows: the more one knows about the *case histories* of other simulations, the better he is equipped to build his own. In other words, *this book is really important.*

THESIS III: Verisimilitude is a virtue "devoutly to be wished."

ANTITHESIS III: "What's in a name? That which we call a rose by any other name would smell as sweet.

Now we are probably putting the case too mildly. The question of verisimilitude is not only whether it adds something or not, but to what degree it is harmless and does not mislead. If it is primarily structure that is being simulated, as in the extreme case of "the island," verisimilitude would be more appropriate than when output is being simulated, as in the case of "the bridge." In a way, the ideal bridge consists of simulation without awareness, which is the diametrical opposite of verisimilitude. An output of the simulation may be produced and may resemble the outputs of a simulandum *without the player's knowledge of what it is that he is simulating*, or that he is simulating at all. On the other hand, in simulations of structure the rules of the game very often disclose its purpose.[4]

There is, however, a clear danger in all this. If the player is called a farmer and the game is explicitly presented as a game which simulates an economy, he may bring into the game all his ideas and knowledge about economics and the behavior of farmers. He may then do certain things not because they grew naturally from the simulation, but because of this external experience with the simulandum. This danger is particularly great when the player himself is unaware of the external source of his ideas and behavior, and attributes them to the rules of the game. The scientist himself may not pay attention to this projection process, and mistakenly concludes that his simulation is even more valid than he thought, since it reproduces additional facts which are true of the simulandum. This pitfall may be termed *artificial validation mediated by verisimilitude.*

Using our analytical framework, this process may be presented as follows: The elements which contribute to the verisimilitude are themselves corresponding elements. So far so good. Some such elements are, due to their labeling properties, cognitively related to other elements. A corresponding element which is a concept (such as a name of a role) can serve as a jumping board for other, simulandum-specific elements introduced into the simulation. At a later stage they are recognized and identified as either "previously unknown elements" or as "an independent test of validity." In its extreme form this makes the simulation a role-playing situation, or a miniature replica of real life. Such indeed are many of the games children play. In their effort to master the complexities of adult life children simulate the adult world chiefly by resorting to verisimilitude.

This problem is closely linked to the choice of role-unit in the simulation. In practically all game simulations the role of a player is a coherent role which corresponds to a role in the simulandum. The scope of a role overlaps with a human unit. Taking as an example the Community Response Game, we have roles such as telephone operators, a policeman, a fireman, etc. All these are coherent roles and relate to human units. Nobody is playing the role of traffic jams, of panic, of anxiety, or of the disaster itself. Such roles may be, of course, completely inappropriate in this particular example,

[4] Interestingly enough, there has been practically no attempt at all to simulate without awareness, which further confirms the universal acceptance of verisimilitude as an asset.

but the point should be clear. By breaking the roles into artificial units, each representing a theoretical construct, the simulation can be transformed into something entirely different, verisimilitude can be practically eradicated, and a whole set of new issues can be investigated. The simulation of the dream work which will be described in the second part of this chapter is an attempt in this direction.

THESIS IV: A game simulation is just a means for studying a phenomenon, and not a goal in its own right.

ANTITHESIS IV: The spirit is willing, but the flesh is weak.

One may argue that this looks like giving too much credit to the spirit. Let us not forget for a moment the endless pains and frustrations one has to bear before giving birth to a simulation. The designer's attachment to it is, therefore, completely natural and obvious. It is not just one of the many possible ways to simulate a given thing; it is *our* simulation, and we definitely care about its future! True enough, during its construction we are only too familiar with its many imperfections, but by calling it the first version, or a preliminary attempt, we save the day. If we are lucky and find out that the validity of our simulation can be actually demonstrated for the world to see, the marriage between it and us is finally sealed.[5] In the interest of science, one is tempted to argue that a simulation should be immunized against such misfortune, and that its validity should remain untested, or preferably, untestable. This may keep open the two-way street that has been mentioned earlier. It is, however, only on rare occasions that after the construction of the simulation one remains genuinely interested in the simulandum. Consider the case of somebody who actually sold his simulation and is making some profits (repeat: profits) with it. His scientific spirit may still be willing, but his flesh, alas, is weak. Let us, therefore, face the truth. A game simulation is not just a means, but an end in itself. We assume that at this point the observant reader is guessing that the main purpose of our own simulation of dream-work is financial gain. He is one hundred per cent correct.

THE CASE HISTORY

Although we began this chapter by stating that "telling the story of a simulation, from birth to maturity, is extremely difficult" and that "one should never believe a single word about simulation construction," we

[5] Editor's note: The reader may note the incestuous metaphor of this paragraph.

will attempt this almost impossible task and describe some steps in the construction of our simulation. We shall use this description to illustrate some of the points made in the first part of this chapter; the rest depends upon the reader's will to believe.

The Rise and Fall of the Great Simulation

Our starting point was the attempt to simulate the psychoanalytic theory of personality. In simulating the structure of personality according to psychoanalytic theory, we confronted a rather complicated simulandum. Psychoanalytic theory, even if limited only to the Freudian version, is so complex that no single study may hope to investigate it thoroughly. Many of its elements are unknown, contradictory, or do not lend themselves to direct observation. We could not and did not claim maximal knowledge of the simulandum; on the contrary, to a certain degree it was our ignorance that drove us into this venture. We looked for a tool that might help us teach the theory to others but very soon found that we were dealing with a tool that might help *us* understand the theory better. Thus, the aims of the simulation were of types (S_1O_1) and (S_2O_1) as defined above, namely "to teach the researcher and the player more about the theory of the simulandum." These being our aims, we first attempted to simulate the structure of the simulandum in a way that would achieve maximum correspondence.

At the start the task seemed very easy and the theory quite clear. The first simulation included the following elements: the roles of Id, Ego, and Superego, their resources, aims, and functions. In the game three players—Id, Ego, and Superego—coped with given instincts and environmental pressures and tried to arrive at a decision regarding their next step.

This simulation was soon dropped. In fact, while it resembled some bargaining simulations, its major drawback was *over*-correspondence. The simulation contained many of the necessary elements, but it lacked the gaming property (simulans-specific elements). People could have learned something from this simulation, but would hardly have enjoyed it. Essentially, the deficiency was that all the active roles in the simulans were in the Ego's part. We felt that we needed another simulation in which the focus of attention would be the Ego, and this second attempt turned out to be the "Great Simulation" or "The Monster" presented in Figure 5.

The game was to be played by two players: the Conscious Ego (CE) and the Unconscious Ego (UE) (Freud, 1964, Vol. 22, p. 78). This division may be considered as the most important element common to the two systems. From the simulandum's standpoint, the distinction be-

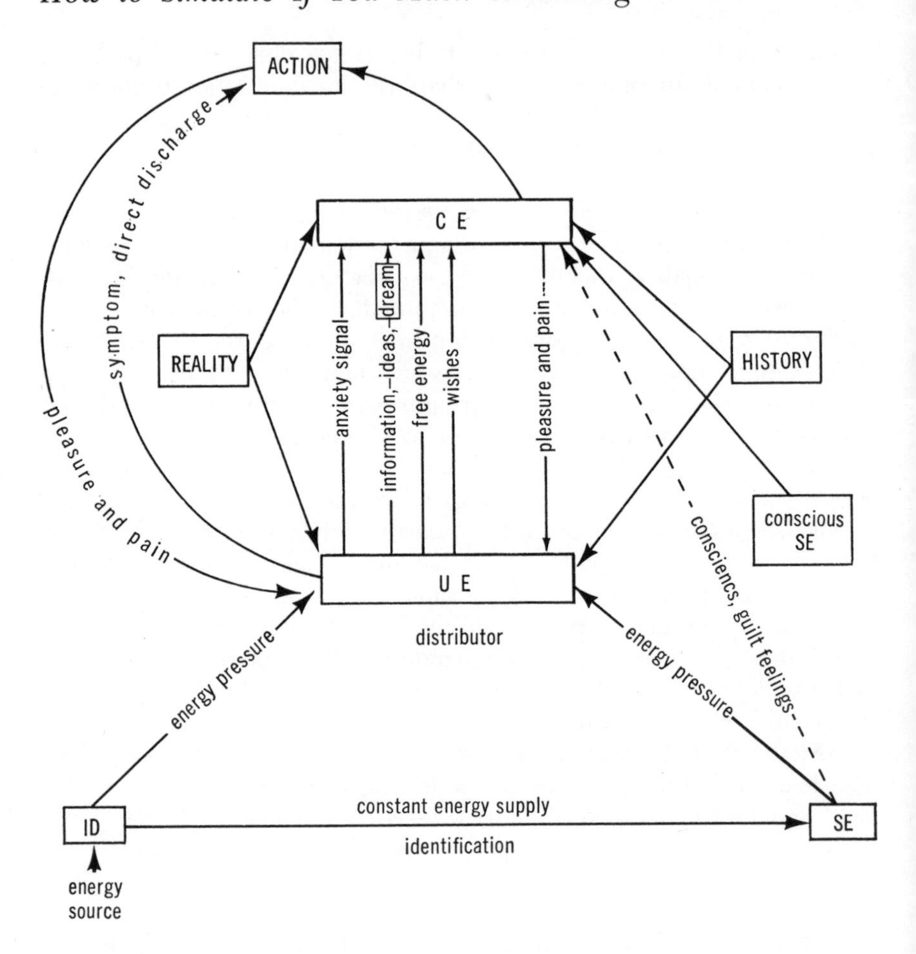

Figure 5: The "Monster"

tween the conscious and unconscious parts of the Ego is perhaps the greatest insight of Freud's theory. From the simulation's standpoint, this division enabled us to define two active roles in the game.

It would be very tedious to go into the details of this game. Suffice it to say that we apparently succeeded in our aim: to create a high correspondence between theory and game, at least with regard to the many details of the process. However, one simulation-specific element which was included to handle the game properties of the simulation led us to be less satisfied with the adequacy of the simulation in this form. Here we refer to the fact that UE and CE, who are two different players in the game, are two systems *within* the person according to the theory. It is naive to believe that two persons, posing as two parts of the same individual, will give in their behavior the "true" flavor of interaction within the person. Furthermore, UE's role must be played by a wakeful, conscious person—and the rules of unconscious behavior are totally alien to a wakeful, normal adult. These elements posed a great danger to the validity of the simulation.

After considerable effort The Monster was almost ready, except for the problem that the Unconscious acts according to primary process and the Conscious acts according to secondary process. Freud did not directly define the primary process, since a wakeful person has no access to this though form. In the simulation, however, we had to assign the role of UE to a wakeful person and had, therefore, to formulate explicitly his action rules. How to present a rational set of rules that will produce the most irrational of human products? When faced with this problem, two conclusions seemed evident: first, that The Monster cannot exist without primary-process action rules, and second, that the task of formulation of these rules is so important that it deserves a simulation of its own. Some attempts to formulate primary thought processes are known in the psychological literature (Arieti, 1948; Matte-Blanco, 1959), but these were not sufficient for our needs. We thus embarked upon the project of *Simdream* which is the subject of the next section.

The moral of the story so far reads: Some theories are for snobbish reasons made deliberately complex, so as to avoid being simulated.

SIMDREAM—AN ATTEMPT TO SIMULATE THE "DREAMWORK"

At this stage of our case history, the changed simulandum (with its focus on primary process) led to a different simulation technique: We attempted to simulate the *product* of a process, rather than the process itself or the structure determining the process. In other words, we looked for a rational set of rules that would produce artificial dreams. According to the claim that "two things that look alike are probably more alike than they look," we were also hoping to gain through our simulation some new insight or working hypotheses regarding dream theory and the actual nature of dreams.

In spite of our focus on the product, we had in mind the Freudian theory (Freud, 1964, Vols. 4–5) of the dream-work, and tried to create in the simulation a set of rules which would correspond as much as possible with the explicit elements of the simulandum. Simdream is, then, some mixture of "bridge" and "island" simulations.

The following are the corresponding elements and their functions in the game.

Ideas

These are the basic stuff that dreams are made of. Simdream has as its basic material a series of cards, each representing an idea. Ideas are grouped according to their common theme, such as Father, Mother, Friend, Animals, etc. Theoretically, a theme is a category of unconscious storage of all ideas related to it.

Aim of the Dream-Simulation of Tension and of Censorships

Dreams, as Freud postulated, are aimed at the reduction of unconscious tensions. These are repressed wishes and ideas which have been aroused by recent experience, and their direct expression will be strongly opposed by the Censor. By taking advantage of the weakening of the Censor during sleep, it is possible to reduce these tensions. But repressed ideas are usually anxiety-loaded, and expressing them directly, even in a dream, may arouse enough anxiety to endanger the sleep itself. In the simulans, one or more of the themes are chosen to be "tension-themes." By picking out an idea from a tension theme and using it for the dream, a constant amount of tension is reduced. Censorship and anxiety are simulated by attaching to each idea a censorship score. (These scores run from -10 to $+10$.)

Residues

These are ideas about recent events which have not yet undergone repression, and may be used as undangerous vehicles for more dangerous material. Accordingly, Simdream has a theme of residues, each residue having a small negative censorship score.

The creation of the primary version of Simdream was, in fact, based mainly on these corresponding elements. Following the composition of the rules of the game, we may be able to point to some other common elements that emerged.

In its first version Simdream is a solitaire. The player is confronted with the themes, some of which are tension themes. He does not have the information about the content and the censorship score of any particular idea prior to its selection. The only information he has is the sum total of censorship scores for all ideas in a given theme. Some themes are, therefore, more dangerous than others. Usually the tension-themes have particularly high censorship scores. The selection of the theme is determined by the player. *The selection of an idea within a theme, is however, random. This is the core of Simdream and may be considered either as a simulation-specific set of elements or as an hypothesis regarding the "undiscovered country" of unconscious thought processes.* The player draws ideas from the different themes, and the amount of tension reduction and the cumulative censorship scores are noted. This string of ideas is the basic simulated dream, and we may turn now to additional corresponding elements.

Ending a Game

In the first version of Simdream, there are three different possible endings:

(1) The anxiety threshold has been crossed, which means the player has awakened due to anxiety. This will happen if the cumulative censorship score has been higher than a certain positive value known beforehand to the player. An anxiety dream does not reduce any tension in the simulation, and tension is re-attached to the particular theme from which the last idea has been chosen.

(2) If the censorship has been successfully avoided by obtaining a censorship score below a given threshold, the dream is successfully terminated. If there are any additional tensions to be reduced, the player may immediately start a new dream.

(3) If neither of the above two possibilities did occur, the dream ends after the selection of 10 ideas. This is one of the simulation-specific elements, and it has no direct rationale in the simulandum. It enables us, however, to keep the length of dreams within limits and allows for better interdream comparisons.

Secondary Revision

It is only in rare circumstances that the final product of the dream work consists of discrete ideas following one another. The operation of secondary revision arranges the raw material of the dream into a partially coherent unity. Concerning this operation Freud writes: "The easiest way of forming an idea of its nature is to suppose, though the supposition probably does not meet the facts, *that it only comes into operation AFTER the dream-content has already been constructed.* Its function would then consist in arranging the constituents of the dream in such a way that they form an approximately connected whole, a dream-composition." (Freud, 1964, Vol. 5, p. 666.) From this and from other passages it is not clear just when exactly the operation of secondary revision takes place. In Simdream we are trying out two different ways. One set of instructions tells the player to arrange the material in a connected framework simultaneously with the generation of the dream itself. This means that he is revising the dream without having access to any of the future ideas that would fall to his lot. The second approach is for the player to wait until the dream ends and then go over its constituent ideas and attempt to integrate them. In both versions the player must keep to the sequential order of the ideas. The selected phrases should be changed as little as possible during the secondary revision, but if the coherence of the story requires it, minor changes are allowed. The player is encouraged to add as little as possible to the raw material, and try to achieve integration by good editing rather than by adding new ideas.

We must confess that this is the weakest part of Simdream and might, perhaps, be discarded altogether. The previous steps of dream production were completely formalized and can, in fact, be played by a computer. The secondary revision is a creative product and can be achieved in many different ways. Players who are generally more creative are also capable of producing more "dreamy" dreams when revising any set of selected ideas. It is probable that the human player brings into the gaming situation his expectations regarding the image of a dream, and revises his string of ideas according to this implicit knowledge more than according to out set of instructions. In principle it should be possible to formulate exact rules for this stage also, but this task will be left for another version of Simdream.

Displacement and Condensation

Displacement and condensation are descriptive concepts used by Freud to summarize various strategies of compromise between the unconscious urges seeking release and the forces of repression censoring these attempts (Freud, 1964, Vol. 22). Although not explicitly included in the basic rules of the game, we felt that any worthwhile simulans of the dream-work must include these phenomena. How do they appear in Simdream? Analyzing the possibilities within the framework of the simulation, we discovered that displacement is a basic phenomenon, whereas condensation may occur only at the stage of the secondary revision. The selection of ideas within a theme is random. This makes it costly for a player to utilize only the tension-themes, since their censorship scores are relatively higher than those of other themes. In order not to cross the anxiety threshold it would be rational for him to select ideas from themes with a better over-all censorship score or from the day's residues. This gives him a chance to improve his cumulative score and once more return to the dangerous theme to continue the task of tension reduction. These ideas from non-tension themes serve the purpose of concealing the source of the dream and simulate displacement. The greater the number of ideas selected from outside the tension-themes the greater the amount of displacement in the dream.

The notion of condensation can be translated to read as follows: maximal tension reduction with the minimal number of ideas. Since the tension reduction of each loaded idea is constant, this additional principle is simulated by evaluating any amount of tension reduction according to the number of ideas selected. Thus, for instance, it would be safe but uneconomical to utilize all the residues that are available. The art of dreaming becomes a rather risky venture and the player has to be good at "brinkmanship." But the main art of condensation is apparent in the secondary revision, where the player is reinforced for the shortest possible version, even the expression of several adjacent ideas in one image. These hunches about the theory of the simulandum gained through exploring the simulation clearly demonstrate our earlier points about the importance of learning during the construction of the simulation, even before it was ever tested out.

Symbolization

Finally, it is worthwhile to discuss one of the simulandum-specific elements which, to the layman, is one of the main points in psychoanalytic theory of dreams: the apparent content of the dream is a symbolic means to convey latent content. Freud postulated some universal symbols and others which are idiosyncratic. In the first version of Simdream no provision was directly made for this element. It is, however, obvious that we have succeeded in simulating dreams even without this element. (Chapter 1 contains a detailed example of one simulated dream.) In the next version, we may deal directly with this problem. The possible solution could be as follows: for each idea we may have an alternative symbolic expression on a card attached to it. A player may choose to use this symbolic alternative when his cumulative censorship score is high, and thus reduce the danger of awakening, but at the same time discharge a smaller amount of tension. Another improvement may be to ask each player to create his own list of the day's residues. He, then, may try to camouflage a dangerous idea by expressing it through one of his residues. Another player, the Judge, will decide how successful was the disguise, and a third player, the Analyst, may later try to analyze the dream into its primary givens and ideas.

Let us now summarize the critical periods in the history of our simulation:

1. Decided to make money.
2. Thought that Freudian theory is sufficiently popular to suit our purpose.
3. Stereotypically divided the personality into three roles: Id, Ego, and Super-Ego.
4. It didn't work. Id and the Ego had nothing interesting to do. A boring game.
5. The conscious ego (CE) and the unconscious ego (UE). Much better. Two players with a lot of dynamism between them.
6. Too much dynamism, impossibly complicated. A monstrous game.
7. How to rationalize the irrational? How should UE play?
8. That is an interesting problem. Let us try out hand with the primary process.
9. Dreams are the chief product of the primary process. Besides, everybody dreams. Remember the money.
10. Partial randomness is the solution to the primary process.
11. Simdream is a dream, is a dream.

REFERENCES

ARIETI, S.
1948 "Special logic of schizophrenic and other types of autistic thought." *Psychiatry*, 11, 325–328.

BOOCOCK, S. S. AND E. O. SCHILD (eds.)
1968 *Simulation Games in Learning*. Beverly Hills, Calif.: Sage Publications, Inc.

BREZNITZ, SCHLOMO AND AMIA LIEBLICH
1970 "The Unconscious plays patience: An attempt to simulate the dream-work." *Simulation and Games*, 1, 5–17.

COLBY, K. M.
1963 "Computer simulation of a neurotic process." In S. S. Tomkins and S. Messick (eds.), *Computer Simulation of Personality*. New York: John Wiley and Sons, Inc.

FREUD, S.
1964 *The Interpretation of Dreams*. Standard edition, Vols. 4–5. London: The Hogarth Press.

FREUD, S.
1964 *New Introductory Lectures to Psycho-Analysis*. Standard edition, Vol. 22. London: The Hogarth Press.

GUETZKOW, H. (ed.)
1962 *Simulation in Social Science: Readings.* Englewood Cliffs, N. J.: Prentice-Hall, Inc.

GUTTMAN, L.
1959 "A structural theory for intergroup beliefs and action." *American Sociological Review,* 24, 318–328.

INBAR, M.
1968 "Individual and group effects on enjoyment and learning in a game simulating a community disaster." In S. S. Boocock and E. O. Schild (eds.), *Simulation Games in Learning.* Beverly Hills, Calif.: Sage Publications, Inc.

KIBBEE, J. M., C. J. CRAFT, AND B. NANUS
1961 *Management Games.* New York: Reinhold Publishing Corporation.

KOESTLER, A.
1966 *The Art of Creation.* London: Pan Books.

MATTE-BLANCO, I.
1959 "Expression in symbolic logic of the characteristics of the system UCS." *The International Journal of Psychoanalysis,* 40, 1–5.

MILLER, G. A., E. GALANTER, AND K. H. PRIBRAM
1960 *Plans, the Structure of Behavior.* New York: Henry Holt and Company, Inc.

POE, E. A.
1951 *The Philosophy of Composition.* The Viking Portable Library. New York: The Viking Press.

SCHILD, E. O.
1968 "The shaping of strategies." In S. S. Boocock and E. O. Schild (eds.), *Simulation Games in Learning.* Beverly Hills, California: Sage Publications, Inc.

UHR, L.
1960 "Intelligence in computers: The psychology of perception in people and in machines." *Behavioral Science,* 5, 177–182.

FREDERICK L.
GOODMAN

Chapter 6

Coaching: An Example in Nested Games

Oftentimes the simulation of a very simple process requires special ingenuity. The author started with a practical aim: to develop a training device for school counselors. Early in the design process he concluded that his aim would best be achieved by simulating essentially the process of communication in advisory settings. To achieve this modest goal he found that he needed recourse to such solutions as a game within a game, individual roles played by teams, and an overall game lacking a clear goal. Substantively, the game is relevant not only for those interested in the communicative process in situations defined as largely cooperative, but also for those studying formal organizations.

—The Editors

Coaching: An Example in Nested Games

The origin of this simulation lies in a request to develop a training device for use by school counselors concerned with improving the information systems which serve them and their counselees. From the outset it was clear that the project could be of interest both to those who were primarily concerned with counseling and to those who were primarily concerned with the design and operation of information systems. What was not clear at the outset was the idea that counseling is very much a matter of improving the flow of information to and from counselees and that any process of information system development is very much a matter of improving one's ability to counsel others.

The breadth or generality inherent in the simulation probably stems from the designers' conscious reluctance to begin by specifying the objectives of the simulation in a detailed way. It may be accurate to say that the simulation developed more as a matter of emphasizing what it *should not be* than what it *should be*. To illustrate this point, early discussions led to the notion that the simulation should be relatively "pure," but that assertion is meaningless until one dwells on the kinds of contamination which should be avoided. Most important was the idea that the simulation should not be contaminated by the assumption that the designers knew how counseling really should take place. Similarly, the terminology associated with any particular sets of people, records, tests or goals should not be permitted in the simulation.

Frustrating though these restrictions were, they forced the examination of the most basic elements of any counseling situation: a set of people doing roughly what children in school do and another set of people charged with improving the performance of the first set. Viewed another way, the elements were taken to be the *images* which members of each set had of themselves and of each other and the *messages* which flowed from person to person with the potential for modifying the images. Although this view of the counseling process may seem a bit abstruse at first, it has the virtue of turning out to be simple yet quite comprehensive. Certainly every person must have some image of himself: who he is, where he is, how he thinks he is seen by others, and so forth. It is also likely that the image that person A has of person B is different from person B's image of himself. Of course, B is likely to have an image of A which differs from A's image of himself. All this is likely to be true whether both A and B are students, or both are counselors, or A is a student and B is a counselor. In addition, if A and B can be described as "communicating with each other" it is likely that their images of themselves and of each other are changing as a result of the messages which are passing between them.[1] This view makes no claim for the accuracy

[1] Much more can be said about the interaction of images and messages, and much of it has been said in Boulding (1956).

of the images one holds of himself or even for the notion that the process of image building is a conscious phenomenon. The challenge posed here is not to write comprehensively about such a conceptual framework but to acknowledge the role that such a framework played in the development of the simulation and proceed to a description of the means by which such matters were operationalized in the simulation.

OVERVIEW

The most important single step in the development of this approach was the realization that the goal of having one set of people help another set might be achieved very effectively if the overall activity were viewed as "a game within a game." The core game (the game within the total game) should occupy the set of people analogous to students; the others, the counselors, could then play at improving the performance of those engaged in playing the core game. The fact that the role of the counselors is left ambiguous, that they are not simply winning points by playing the core game but are left to determine the nature of the game they are playing and what it means to win it, became the major feature of the overall simulation. The choice of the core game remained a critical factor, but the essential character of the simulation was set when it became clear that it was going to be possible to build a simulation which did not require the designer to specify the criteria for victory, but to leave this decision, in every run of the simulation, to those involved as players. This was the route to the "pure" game referred to above, a game that did not assume that the designers really knew how counseling should take place. The importance of this aspect of the simulation emerged only slowly in the minds of those associated with the game. It now seems overwhelmingly important for people who counsel students to examine the nature of the activities they are engaged in, to establish their own criteria for success. The only claim made for this simulation is that those playing it will end by discussing what it really means to be a good counselor, what an effective information system should do, what the difficulty of actually providing the services one envisions, and so on. The game itself quickly recedes in importance during the discussions which follow its play, and people frequently talk directly about their own jobs and their own problems.

It was quite conceivable that any one of a variety of games could be used in the role of "core game," depending on the nature of the situation one faced. Given the view of counseling to be dealt with here, the quest was for a game which allowed one to deal as directly as possible with the unfortunately vague concept of "image." It looked as though some sort of logic game might do, a simple version of checkers, for example. The reason for starting in this direction was the notion that the closest synonym to "image" which might conceivably yield to operational or behavioral definition was the word "strategy." My strategy vis-a-vis an opponent would, of necessity, involve an image of where I was relative to him, what I had done and could do, what he had done and might do, what was worth doing, and so on. Similarly his strategy would involve his self-image and his image of me. As we communicated, that is, made moves against each other, these strategies might change. The "move" would be analogous to the "message" and the "strategy" would be analogous to the "image." In retrospect, the analogy seems far from perfect, but it proved to be useful in the design of the simulation.

The selection of a particular logic game came very rapidly. Within a day of the time that the word "strategy" had begun to play a key role in the design of the simulation, a conversation with Layman Allen, developer of *Wff 'N' Proof, Equations,* and other games, led to a quick solution to the problem. Allen immediately realized that the game called "Tac-tickle," developed by Harry D. Ruderman and marketed as one of the games in the *Wff 'N' Proof* series, would serve the purpose admirably. The accuracy of this insight illustates an important principle in the design of simulations that was to be learned many times over in the design of this particular one: there is no substitute for collaberation among like-minded people, each with an awareness of different games and different kinds of solutions to simulation problems.

"Tac-tickle" is a simple combination of tic-tac-toe (noughts and crosses) and checkers. Played on a board divided into five rows and four columns, each player gets four pieces. Instead of arranging them four in a row across either the top or the bottom of the board, each player places two at the top and two at the bottom. They are alternated so that if the top row contains them in the order A,B,A,B, the bottom row must read B,A,B,A. The game can be played with any kind of markers, such as coins, buttons, match sticks or pieces of paper. The pieces are moved one square at a time, taking turns moving either forward, backward, left or right, but not diagonally. The object of the game is to get three of your pieces in a row (in any direction including diagonally) before your opponent can do so. The reader should draw a board and play the game with someone to realize the engrossing nature of such a simple format.

When used as the "core game" in the counseling simulation, "Tac-tickle" is played by six players, each of whom has five boards in front of him. Continuing to refer to players by letters, this means that A sits with five boards in front of him, one being the board on which he may play with B, one being the board on which he may play with C, and so on for D, E, and F. In front of B, of course, are five boards for games with A, C, D, E, and F. Players C, D, E, and F are similarly equipped.

This general layout involving six players, analogous to six students, has remained stable from the time of the first conversation about "Tac-tickle" to the present. That each player should engage in games with others simultaneously, playing by announcing his moves to the opponent as he might if he were engaged in a game of checkers or chess by mail, was also immediately clear. Very early in the design stage, certainly before the first physical boards were drawn up, an important scoring principle was developed. In order to promote a style of interaction based on cooperation instead of competition, the principle of awarding, say, two points to any player who lost a game and five points to anyone who won a game was adopted. This would mean that two players might agree to take turns being beaten in order to accumulate seven points each in a relatively short time. Certainly, children in school cooperate as well as compete, and it seemed desirable to have them do so in the core game.

If one returns to the initial conceptual framework involving the word "image," one can see how player A has an image of B's board: the one right in front of him. He also has an image of "his" board in front of B. The two boards should be the same, at least if the boards started out in a matched fashion and if all the moves sent back and forth between the two were interpreted correctly. But this is only the simplest image that A can have of B and of his relationship to B. Assuming a game is underway between the two, there is not only the static image of where the pieces now are; there is a temporal or historical image of the way each piece got to its present position. There is an image of the future, characterized by statements such as "if I move there, he will move here," and so on. Then there are the general images that A has of B such as, "he's a good player, but I can beat him," or "we are partners in a sense and if I let him beat me this time, he will let me beat him next time and we'll both get quite a few points quickly," or "I won't play with him any more, he seems to be mixed up," or "he's the highest scoring player in the whole game; I wonder if I can beat him," and many, many other possible images. Clearly the format produced a promising range of inter-personal relations with which counselors might concern themselves. Many problems remained, however, before this germ of an idea became a full-fledged simulation.

It was not enough, for example, to assume that errors would creep into play as a result of poor listening, inaccurate statements, misinterpreted motives, or generalized "falling behind." All these possibilities for errors existed, but additional sources of potential errors had to be built in to make the counselor-counselee more realistic in the average play.

To do this the players were told that they could not safely make the assumption that the boards would always be set up in the "matched" fashion referred to above, a fashion which would allow each move to lead to an accurate corresponding move on the companion board (presuming both players followed instructions properly). The players were told that their boards would sometimes be confused "on purpose" (as explained later) to increase the probability of error—with the resulting need for clearheaded cooperation and help to sort out the problem.

DEVELOPMENT

No one can recapture exactly the order in which ideas emerged and fit into place en route to a finished work. Much of what seems quite orderly and rational when viewed in retrospect is likely to have been the result of stumbling trial and error. One thing is clear: the highest priority was given to actual trial runs of the simulation at early dates, rather than to completing the design in a theoretical sense before exposing it to practical trials. This approach required two things: first, access to people who were willing to give up two or three hours to trying the game, when there was a distinct possibility that it would not work very well; second, intensive effort on the part of people willing to make the artifacts necessary to try even the simplest of prototypes, when there was a distinct chance that a particular set of artifacts would be discarded after one trial. The fact that the final version of the simulation has more than 1,200 pieces which are moved on more than 150 small playing boards indicates the extent of this development commitment. Trial and error can be very expensive.[2]

It is difficult to state precisely how much time the development of the simulation required. From one point of view, the intensive development period took only two months, from the previously mentioned conversation with Layman Allen in mid-January to the first public play in mid-March, 1967. This work, however, had been preceded by about four

[2] Fortunately, this project had the support of Professor Garry Waltz of the University of Michigan, who was in a position to help with both requisites mentioned above: people to try the simulation and people to help make the artifacts. Indeed, it should be stressed that the project not only had his continued support, it was very much born out of his desire to see that something of the kind be created to help counselors and his insistance on the point already stressed: that assumptions about the nature of counseling should be carefully controlled and, if possible, avoided. Only through his skillful blending of resources, made available through his work with the American Personnel and Guidance Association, the guidance and counseling clearinghouse in the U. S. Office of Education's Educational Resources Information Center (ERIC) and other projects which he has spear-headed at the University of Michigan, could this project have survived the development period.

months of sporadic speculation about the nature of the simulation, during which the overall idea of "a game within a game" and the "image-message" format slowly evolved. At the other end, the first public play in March, 1967 did not mark the end of the development period. Play in the months which followed led to one minor improvement after another. It was not until June, 1968 that the present version, with its lightweight, easy-to-manage boards, was finally assembled. Given this history, the present version cannot be called the final version. The simulation is so open-ended in character that modifications and adaptations are likely to continue as long as there is any interest in the game.

WORKING OUT THE MODEL

The first trial run was based on the principles previously described, and played on paper boards with paper markers. At this stage the game used nine participants: six "students" to play the core game and three "counselors" to improve their performance. Practical and theoretical problems abounded. Students were told to make three moves per round, each against a different opponent. The reader will recall that each student may engage in games with every other student. To increase the sense of competition and cooperation, it was decided to force the players to ignore at least two players on any one round, hence the "three moves per round" rule. (This feature has remained in the current version.) Each move was written on a slip of paper, which was picked up by the game director, taken to a central board to be recorded on both sender's and receiver's boards, then shown to each of the counselors, and finally taken to the opposing student, who kept it. In the first session, a carbon copy of the message was retained by the student initiating the move. A's moves had to be completely delivered before B's could be collected, for B's move might be influenced by the nature of A's move. The mechanics were so cumbersome and the pacing so slow that the players found themselves thoroughly bored. Equally disastrous from a practical point of view, the paper slips used for markers had an unfortunate propensity to become hopelessly confused and finally (in a sense, mercifully) to blow away.

These were difficulties that one might confidently expect to solve, although the pacing problem did look extremely tough. A far more discouraging aspect of the first play was the affirmation of the fear that the counselors would not have a basis for advising the students or helping them in any way. There was a distinct possibility that they would know less than the players of the core game knew about what was transpiring or was likely to transpire. This difficulty was anticipated, of course, but the possible solutions to it needed considerable experimentation.

The basic advantage that counselors were to have had was to stem from the fact that they could see the "big picture": who was playing whom, what strategies were evolving, and so on. For this purpose, they were given copies of all the players' boards. Another advantage was to have stemmed from the fact that counselors were to be permitted to communicate more freely with other players than were the students, who were playing against each other. This advantage could be granted by virtue of an arrangement which has not yet been described. Apart from the announcements of moves on the part of players, there was to be no communication among players except in writing, and the written messages were to be paid for in roughly the fashion that one would use in sending a telegram. Counselors would simply be given more funds to pay for their messages than students would be given.

The notion of constraining communication among the players, both counselors and students, was introduced in order to develop many aspects of the simulation in addition to the one just mentioned. If attention is to be focused on the information system aspect of the game, players must be directly confronted with the notion that information is seldom, if ever, free. There are costs associated with generating, storing, processing and disseminating information. This idea was emphasized from the outset both by charging for certain types of messages and by putting limits on the amount of time that players were given to perform their tasks. Naturally, both these techniques had the effect of causing players to establish priorities, either explicitly or implicitly, for dealing with the problems they encountered.

The problem of giving the counselors an advantage over the players, so that players could benefit from their help, was also approached in another way. If the students could be led to make certain kinds of errors, the nature of which would be hidden from them but made known to the counselors, the counselors might be able to help sort out the difficulties arising from such errors. To avoid "contamination" of building in certain kinds of errors which could be resolved in pat, pre-conceived ways, the error source would have to be very general in character. To meet this need it was decided that the boards on which two players would compete, A's board B and B's board A for example, could occasionally be set up in such a way that any move announced by one player would have a slightly different effect on the two boards; that is, after the move the pieces on one board would be in a slightly different position from those on the other board. This is the way the confusion was set in "on purpose." The counselors would know how the boards were set initially; the players would not. (This idea has survived to the present, but with many modifications.)

Two problems arose immediately. If, on the one hand, many boards were set up in a fashion designed to produce confusion, the confusion was likely to become complete chaos very quickly. On the other hand, if the counselors knew about this possibility and realized its implications —which they were very likely to do—they would simply tell each player what his opponent's board looked like and thereby wipe out the whole advantage which they were supposed to have been given. A solution to these problems will be given in due course, but it would be getting well ahead of the chronological description of how the game was developed to discuss it here. In actual fact, attention was concentrated most heavily on solving the practical problems of the game, in order to permit the replays that might yield the insight that would lead to the solution of the theoretical problems.

Paper markers were used initially because games played "by mail," that is, on two different boards (instead of one board with each person reaching out and moving his own pieces), required that each of the four pieces be labeled. Each player was given square markers on which were written I, II, III, and IV for his own pieces and triangles similarly labeled for his opponent's pieces. (Roman numerals were used because initially the squares of the playing boards were numbered from 1 to 20 in Arabic numerals.) If heavier markers were to be used they would have had to be cut into shapes or colored and then labeled. Even so, heavy markers might easily slide, especially if future versions of the game required that the boards would have to be moved during play in order to expedite the transfer of information about the players' moves to the game director or the counselors.

At this point the ideas of using golf tees as markers and masonite peg-board for the playing boards was tried. The tees could be bought in two different colors to differentiate between a player's own pieces and those of his opponents. The tops would be large enough to mark, but the bottoms would be small enough to fit into the pre-formed holes. Large quantities could be purchased quite inexpensively (although, as it developed, not so easily—at least in January in Michigan).

The tees were bought and labeled using four figures: a dot, a square, a triangle, and a circle, instead of I, II, III, and IV, since the figures seemed to provide for easier discrimination when many tees were crowded fairly closely together. The counselor boards still remained an imposing sight, despite this improvement. If the array of two-hundred forty golf tees arranged on thirty playing boards in a space of roughly two feet by three feet was to be of help to anybody, still greater efforts in the direction of visual clarification would be needed. The task of moving the tees in response to the moves the players made was hard enough; the task of interpreting the board to see who needed what kind of assistance was staggering.

Two important but quite different steps were taken to overcome these difficulties. The first was to color-code the boards so that the board upon which player A played against B was the same color as the board upon which player B played against A. Every pair of boards was given a different color. It then became relatively easy to find corresponding boards and see if the markers were arranged in the same pattern. The other step involved a change in the organization of the game as well as in the materials. Instead of requiring each counselor to keep up his own set of boards, the role of the counselor was given to a team. This group of from four to ten players was given one counselor's board and told that they were to work as a team to improve the performance of the six players of the core game. Competition between counselors was maintained by playing with two or three teams of counselors, each striving to improve the performance of the same six students.

Unreal though this inverted ratio of counselors to students may be, the dynamics of the game improved dramatically. Counselors within a team were allowed to discuss their goals, problems, strategies, and reactions as freely as they wished. Only communication between counselors and students and between one counseling team and another was subject to the constraints described above. Not only did this make it possible to process the large amounts of information that counselors had to handle; it interjected organizational variables into the game. The type and extent of leadership within a team, for example, became quite important. The fact that the ambiguous role of the counselor could be discussed freely within the team during play, rather than after, meant that the subtle ideas involved in the game were likely to be made explicit at a time when they could be tested. For example, the idea that counselors should try to maximize the total number of points earned by players rather than "narrow the gap between the scores of the 'best' players and the scores of the 'worst players' " would be an idea that counselors could debate during a session. Thus, many possibilities the players would otherwise have discovered only after several plays of the game began to be discussed and tried out in a very short time.

Ultimately the notion of a group of counselors serving a few players of the core game was the idea that did most to solve the problem of giving counselors an advantage over the players. The importance of this should not be underestimated. In simulations that use the structure of a game within a game, the power of this structure can be expanded by greatly reducing the ratio between the number of people providing the basic set of relationships (playing the core game) and those who are to deal with the basic relationships in some way. Another example would be a simulation in which six "citizens" (playing a core game) would be provided services by a dozen "officials." Essentially what this technique gains is time, for one person's idea leads quickly to another idea on the part of another player. In addition, it probably increases the odds that participants will "see" what is happening, as observations are verbalized. All the advantages of group interaction become relevant. That all the problems of group interaction also become relevant is equally valuable, for a player is likely to work as part of a group in his real job (though not a group which is roughly the same size as, or even larger than, the one it serves).

About the same time that the idea of a team of counselors was being tried out, another important development occurred with respect to pacing. Since there was no need to preserve any kind of secrecy with respect to the players' moves (as might have been the case if the players of the core game were to be given the disadvantage of incomplete information), the basic moves of the game could be called out verbally instead of written down. This change meant that the receiving player, all the counselors, and the game director could adjust their boards simultaneously with no need for individuals to write down each move and have the message delivered to someone else. Another veil was lifted from the initially obfuscated situation.

A routine was quickly established that could be varied, but which has not been varied for well over a year. A player is told that he has thirty seconds to announce three moves, one move against each of three different players. The moves are written on a blackboard or sheet of paper at the front of the room and left there until the end of a complete round; that is, until all players have moved and there has been an opportunity to exchange messages. Therefore, a player must choose to play with some of his fellow players and to ignore others on any given round. The accuracy of what one hears can be verified by looking at the written version at the front of the room. Each participant may adjust his board with the confidence that he is as up-to-date as anyone; yet, he can re-check his moves in relative leisure (during the message exchange period, for example). Thus the game was made to move much more quickly but became much less frantic than it was in some trial runs.

After a trial run fairly early in the development period, before these pacing problems had been solved, a player (actually a graduate student in guidance and counseling) offered the criticism that although the game was beginning to model some aspects of the counseling situation in an interesting way, it was obsessed with the inter-personal problems of students. Students had many problems of other kinds, including, for instance, academic problems. The response to this entirely accurate insight was to rush into place another fundamental aspect of the simulation. From this point on, players of the core game were given the chance to win points not only by winning or losing to each other, but by beating a "master player," simply an assistant to the game director. In essence, the game they were to play was the same one. The "master player" was given his masterly qualities by simply giving him an extra piece with which to play. It would then be possible for him to beat anyone, every time, so his behavior was restrained. He was given a special set of rules which he had to follow; in effect, he was given an algorithm by which to play. The "master player" got no points for winning and did not try to win. The idea was to offer each player an impersonal challenge, a task to be performed strictly at the intellectual level. If a player could figure out the algorithm, he could beat the system consistently and win many points. (For purposes of comparison, it might be noted that a win on the "system" board was worth ten points, a win against another player was worth five points, as described earlier.) Conceivably, he would stumble into a victory without understanding the algorithm very well, if at all. He would then receive his points as a reward, but he very likely would not deceive himself about the nature of his victory.

Counselors were also offered the chance to play against the "master player." If they could figure out the algorithm they could be of great help to their students. This feature, however, raised a point typical of the kind of issue that arises in the game. Should a counselor just tell the students the algorithm, or tell them how to beat the system? Is it somehow better for the student to figure these things out for himself? If so, why? What if one team of counselors is helping students in a way another group has decided is inappropriate?

The introduction of the "master player" to serve as a simulator of the impersonal, intellectual side of a school serves as an excellent illustration of the value of early trial runs. Those closest to the game had become completely pre-occupied with what was to turn out to be but one side of the eventual simulation. It seemed perfectly obvious to a player, however, that a strong bias was being developed. The correction was not difficult once the bias was identified.

To say that the correction was not difficult may be putting the case a little too simply. The algorithm now being used still leaves a bit to be desired. It takes far too much concentration on the part of the "master player" to be sure he is using it consistently. Even so the present algorithm is a great improvement over the first one. (One of these master players was Layman Allen, who had suggested this particular core game in the first place.)

So far, little has been said in this paper about the message-exchange part of the game. Once the idea of charging for messages was accepted, various alternatives were tried. Forms were drawn up, tokens were used to expedite bookkeeping, and various charging structures were considered. Soon, however, all the complicated possibilities were rejected as either unworkable or unnecessary. The basic format finally settled upon involves a charge of one message unit for each word sent, with the cost to be calculated by the sender, written at the bottom of the message and spot-checked by the game director or his assistant. The tokens were done away with and a less time-consuming checking-account procedure replaced them. Each player is given an income of fifteen message units per round; each counseling team receives thirty message units per round. Units that are not used in a round may be accumulated. Each round the game director's assistant simply subtracts and adds the appropriate numbers of message units for each player. If the message is complex, involving for example a diagram, the cost is calculated by the game director, using a fixed charge for having drawn a diagram, plus an additional charge of one unit for each element of information included.

One of the great advantages of the simplicity of such a scheme is that the game director may alter the nature of the game considerably by simply announcing a change in the allotment of the message units. It is extremely useful to be able to put such a flexible tool at the disposal of the director, to speed up or slow down the pace.

Restrictions placed on the routines for picking up and delivering messages turned out to be one of the major ways of giving counselors advantages over students and for getting counselors to concentrate on the important aspects of the game. To make the counselors of maximum use, no written messages were permitted to pass directly from one student to another. But if the students were to send messages to each other through the counselors, the counselor's role would become that of a messenger boy. The answer to this unpleasant possibility is as simple as it is important. During a given period for exchanging messages, there is one pick-up and one delivery of messages. This means that if player A sends a message to counseling team X requesting information from player B, it takes one round to get the messages from A to X, a second round to get the message from X to B, a third to get the information back from B to X, and a fourth round for X to give the information to A, who wanted it in the first place. With a lag of four rounds built in, the chances that A and B will communicate effectively through X, when X is nothing but a messenger, are not very good. This somewhat complicated "delay" feature does not model anything in the actual counseling situation. It is a device to bring the dynamics of the situation around to a desired type of dynamics through a totally artificial means.

This leaves the counselors in just the position they should be, from the point of view of the simulation. If they are to serve A and B, they must figure out what these two are like and what they are likely to want to know, to anticipate their requests and be in a position to provide relevant information in less than four rounds. The counselors must build rapport with their students, in other words. It must be remembered that students must pay out message units if they choose to answer questions which counselors have asked them. The restrictions on communication emphasize in a dramatic way the problem of rapport. If the counselor is to be of service, he must get information from students and this task is likely to require him to explain why he needs to have the information, or more likely, to demonstrate to the student that it is in the student's interest to cooperate with him. Because there are usually at least two teams of counselors competing to establish rapport with students, the situation becomes quite rich in opportunities for skillful handling of people, as well as for skillful handling of information.

It cannot be stressed too often that the entire potential of a game is drastically influenced by details of rules, details of scoring, and so forth. The major problem of giving the counselors scope to counsel was solved at this level, not by adding a new or different dimension to the simulation. In order to familiarize players with the game, all boards are set in the beginning in such a way that any move, adequately interpreted, leads to an exactly corresponding move on the opponent's board. Wins are then verified, points for winning and losing are issued and the players are told how to reset their boards. If the boards are set in the same manner as they were initially, no new problems arise. Sometimes, however, the director will intentionally give the players instructions that will result in their boards being mis-matched. Thus, the stage is set for a whole range of new problems. (It should be added that a win or a loss on a pair of boards which are mis-matched is worth more than a win or loss on a pair of matched boards.) The use of mis-matched boards was viewed as a way to give the students a specific kind of difficulty with which counselors could help. This particular device was selected because it could be introduced to the players gradually to avoid overwhelming them and because it enabled the counselors to discover the source of the difficulty and help the students to overcome it.

Eventually even the boards themselves were rebuilt in order to minimize their size and weight, and maximize ease of use. Not only was the original peg-board and golf tee version large and heavy; it had to be disassembled after each play if the boards were to be moved very far. Fortunately, small plastic boards and pieces were discovered and purchased from a firm specializing in making wall-charts. The prototype now involves 6″ x 12″ player boards and 18″ x 18″ counselor boards. The pieces have "heads" which are shaped to form squares, triangles, circles, and dots. The whole set of boards weighs about what one counselor board previously weighed. The markers may be left in the boards during shipment.

When the boards were re-designed, the names of the players were changed from A, B, C, D, E, F, to A, D, F, H, R, U, to avoid such errors as mistaking the spoken sound "b" for the spoken sound "d." Mistakes of this sort were trivial, but in a simulation which compresses a vast number of variables into a short period of time, wasted time must be cut to the absolute minimum.

It is now possible to run a fairly complete session in three hours, if the goal is to introduce the players to the dynamics involved and allow some time for discussion. Improvements should still be made in the way the introduction period is handled, to permit optional time investment on the part of the players. The full richness of the situation does not come out until two or three hours of actual play has transpired. Since discussion time is an absolute necessity, and since a half-day is frequently the greatest amount of time people are free to invest in such an activity, efforts to streamline the operation are still in order.

Although this discussion has used terminology drawn from the area of school guidance and counseling, more than half the runs of the simulation have been made with groups with other kinds of interests. The terminology indigenous to the simulation itself is totally abstract. It requires no adaptation whatsoever to run the game for groups composed of librarians, educational administrators, or, for that matter, any other kind of administrators. The group of players referred to as "students" can simply be called "library users" or "employees," and the "counselors" can be "librarians," "managers," or "administrators." In its most general sense, the game simulates any situation in which one group of people is responsible for improving the performance of another group.

FINAL REMARKS

After such a rambling discourse concerning the evolution of the simulation, a summary of the design principles which emerged may be in order. Unlike design work in many areas of the social sciences, no attempt was made to develop a comprehensive set of detailed objectives for the task. Instead the procedure was to work toward a general objective, struggling to avoid theoretical and practical pitfalls. Repeated trials were used both to discover the consequences of various ideas and to gather reactions of players and observers. Whenever possible, people who had designed games or had considerable experience with games were used as participants. Constant efforts were made to simplify procedures with emphasis given to color-coding and to avoiding time spent on writing, passing paper or counting and making calculations during the game.

The basic technique of using a game to generate a set of dynamic relationships within a group of people in order for others to have the opportunity to try to improve these relationships emerged as a most promising guideline for future simulations. The technique of dramatically distorting the ratio between those served and those serving in order to promote intense interaction among people who normally play a role in relative isolation also proved to be a promising idea.

Perhaps another technique which might prove valuable in other simulations is that of granting one player a tremendous advantage over others and then placing strategic constraints on his behavior (as in the case of the "master player"). This has the effect of removing attention from the individual idiosyncracies of a person's behavior and focusing it on the abstract nature of the rules used to limit his behavior.

Clearly the technique of restricting resources in an unusual way, in this case by charging for every word passing between students and counselors, forces players to consider priorities and, in turn, values. If a way can be found to permit and encourage groups to develop different systems of priorities, the simulation will sharpen still further the participants' awareness of their own values. It is of great importance, however, to stimulate participants to discuss their actions and intentions in order to get the full value of such considerations.

Finally, if games can be brought to the point at which players will ask themselves what the purpose of the game is and what it means to win, the designer may have gone a step beyond the kind of simulation which subtly imposes his own value system on the players. The more games are used as instructional aids, the more important it may be to design the kind of game which encourages the player to reflect on the basic nature of the game he sees himself as playing.

The startling brevity of the list of principles emerging from such a complex situation is a testimony to the infancy of work of this kind. The conclusions remain intuitive and tentative, although hopefully not trivial. Efforts to elaborate on them at this stage seem an indulgence in the most idle type of speculation. They are to be taken as very practical suggestions growing from a very practical approach to some very theoretical areas of human thought and communication.

REFERENCES

Boulding, Kenneth
1956 *The Image*. Ann Arbor: University of Michigan Press.

DENIS G. SULLIVAN
(with the collaboration of
ROBERT NOEL)

Chapter 7

Inter-Nation Simulation: A Review of Its Premises

INS is historically one of the first simulation games, as well as one of the most widely-known and used, here and abroad. It was developed both for research and for teaching on the college level. The time which has elapsed since its origin has permitted these authors to make a critical evaluation of their experiences and decisions. As a result of this hard look, they contribute reflections to the theory of simulation design, notably with regard to ecology and validity.

—The Editors

Inter-Nation Simulation: A Review of Its Premises

What follows is not a historical reconstruction of INS.[1] We made many choices, some of which we were aware at the time, and some not. Rather than to describe and justify history, our paper reflects the changes in our thinking since the early days of INS. Its critical cast should not be interpreted as a rejection of simulation, nor of the particular simulation we are reviewing. The creation of INS was a response to the evident needs for the transformation of international relations into a discipline based upon reliable cumulative knowledge.

In 1957–58 two major difficulties faced the discipline and, to some extent, still do. The first problem concerns the extremely small number of cases upon which to erect theoretical structures. The disciplinary response has been to extend the number of cases by reaching back into history, but this solution creates as many new problems as it solves. Are findings based on one historical period generalizable to another? What are the relevant parameters? Simulation offered the possibility of establishing parameters and examining over a large number of trials the kinds of interactions making up international behavior.

The second group of problems to plague International Relations have been concerned with data access problems. Partly because of the small number of cases and partly because of the anecdotal nature of diplomatic reports, most propositions concerning international behavior have been verified only offhandedly. Increasing the difficulty in analysis has been the *ad hoc* nature of the reports. Foreign policy documents as justifications for past behavior are subject to the vagaries of all known psychological defense mechanisms: rationalization, bolstering, denial, etc. Simulation would allow the gathering of behavioral data by observation and the exploration of intentions before behavior. For these reasons we felt that simulation would solve two of the major problems in the discipline and thus stimulate theoretical advances.

Before simulation the research alternatives seemed to fall into two classes: natural population observation and experimentation. Natural population observation has the advantage of external validity; the observer is studying samples of behavior from the population to which he wishes to generalize. But, on the other hand, experimentation has the advantage of internal validity; one can be more confident that the imputed cause actually did cause the event.

Simulation belongs in one of a series of half-way houses Campbell

[1] The authors are deeply grateful to Harold Guetzkow and the International Relations Program for a chance to participate in a new venture in the discipline. Both of us remember the intellectual stimulation derived from the project and the general atmosphere in the Political Science Department at Northwestern with a sense of profound gratitude. We have assumed in this paper that the reader is familiar with the general outline of INS. For those who wish further familiarity, see Guetzkow (1963).

(1963) has described as quasi-experimental designs. One sacrifices some, but not all, internal validity to increase the representativeness of the samples of behavior. At the same time one retains some of the power of experimentation to assess causal relationships. We think, now, that one of our principal failures was not to explore more thoroughly the distinction between simulation and experimentation.

DECISIONS IN CONSTRUCTING INS—WHAT TO PROGRAM AND WHAT NOT TO PROGRAM

To begin with, certain parts of our knowledge about international relations are reasonably firm, other parts unknown. If we take the logical structure of what we do know and coordinate these terms with the elements of the simulation, then we can explore the behavior of the sim-

Chart 1 Glossary of INS Terms

1. ***Decision Maker:*** each nation has either two or three decision makers: a central decision maker holding office on the sufferance of a probability of holding function, two external decision makers or foreign ministers, and an aspiring decision maker who attempts to gain political power.

2. ***Validators:*** an undefined group which the decision maker must satisfy if he wishes to remain in power. The satisfaction of the validators as produced, in part, by the kinds of decisions the decision maker records on the decision form.

3. ***Decision Latitude:*** It relates the ways in which the satisfaction of the validators affects the political power of the decision maker. At a certain cost the central decision maker may alter (increase or decrease his decision latitude).

4. ***Revolution:*** when validator satisfaction drops below a certain level, a revolution may be triggered which, if successful, results in the loss of political power for the present decision maker.

5. ***Basic Capability (BC):*** It is a measure of the nation's capacity to produce goods and services and may be devoted to:

6. ***Consumption Satisfaction (CS):*** a measure of the standard of living in the population, or to:

7. ***Force Capability (FC):*** military goods and services.

8. ***Trade and Aid:*** Nations may engage in trade involving FC's, BC's, and CS's. There is no money or private economy in the game. Therefore all trade is by barter.

9. ***International Agreements:*** The nations sign an agreement which is registered with the researcher.

10. ***War:*** After war is declared, and the nation attacked has had time to respond, various negotiating possibilities are explored for its termination, and if terminated, consequences are computed by the researcher.

11. ***Communication:*** Regular communication is by written message. A statistical Report publishes the varying states of the nations in terms of the variables described above, and the World Times keeps decision makers informed about world events from time to time.

ulation with respect to increasing our awareness of what we do not know. Secondly, we did not want to program the behavior of the actors in a way that would make trivial most of our results. For example, we did not want to prescribe goals of major actors in a way that would determine their behavior along a cooperative-competitive dimension. We wanted, rather, to explore the ways in which goals of actors would be shaped by their simulated international environment. Thirdly, we wished to gain knowledge about international, not intra-national behavior. These three criteria implied (we thought) (1) national actors free to choose their own goals and sub-goals, (2) an intra-national environment programmed to their decision-making efforts, (3) a domestic and international economic system programmed to produce decision consequences. (A glossary of basic INS terms is presented in Chart 1.) Therefore the national actors were left free to determine their goals and sub-goals, with the domestic environment programmed to feed back consequences and the unprogrammed international environment (the other decision-makers) free to react.

These decisions reflected what we thought were the priorities in developing theory about international behavior. The behavioral and group characteristics which we thought most needed theoretical development were left unprogrammed. We hoped we would find in the dynamics of the simulation process an account of their development which could be generalized to the larger international system.

SOME MORE SPECIFIC PROBLEMS IN THE DESIGN OF INS

We wished to construct the simulation so that the unprogrammed behavior could be explained by what went on in the simulation, rather than by what the participants brought to the simulation. The solution to the problem determined, to a large extent, the level of abstraction in the game. We attempted to make the simulation highly abstract so that the participant would play his role with the information we provided, not with vague notions of how "X" country might behave. For INS this meant that a participant playing the foreign minister of UTRO would define his role only in terms of the information provided in the simulation. To achieve this goal of controlling role interpretations, we deliberately used names of nations that could not be identified with a particular nation.

What we hoped to avoid was the following kind of thinking by participants: "Now, what nation is what? . . . That must be Nigeria. . . . How does the foreign minister of Nigeria act out his role? . . .

Pan-Africanism—will get all the small African nations together and form an alliance." If this thought process occurs, one can hardly claim that the dynamics of the simulation have accounted for the player's behavior. What he is doing is playing the role with which he has identified UTRO. The same kind of thinking can also result in the formation of expectations about UTRO by the foreign ministers of other simulated nations. With a minimal amount of information, they may be trying to guess what kind of nation UTRO is. As they read the scenario, they may come to the conclusion that UTRO is a poor underdeveloped nation, like Nigeria, and react accordingly. Although identification of this sort may promote role empathy useful for educational purposes, it wreaks havoc with simulation as a research device.

The methodological problem is similar to the anthropologist's concern with the effects of cultural diffusion.[2] Two universes are presumed independent when, in fact, they are linked by diffusion. In INS the identification of the game as INS and the role descriptions lead to role modelling of the system for which the simulator is attempting to develop theory. The fact that the unprogrammed part of INS looks like a piece of the international system may speak well for the role models chosen, because it is not the existence of a simulation dynamic that has its parallel in the international system. (See Hermann, 1967.)

We now feel that the attempt to control role interpretations by raising the level of abstraction in the game should have been investigated more thoroughly on the empirical level. If we had used particular nations at a particular time, we would have known the kinds of inferences the participants might attempt. But with the high level of abstraction in INS, we lost control over role interpretations.

A second set of problems touches more directly the ever present problem of external validity. Of course, the basic test of external validity is the correspondence between the propositions discovered as a result of the operation of INS and those concerning the behavior of the target system. But there is a second kind of external validity which we feel is logically prior to the basic test. We have chosen to call this "micro-validity" because it involves comparability between segments of INS and the corresponding segments of the target process. We have invented the term "micro-validity" instead of following the convention of experimental psychology. For example, take an experiment involving the behavioral consequences of differing levels of fear evoked by experimenter messages. Before the experimenter examines the hypothesis being tested, he must first assess the effectiveness of his manipulation. Does the expe-

[2] There are a number of good discussions of this problem. For a modern treatment see Whiting and Child (1953).

rimental group have a higher level of fear than the control group? He assesses this before exploring the hypothesis for a very simple reason. If, in fact, the experimental group shows no more of the hypothesized behavior than the experimental group, the results are open to two interpretations; (1) the hypothesis is false or (2) the experimental treatment did not work. By checking independent evidence as to the effectiveness of the experimental manipulation he can rule out the second interpretation.

Simulators are faced with logically similar problems, but must take into account additional factors. If a simulator is interested in evoking in decision makers a certain level of fear, he must show that (1) his manipulation is effective, and (2) the level of fear is roughly the same as that found in the target process under the appropriate condition. The addition of requirement (2) constitutes the justification for the introduction of our term "micro-validity."

Achieving micro-validity is an exceedingly complex task involving relations among the various dimensions of the simulation. Take, for example, the problem of controlling the feeling of task pressure. It is, we think, a characteristic of international system roles that their incumbents have too little time to do the things they must do. Their perspectives tend to be short-run. The systems they deal with seem to be on the verge of going out of control. The rush of events sets the agenda. Simulation of the problems of information overload and the feelings of lack of control depends, to a large extent, on the handling of time. Simulated time may be rushing ahead at a month a minute, but messages are read at the same old speed, and meetings may take as long as they do in the international system. Time is truly out of joint in simulation.

The division of task pressure into its foreign and domestic components involves even more complex considerations. The swell of domestic crisis may shift the decision maker's attention to domestic affairs, with intermittent glances at the international scene. There seemed to be three general ways to approach this problem. The international system could affect the domestic system, requiring the decision maker to attend to domestic problems; the domestic system could have a dynamic of its own requiring periodic attention by the decision maker; and the laboratory ecology could be manipulated. We integrated all three approaches. First, we developed a security function relating events in the international scene to the security of the nation and then related national security to the decision maker's probability of continuing in office. Second, we developed a domestic satisfaction index, based on the satisfaction of those most powerful in the domestic system, and related it to the decision maker's probability of remaining in office. Third, we used instrumentation to require the central decision maker to spend a certain amount of time doing housekeeping work related to the domestic system. By developing relations among the three components of simulation, we attempted to simulate task pressures.

In most cases, however, the eventual decision as to the structure of the simulation came about in the following way. Parts of the physical apparatus of the simulation were coordinated with terms in the conceptual structure. Participants were instructed to "pretend" that an element coordinated with a conceptual structure term was the corresponding element in the international system. For example, in the early experimental runs international space was not physically partitioned into national units. Participants occupied a nation by sitting at a table and could easily communicate across imaginary national boundaries with other decision makers. The capacity for communication was oddly incongruent with the notion that each table and set of chairs represented a nation. Therefore, in later simulations the international space was physically partitioned to increase the capacity to "pretend." This change made it impossible to communicate easily and thus heightened the nation-like illusion.

Many of the early decisions, which involved more complex considerations than the above example, were made simply to get the simulation running. After a run, a variety of adjustments would be made to increase the "credibility" of the pretense. Thus little work has been done on the "micro-validity" problem as contrasted with the "macro-validity" studies already published comparing traditional propositions to those from INS.

We originally thought about the validation problem in the macro-sense but, since then, have come to the position that micro-validity studies are logically prior to macro studies.[3] There are two aspects to the micro-validity studies. The laboratory setting includes all those activities and physical elements explicitly coordinated with terms of the target process language plus other activities and elements necessary to make the simulation work. The second set is in some sense hidden because research reports on INS are usually made in the language of the target process. For example, the use of a loudspeaker to keep all nations informed of time flow in INS periods and various decision form requirements is not part of the target process but may have a dramatic effect on the behavior of the participants. To choose another example, the im-

[3] Stoll and McFarlane's (1969) study of the Parent-Child simulation game is implicitly a micro-validity study. They demonstrate how sex and friendship of player dyads affect the interaction processes of the game. Thus before generalizing from the game to real-world family interactions it will necessary to eliminate the role of player characteristics on game process.

mense volume of paperwork requires that INS time be divided into periods so that communication and decision forms may be updated. While forms are being updated, decision maker attention is focused on allocations in the domestic system. Although one may be able to think of analogues to this process in the international system, its original justification was one of orderly housekeeping.

A third set of assumptions made in the creation of INS involved the notion of consequences and entry into and exit from INS by the participants. The two problems are intertwined in ways we did not realize when we first established INS. In Erving Goffman's (1961) terms participation in INS is a game encounter in which participants accept, for the duration of the game, the rules of irrelevance. The small space—a cubicle with a table and chairs—is a nation just as different colored bottle tops may be used as pieces in a game of checkers. The conceptual structure places a "frame" around a set of objects and activities and the meaning of those activities is specified in terms of the frame. Games of this sort are, as Goffman points out, world building activities. As the participant enters INS he learns a set of "transformation rules" which specify how his real-world characteristics will be expressed in the setting of INS.

For example, the transformation rules for a run in INS for State Department personnel might specify that they take roles within each nation equivalent to their actual position in the hierarchy of the Department. An INS run for players recruited from different nations might encourage them to consider their actual nationalities in making decisions within the game. On the other hand, players might be instructed to ignore their real-world characteristics and, as proof of the irrelevance of these characteristics, players could be assigned to positions and nations through a randomizing process. Presumably, the participants accept the transformation rules as specified by simulator, but it is quite possible that a variety of latent transformation rules would have to enter the encounter. Members of fraternities may be more likely to ally with their brothers, males with females, liberals with liberals, etc. To the extent that these latent transformation rules are powerful and run against explicit transformation rules, the simulation is corrupted. We were aware of this problem and attempted to solve it by writing convincing scenarios to promote identification with the explicit transformation rules of INS for a particular run.

But we now think that in attempting to maximize the acceptance of explicit game rules we may have sacrificed an important value in simulation. Implicitly, many of the features of INS were constructed with the view that decision makers would be confronted with a variety of dilemmas. For example, an effort to increase military capability would subtract from a decision maker's capability to sustain validator satisfaction, and this situation should prove a dilemma to the participant, regardless of its effect on his probability of continuing in office. A decision maker given a role in a small poor nation should identify with his country's aspirations to develop, not simply look upon development and validator satisfaction in terms of his probability of losing office. But the more successful we were in developing, in Goffman's words, "a locally realized world of roles and events . . . (cutting) the participants off from many externally based matters . . . ," the more likely the participants were to view INS as a game in which some combination of a role-inferred goal and probability of office holding was a goal to be maximized and all other activities and outcomes subordinated to it. Thus war, nuclear or otherwise, became an event lightly considered by the participants.

It is only when the participant sees his actions in INS as reflecting his real-world attitudes that such events can have strong incentive power. Thus if the participant believes his behavior will reveal his attitudes toward politicians, his intelligence, or his commitment to world peace, the dilemmas become real to him. But a condition for strong incentive motivation is that there be a connection between his roles in the world outside INS and inside INS. One might predict, then, that if the dilemmas contained in INS were real to the participants, their attitudes toward each other outside INS might be altered in ways predictable on the basis of their INS experience. And we now feel that this relationship between within-INS activity and outside-INS activity might be turned to our advantage. If we explicitly accept and promote a real world simulation link as a method for assuring appropriate motivation, then the basic test for the effectiveness of the manipulation would lie in correlations between shifts in attitudes and beliefs among INS role actors and the same group outside INS.[4]

In designing INS our thoughts ran in different directions. We attempted to find analogues of consequences to induce appropriate motivation. As long as programmed consequences are in the form of numbers, hand or computer calculated, they have little meaning for the player. We considered substituting poignant descriptions of poverty when validator satisfaction decreased or requiring the participants to watch the death of a number of guinea pigs proportional to the number of dead in war, etc. But, at least in the early days of INS, we were unable to hit upon a satisfactory solution.

[4] Noel reports in his description of the early INS runs at Asilomar (with foreign service officers) that many of the professionals in the game had "their reputations on the line." See his full description in Guetzkow (1963).

A fourth set of assumptions concerned the relationship between the programmed intra-national environment and the inter-personal international environment. One aspect of this problem—the time dimension—struck us early as a severe problem. It was quite easy to set up functions tracing the effects of decision maker investment choices on validator satisfaction and probability of office holding over time. But we knew if we brought the time interval down to a period appropriate for the inter-personal relations in the international system, nothing would happen of significance in the domestic system. If one has the equivalent of a National Security Council meeting in the simulation, it may take exactly the same amount of time it does in the real system. But in terms of the domestic system, the equivalent of six months may have passed in ten minutes.

The time imbalance between the programmed domestic and the relatively unprogrammed international environment was, as one would suspect, the most pronounced in areas of message exchange, inter-nation negotiation, and decision making—precisely those areas which the simulation was designed to explore. To bring the two areas into time congruence would have required a quite different approach. INS was designed to explore macro-international events, changes over reasonably long periods of simulated time. From this perspective, changes within nations concerning investment effects, validator satisfaction, etc. were relevant. But the most obvious solution to the problem of time imbalance would mean a relatively fixed domestic setting with changes occurring on a qualitative level—streams of events determined by probabilities for the kind of system at a particular point in time. We reject the idea that GNP doubles while the negotiating team is having lunch in Paris, but we do know that they may read about a riot, demonstration, etc. in their equivalent of the morning New York Times. This solution makes more difficult the use of simulation in developing hypotheses about intra-national and international changes. In maintaining the discontinuity between simulated domestic system time and partly real international time, we simply hoped for the best.

A fifth set of assumptions concerned the simulation of the decision maker's limited control of domestic and international events. We felt quite confident that the decision makers of other nations would prove sufficiently recalcitrant to evoke the appropriate feelings of limited control of the flow of international events. We wanted to avoid evoking the following kind of response to the programmed output from the domestic system: domestic system in equilibrium, problem posed . . . information displayed . . . solution proposed . . . alternative chosen . . . consequences calculated . . . output fed back to decision maker . . . problem redefined in light of past decisions and new information . . . problem posed.

This kind of model, we felt, would produce in decision makers a sense of control and rationality not characteristic of the system being simulated. The principal mechanism we used to avoid a heightened sense of control was a stochastic model that made somewhat unpredictable the consequences of decisions. Attached to the stochastic function were descriptions of riots, demonstrations, etc.; however, reviewing the procedure, we now find it inadequate for several reasons. There was no provision for creative response to qualitative events attached to the stochastic model. Therefore, pressures were not increased for the decision maker to turn his attention away from international events to considerations of the appropriate domestic response. In addition, the time-period-decision-cycle form tended to reinforce non-dynamic shifts in the decision maker's attention span.

A sixth cluster of problems surrounded the treatment of communications. From the beginning, we were aware that in avoiding a small group experiment atmosphere we would have to rely quite heavily on written communications. There were also a number of other assumptions supporting reliance on written communications. First, we hypothesized that written messages would increase the amount of role differentiation within the national unit. Second, we hoped that a high volume of written communication would heighten role identifications and, thereby, make the simulation more "real." Third, we wished to come as close as possible to the ratio of written to oral communications in the system being simulated.

After a number of trial runs of the simulation, we realized that our assumptions on communication were rather incomplete. Given the level of communication introduced by us, the simulation simply would not run! There was no way for decision makers to find out what the state of the world was except from *other decision makers.* The essence of communication in the real international system is multiple sources of information; real decision makers have independent and multiple ways of verifying propositions about the international and national systems. INS seemed to require the introduction of a third independent, and partially correct, form of communication: the world newspaper. In a sense, the world newspaper represented for each participant the mix of strategies normally available in the international system for keeping informed and informing others. It also assumed an increasingly important role in performing other functions. The archives of the world newspaper contained a record of events occurring in INS, but the articles actually appearing in its pages could be written with an appropriate amount of distortion and leakage. Thus the world newspaper could perform espionage and selective perception functions.

A seventh area of problems and assumptions we had to consider involved what we now call the level of aggregation for the programmed variables in INS. Simply for reasons of computational simplicity and theoretical parsimony we wished to minimize the number of variables making up the intra-national process. We used rather conventional categories—economic, cultural, and political—as reference standards in developing the system of interacting variables. The fundamental dependent variable became probability of office holding. Proceeding as if we had done a complex factor analysis to locate fundamental variables in each domain, we defined what Harold Guetzkow has come to call "prototypical" variables—basic capability, validator satisfaction, decision latitude, and so on. Basic capability was initially cast in terms of economic determinants and thus could be increased by investment, converted to consumer satisfaction, or used to generate military capability. We adopted the policy, then, of taking a small number of key variables and waiting to see if the results of a trial run of the simulation would force us to differentiate them.

It was in this way that we responded to the problem of the interface between the output of the programmed part of INS and the response of the participants to that output. However, in following this procedure we created some unnecessary artificial features. Take, for example, the concept of basic capability. It becomes, as part of the conceptual structure of INS, a stimulus object in the game. Our hypothesis had to be, then, that there are aggregations performed by decision makers and their staffs in the real international system which correspond to those we used to determine basic capability in INS. But participants in the real international system must employ their own aggregation procedures. One might claim, of course, that the variables used in INS are roughly the same as those actually used by real decision makers. Basic capability does correspond, to some extent, to the notions of national power found in the popular press and conventional textbooks. But INS does not allow the exploration of many of the information searching and processing operations which might prove of major interest in developing a theory of international behavior.

The final cluster of problems concerns setting the level of abstraction in INS. It seems appropriate to conclude the paper with this problem because it raises in a new frame many of the issues discussed earlier.

We mean, in part, by level of abstraction the amount of detail with which the international situation and national characteristics were specified. In some ways, the levels of abstraction and aggregation are intimately related. The use of prototypic variables meant that systems were described to participants at a high level of generality. In using names not identifiable with existing nations and descriptions involving a high level of aggregation, we made it more difficult for the participant to identify a nation historically, in order to avoid the unwanted effects of role modelling.

A second reason for the high level of abstraction involved the notion of parsimony. We did not want to clutter the simulation with a large number of variables whose relationships could be expressed more simply. In this purpose we failed to differentiate between the way the programmed part of the system worked as a model and the way it was perceived by the participants. It would have been easy to aggregate several variables within the model for the computation of environmental consequences and to de-aggregate the variables as we fed the information back to the participant. Of course, the response choices of the decision maker would have been enriched, but this might have been turned to our advantage.

A third reason for the high level of abstraction flowed from the notion of generalizability. The more detailed the simulation, the narrower the scope of the propositions emerging from it. Because the nature of the simulation required many replications to provide evidence for a proposition, we wished the propositions to be as powerful in their implications as possible.

Fourth, we felt that moving in the opposite direction—towards the reconstruction of historical periods like those employed in Rand crisis gaming models—we would suffer a loss in reliability. For example, providing details as to weapons would require, in a meaningful reconstruction, the use of judges to decide losses and gains in the event of war. It would have complicated the simulation immensely to have had to deal with inter-judge reliability problems both within an INS run and across replications.

Fifth, we anticipated that it would be quite easy to increase the richness of the simulation and therefore its capacity for Rand-type exercises. We felt that it was of a higher priority to produce a workable simulation on a rather general level.

CONCLUSION

The creation of INS came at a time when there had been little prior work in simulation. Each step in its design was a step into an unexplored region. We had to learn by trial and error, and many of the assumptions and problems discussed in the above pages require restatement and new solutions.

REFERENCES

BRUNSWICK, EGON
1930 "A conceptual framework for psychology." In *International Encyclopedia of Unified Science*, 1.

CAMPBELL, DONALD T.
1963 "Experimental and quasi-experimental design for research and teaching." In N. Gage (ed.), The Handbook of Research on Teaching. Chicago: Rand-McNally.

GOFFMAN, ERVING
1961 *Encounters*. Indianapolis: Bobbs-Merrill.

GUETZKOW, HAROLD ET AL.
1963 *Simulation in International Relations*. Englewood Cliffs, N. J.: Prentice-Hall.

HERMANN, CHARLES F.
1967 "Validation problems in games and simulations with special reference to models of international politics." *Behavioral Science*, 12, 216–233.

ROSENBERG, M. J. AND R. ABELSON
1960 "An analysis of cognitive balancing." In C. Hovland and M. Rosenberg, (eds.) *Attitude Organization and Change*. New Haven: Yale.

STOLL, CLARICE S. AND PAUL T. MCFARLANE
1969 "Player characteristics and interaction in a Parent-Child simulation game." *Sociometry*, 32, 259–272.

WHITING, J. AND I. CHILD
1953 *Child Training and Personality*. New Haven: Yale.

GERALD ZALTMAN

Chapter **8**

Simulations for Learning: A Case in Consumer Economics

Consumer is an intriguing game. Though simple in structure, it teaches about a range of issues: types of utilities; cost of credit; legal consequences of contractual commitments. It is also unusual in that it accommodates up to seventeen players who proceed at their own rates while maintaining interdependences. Zaltman analyzes the history of the game within the framework of both required and desirable criteria for pedagogical simulations. He concludes with suggestions helpful in estimating the extent and type of field-testing a game will need.

—THE EDITORS

Simulations for Learning: A Case in Consumer Economics

This paper is essentially concerned with the problems and considerations involved in constructing a simulation game for teaching. Insofar as the problems and criteria involved in the construction of social simulation games as teaching tools are similar to those involved in constructing other kinds of simulations, this paper may also have some relevance for the construction of simulations with other objectives. In the discussion to follow, examples will be provided from one particular game, Consumer. This game exists in two versions—a board (all-man) game, and a computer-based (man-machine) game. The board version is the most thoroughly tested and will be the basis for discussion.

The basic activities in constructing a simulation for pedagogical purposes are:

1. Defining the instructional objectives of the game
2. Defining the target audience
3. Defining the model and theoretical assumptions of the underlying social processes to be taught
4. Operationalizing the model
5. Testing the simulation

The entire game building enterprise involves trade-offs. Few procedures can be considered unchangeable. For example, it may be necessary to take some poetic license with the model in order to better achieve some instructional objective. Or, after field testing, it may be found necessary to restrict the intended audience in order to make the game more playable for some particular group. However, not all changes involve compromises. The processes of operationalizing and testing a model may highlight inadequacies in the model or its assumptions and suggest further necessary changes. From an instructional standpoint, we decrease the likelihood of teaching the wrong things. From the standpoint of theory construction, we have further refined one formulation of the functioning of a social process.

INSTRUCTIONAL OBJECTIVES AND INTENDED AUDIENCE

No attempt will be made here to describe or document the extent to which consumers in all socio-economic groups experience problems in using credit. Suffice it to say that the problems are widespread and all too frequently cause serious trouble. (See for example, Troelstrup, 1965; Mors, 1965; Caplovitz, 1961). The major objectives of Consumer are oriented toward these problems.

Briefly, the game is structured in such a way as to encourage consumers to:

1. Weigh the added cost of financing a purchase against the additional value of possessing the item immediately;
2. Consider the opportunity costs of the purchase, that is, to determine whether there is another use of their money that will yield greater utility; and
3. Guard against unanticipated events not generally covered by insurance.

As a result of interactions in the game between consumers and credit agents, players learn:

1. To compare the interest rates charged by different financial institutions;
2. To expect credit rating to affect the ability to borrow;
3. To understand fully the implications of contracts before signing; and
4. To appreciate the mechanics of that sector of the economic system concerned with consumer credit.

At the outset I decided to develop a game for use among adolescents with varied learning abilities and different social backgrounds. I later discovered that with some modifications the game could also be used successfully among adults of differing backgrounds and capabilities. Thus the audience for the game became a large and heterogeneous one.

THE MODEL

Like most other social simulation games, Consumer makes a key theoretical assumption concerning behavior: It assumes behavior by purposive, goal-oriented, self-interested individuals.[1] The selection of roles and structuring of relationships among players form the essential components of the game model. There are two competitive roles in Consumer: three players take the roles of credit agents (a bank loan officer, a department store credit manager, and a finance company loan man-

[1] This excludes a number of alternative theories which would have resulted in a rather different game structure. This assumption about individual behavior is not peculiar only to theories about economic behavior. It also underlies theories of behavior in several other social contexts as evidenced in the work of the exchange theorists in sociology and social psychology. (See as an example the model discussed by the Gullahorns in this volume—Editors.)

ager), and as many as twelve players take the role of consumers. In addition, there are two purely administrative roles: a salesman and a coordinator (who also functions as a judge in case of disputes).

A general problem is simulation games is that some roles (seldom more than one or two in any simulation) are necessary for the functioning of the game but may be boring for the players. Hence, the players in these roles may lack motivation. This problem of passivity among students has long been of concern to educators trying to heighten involvement in the usual lecturer-audience classroom setting. In simulation games it is usually handled on an *ad hoc* basis in each game session. For example, passive roles are good positions in the first play of a game for students who lack self-confidence or who are easily discouraged by competition. These roles are good introductory positions from which to move such players into more challenging roles. Also, as different levels of complexity are added to a game, formerly passive roles may become quite active. An example of this in Consumer is the role of salesman (to be discussed later).

The behavior of purposive, self-interested actors in a game is determined partly by the goal-specifying rules. In Consumer the consumer's goal is to maximize the satisfaction obtained from his purchases; the credit agent's goal is to maximize returns from the business he conducts. In pursuing these individual goals, it becomes evident to consumers that a relationship with the credit agent may be profitable, and vice versa. Thus, mutually beneficial exchange relationships develop between players in different roles who are trying to further their own self interests. As in real life, some exchange relationships are better than others, and mechanisms are included to allow consumers and credit agents to discriminate among differentially profitable relationships. (Players don't have to exercise this judgment, although sooner or later they usually do.) Perhaps most importantly, players are not *required* to enter into any exchange relationships; that they do is the result of motivations provided by their respective goals. Formal provisions concerning the relationship come into operation only after the decision to enter into an exchange relationship with another player is made.

The structural model of relationships between credit agent and consumer is at once cooperative and competitive. The individual goals of players in the two roles make cooperative exchange relationships desirable and mutually profitable. The conditions of the game serve to establish a "bargaining range" within the limits of mutually-profitable exchanges. An essentially competitive relationship develops in determining where within this range a formal agreement will be concluded. The competition revolves around such factors as what collateral the consumer should put up and what special provisions should be added to the contract to cover various exigencies. How hard a bargain the credit agent or consumer is able to strike depends upon such things as his negotiating skill, the availability of alternative relationships, and an understanding of the utility the other player is placing on the present transaction. For instance, a credit agent will be in a relatively good bargaining position with a particular player if there is a sizeable demand for his money among other consumers and if he knows that the borrower is having a difficult time securing funds from other sources. This, of course, means that those who have more information about the economic state of affairs of other players have an advantage over those who do not.

The game further assumes that a consumer places differential priorities on items: there are some goods and services that are more desired

Table 1 Schedule of Utility Points Assigned to Purchased Items Over Time

	Months (Game Rounds)			
Item Purchased	*1–2*	*3–4*	*5–6*	*7–8*
Kitchenware	27	25	23	21
Refrigerator	240	200	170	150
Bed	100	75	50	25
Chair	34	30	27	25
Sewing Machine	55	55	55	55
Clothes	40	40	40	40
Rug	45	45	45	45
Vacuum	52	60	68	76
Vacation	56	60	64	68
Table	22	25	28	31
Washing Machine	135	150	165	185

and consequently those purchases are preferred earlier than others. In other words, our self-interested, goal-oriented consumer can be expected to have a psychological structure or schedule of rewards reflecting his time-ordered preferences for various items. This is simulated for all consumers by assigning each item with a different specified schedule of utility or satisfaction points. (See Chart 1)

Consider first those goods and services which are very important because their functional need is great; for example, the need for a refrigerator when none is present in the home or apartment. In this instance there is a cost involved in going without the needed item. To simulate this dissatisfaction resulting from deferred gratification, the number of utility points received for the purchase of such goods decreases as the game proceeds. If a refrigerator is purchased (the price being $200) in the first or second month of the game, the buyer receives 240 utility or satisfaction points. Only 150 points are received if the purchase is made during the last two months in the game. This does not mean that a refrigerator is any less useful in one month than it is in another. Rather, if it is an important item, as it is assumed to be in this game, then there is also an important "cost" or dissatisfaction incurred by going without it.

Other goods and services sold in the game increase in utility or satisfaction points as the game proceeds. The satisfaction points start at less than the dollar cost of the item and exceed the dollar cost at the end of the game. Thus, a week-end vacation which costs $60 yields 56 satisfaction points if deferred until the end of the game. One reason for such structuring of this group of items is to teach about opportunity costs. When a consumer foregoes one purchase in order to make a less satisfying purchase, he suffers an opportunity cost which is the difference in satisfaction between the two items. Since it is possible to purchase all the items in the game, an opportunity cost occurs only when buying a particular item means postponing a more rewarding item until a time period in which the utility or satisfaction points have dropped. During field testing I learned that this wasn't always clear to all players for whom the game was intended. Therefore, I decided to take some poetic license with the structuring of utility points and lowered the utility points for some items when purchased early in the game. In effect, players are over-penalized for purchasing a less-needed and therefore less-rewarding item early. This was found to be necessary to facilitate discussion of the opportunity cost concept among younger players and older slow learners.

Quite apart from consideration in teaching the opportunity cost concept, a schedule of increasing satisfaction points in consistent with the time-ordered psychological preferences consumers may have for some items. There are some items for which our needs or desires are cumulative in the absence of satiation. While the need for a refrigerator may be no less in December than it was the previous March, the need for a vacation may be greater in December than in the previous March if there were no vacations in between. Also, some items become increasingly important over the family cycle as a result of changes during the family life cycle. As the family size increases from two to three, etc., so does desirability of owning a washing machine in lieu of using the laundromat. Consequently, the absolute value of owning a washing machine may increase over time.[2]

[2] For a relatively short period of time the game contained a set of "life situation" event cards which described changes in the player's life situation bringing a concomitant change in the utility assigned various items. This was done to make clearer to the player some of the rationale behind the schedule of utility points.

OPERATIONALIZING: THE GAME SIMULATION TECHNIQUE

A model is operationalized primarily by means of a set of rules. The formal social structures in a game are derived directly from those rules. The informal social structures have their origins in the behavioral phenomena which emerge as by-products of these rules. Generally, the fewer the rules, the better the game. The physical equipment used in a game is also important in operationalizing a game. The use of various kinds of rules and equipment in operationalizing a game will be the concern of this section.

The discussion is organized around a number of pedagogical criteria which I have somewhat arbitrarily divided into two categories. The first category, that of the required criteria, includes the following three features: (1) the game must be self-sustaining; (2) the game must be self-judging; (3) the game must contain feedback mechanisms. The second category, that of the desirable criteria, includes the following characteristics: (1) the game should be simple enough to make relevant features salient; (2) the game should contain levels of complexity which can be affixed in a step-wise fashion; and (3) the game should allow alternative strategies.

Self-Sustaining

A simulation game is self-sustaining when the activities or processes embodied in the model function primarily as a result of their mutual relationships with each other. Three operational conditions must be met for the game to be self-sustaining. First, provisions must exist to overcome problems created in the process of abstracting a set of processes from a larger environment and in the process of operationalizing the game itself. Second, the game should be self-disciplining: that is, the formal and informal game structures should be able to correct aberrant behavior. Finally, only action by players should be necessary. After the game starts, participation or intervention by persons external to the game (teachers or administrators) should not be required. Let us turn now to a consideration of these operational conditions.

Social activities and the relationships among these activities are part of a social system. Homans and numerous others have pointed out that a given social system also exists in an environment of other systems

Post-game discussions were found to be equally effective in accomplishing this objective and consequently the "life situation" event cards were eliminated as they added needless complexity.

with which it may have reciprocal causal relationships (Homans, 1950). Consumer behavior, for example, influences and is in turn influenced by other social activities. When constructing a model one necessarily abstracts a system out of its environment of other systems with which it has a causal dependence. The problem that simplification creates is that part of the motivation for action in the game may be the result of processes in other systems which have been "ignored." It becomes necessary, then, to compensate for abstraction without unduly increasing the complexity of the model.

One technique is through the use of *environmental response rules.* These rules represent the likely behavior of relevant but missing parts of the environment. In Consumer processes in such life areas as health planning and the job market are not simulated even though happenings in these areas have important bearings on one's financial needs and the decision to borrow money. Instead of introducing these processes themselves, I took the *probable* consequences of these processes (for instance, being unemployed or having a medical expense not covered by insurance) and introduced them into the game through "chance cards." These cards serve to connect in at least a minimal way the consequences of one or more sets of processes in one system, (the labor market) with the operating model of an on-going set of processes in another system (the credit sector of the economy). These consequences, happening on a probabilistic basis, are inputs important in keeping the simulation dynamic and self-sustaining—they provide part of the impetus for having to make such financial decisions as are necessary in the game. (It is also a relatively easy procedure to alter the chance cards to reflect the differential likelihood of certain events among particular socio-economic groups.)

For a social simulation to be self-sustaining it must also provide mechanisms within the game to correct deviant behavior. Such behavior may have two origins. One type of deviant behavior, *strategic deviance,* has its roots in the intentional structure of the game. For instance, credit agents in Consumer are encouraged through the structure of the game to test the limits of their clients' gullibility and/or carelessness. One result is that the credit agents can be misleading in their advertising and in the contracts they require consumers to sign. Such deviance may be a good short-run strategy. Hence the game must also provide legal proceedings. These are specified by mediation rules which concern conflict situations in which neither party to the conflict has the power to resolve it. In Consumer, the coordinator temporarily becomes the judge and suspends activity in the game. The consumer and credit agent each have one minute to present their versions of the dispute along with whatever evidence they have. The judge, using a set of guidelines provided in the game, makes a decision which is binding on both players. In this way deviant behavior is corrected (to the extent that it is contrary to the legal facts of life), and it is also prevented from disrupting the game for the two players.

Potential conflict situations were deliberately included for their instructional value. Most trouble arises between consumers and credit agents because the consumers are often careless in reading their contracts and filling them out. When a credit agent exploits this carelessness and the consumer discovers it, the consumer will usually institute legal action. The publicized outcome—usually against the consumer—often has a very sobering impact on all consumers. Generally, comparisons of contracts signed after the first court case with those signed before show a great deal more understanding and caution among consumers after the court scene. Afterwards, consumers spend more time reading the contract. They ask for definitions of terms such as collateral and repossession, and they make sure they obtain exact copies of the contract with the credit agent's signature. Thus, the court scene constitutes a very important learning experience for *all* players; the consequences of certain behavior (e.g., being too misleading in advertising or too careless in reading a contract) are demonstrated.

Notably, the behavior resulting in legal proceedings arises informally as a result of other formal structure in the game. The game rules concerning court action simply provide guidelines *after* the situation comes about. An alternative technique would have been to increase the number of behavioral constraint rules: formal rules prescribing the do's and don't's for the credit agents when having a consumer sign a contract, so that they could not be misleading within the framework of the game. This procedure would attempt to teach by having students automatically go through or be exposed to the correct motions. Earlier versions of Consumer were in fact like this latter type. It was found, however, that this approach was a far less effective way of conveying information about contracts. Moreover, it made the game more complicated for credit agents since they had more rules and formal procedures to follow. This structure was both less interesting *and* less realistic.

The second kind of aberrant behavior, *recalcitrant deviance,* is more deeply rooted in a player's extra-game attitudes. It may be intentional, as when the student simply fools around; or it may be unintentional, as when a student has a negative reaction to the element of competition. Nothing in the formal rules of any simulation can require players to cooperate in the conduct of a game session. In this regard, simulations are very much like other teaching techniques: students cannot be forced to involve themselves in whatever manner the instructor may want. The fact that social simulation games seem particularly effective in involving inattentive or hard-to-control students in normal classroom contexts may be explained in large measure by the effectiveness of peer group pressures toward cooperation. If a player fools around too much, the group activity—the social simulation—can't operate smoothly. It is quite interesting to watch how efficient other players are in securing the "deviant's" cooperation in a game session, whereas in other classroom settings the same deviant is often encouraged by his peers to be disruptive.

Needless to say, the game designer should do all he can to augment the inherent qualities of a social simulation in correcting disruptive behavior of this type. One problem I faced in Consumer was cheating. For example, there was a tendency in early versions for some players to take product cards from others or alter credit information on their own record sheets. Such deception was corrected by the simple device of having those in non-consumer roles use special color-coded pencils. It then became an easy matter when a complaint or suspicion arose to compare the items circles in green by the salesman on a consumer's record sheet with the product cards displayed in plastic envelopes. (The two should be identical; if a player has more items than those circled by the salesman, he has items which don't belong to him.) Also, the coordinator can determine whether a monthly installment due the Finance Company, for instance, has been properly paid by observing whether an orange check mark has been placed in the appropriate square. If nothing has been checked or if another kind of marking has been placed there, then that installment has not been taken care of properly. The player will not be allowed to continue into the following month until he has either told the coordinator he intends to skip that payment (in which case the coordinator records it for the Finance Company's knowledge) or until he has settled the matter with the Finance Company.

There is another form of recalcitrant deviance—this one, however, is unintentional. Some students try to avoid openly competitive situations or withdraw from such situations as soon as they begin to fall behind. It is important, therefore, that structures exist in the game that minimize both forms of withdrawal. The obvious countervailing structure is a cooperative relationship. Cooperation provides for mutual reinforcement and puts social pressure on a player to continue active participation in the game session. when others' strategies are dependent upon his. Consumer can be readily adapted to prevent player withdrawal by having multi-member consumer units. I found this device to be especially effective among junior high school groups and others who are easily upset by adverse chance cards. Another technique is to have players proceed through the various months of the game at the same time rather then have them work at their individual speeds. This can minimize feeling of "falling far behind" induced among slower players by those who complete the game quickly.

Yet Consumer may still have problems of withdrawal because there is a relative lack of interdependent strategies among players in the same role. This is not to say that players in the same role do not cooperate. To the contrary, they often do, but this informal behavior is the indirect result of informal relationships between consumers and credit agents. The credit agent is sometimes seen by consumers as a common challenge or adversary about whom it is worthwhile to exchange information. Also, aggressiveness on the part of credit agents may overcome withdrawal or hesitant behavior on the part of consumers. A consumer sitting down inactively is an easy target for credit agents to approach. Even if a borrowing transaction is not consummated, the interaction between the two players is usually sufficient to motivate the consumer to become more active. This is partly because a credit agent may outline for the consumer what appears to be good competitive strategy.

Self-Judging

To be self-judging, the scoring system should lie entirely within the model or structure of the game. Points must be earned or lost solely on the basis of what happens in the game and not by a teacher's evaluation of a player's performance. Points are not the only means by which success or goal achievement in a game may be measured, but they are the most frequently used means.

Furthermore, it should be evident to players that their standings at the end of a game are a direct result of their actions in the game. Whether it is "more" or "less" is partly influenced by the player's perception of the role of chance or luck in the game. It is important in Consumer that students not perceive the game outcome to be overly influenced by the environmental response rules, over which they have little control.

There are two types of environmental response rules. One, mentioned earlier, is where the likely response of the environment is determined throughout the game. It assumes or is concerned with one-way causation. For instance, there is a certain probability that a chance card will be drawn saying, "Your spouse in unemployed; receive only $50 next month." This probability can be adjusted to reflect reality for the particular group playing the game, but once fixed, it remains constant throughout the session. The second type of environmental response rule is more concerned with instances characterized by reciprocal feedback relationships between the model being simulated and relevant but missing parts of the environment. There are no instances of this type of rule operationalized in Consumer. Being employed or unemployed influences the need to borrow money but borrowing money doesn't influence one's employment.

The likelihood of a player attributing his performance in a game to luck or chance seems smaller with the latter type of environmental response rule, if only because the player is better able to understand the derivation of the probabilities contained in those rules.[3] The environmental response rule in this case constitutes a particular feedback mechanism. When the first type of environmental response rule is the sole or dominant type in a game it becomes important to place greater emphasis on other feedback mechanisms. Players should not be allowed the opportunity for excusing their performance over a series of plays as a result of bad luck. Feedback mechanisms are countervailing forces to the chance elements by making more salient the fact that the consequences in the game are primarily a function of the choice of actions or strategies, including responses to chance cards.

Feedback

It is essential that an educational simulation game be constructed so that a player is able to evaluate the effectiveness of particular strategies. The efficacy of social simulation games lies largely in the fact that they demonstrate to players the consequences of behavior by having them experience those consequences. Most easily, at the conclusion of a game session one can have the players receiving the highest and lowest scores describe their strategies and experiences. It is desirable, however, that some mechanisms exist whereby players are able to evaluate their strategies during the course of the session. Positive and negative reinforcements in the course of a game session will guide game behavior toward the more rational behavior patterns that the simulation is designed to teach. For example, as a player receives feedback to the effect that payoffs on a particular strategy are low, he will begain to search for and test alternative strategies. As a consequence, players will pay extra attention to the rewards and penalties attendant upon the strategies of others and thus learn from other players' experiences as well as from their own.

Feedback in Consumer is largely public. All products bought by consumers are represented by cards which are placed in a plastic dis-

[3] A very good example is Boocock's *Life Career* (1969), described elsewhere in this volume.

play holder upon purchase. The holders are located together in a central part of the room. Simple inspection of the product cards helps a player decide, for example, whether he is purchasing items in the best sequence. Another form of feedback in the game, discussed earlier, is through court action. This procedure is a way of telling each player whether his behavior in borrowing transactions is presenting any undue risk.

Finally, the use of record forms provides feedback during the course of a game. Consumers have a simple record sheet. One section, filled in by the credit agents, contains information about the number of borrowing transactions a consumer makes, the terms of the different transactions, and the consumer's repayment history (whether installments have been missed or whether repossessions have occurred.) This sheet was initially intended to serve two functions. One was to simplify certain bookkeeping tasks, and the other was to simulate a credit rating service. A credit agent could determine quite quickly whether a consumer was a good credit risk or a poor one by inspecting the information in this section. The responses of the credit agents to this information provided feedback to the consumers as to how well they were preserving their borrowing power. In addition, it also developed that credit agents used this same set of information to keep track of how well their competitors were doing since these sources of credit were also recorded. Credit agents were thus provided with feedback mechanisms about their relative standing and about their differential inclinations to assume risk.

Levels of Complexity and Simplicity

Different levels of complexity of games enable the instructor to start a session at the level providing the optimal challenge for his class. Additional levels may then be added in a step-wise fashion so that the student is gradually introduced into an increasingly complex learning situation. Also, game sessions at different levels of complexity may be conducted at the same time where participants of widely differing abilities are in the same class. What is important is that the different levels of a game be compatible with one another. The different levels ought not to make different theoretical assumptions about behavior; they should all be consistent with the goal-specifying behavior included in the most elementary level but should accomplish relatively independent teaching objectives.

There are three levels of complexity in Consumer. The first level, which concerns the credit use behavior of consumers, was described at the beginning of this paper and has provided all illustrations used. The second level concerns product differentiation. In this version there are no credit agents. In their place are three salesmen, each of whom represents a different firm or brand line. The items they sell differ in quality and potential for breaking down, wearing out, etc. As a consequence, satisfaction from their purchase may vary from brand to brand. The salesmen compete in trying to make the most sales. Consumers have buying guide literature available if they want to use it. The information contained in this literature is usually but not always accurate, so that effort to obtain additional information prior to buying will usually but not always pay off. In the third version there are both credit agents and salesmen. Pressures on consumers to borrow and buy are greater because the consumer has two sources of influence directed toward him instead of just one as in the other two versions. Moreover, the salesmen, whose goal is to make more sales, and the credit agents, whose goal is to make more safe credit transactions, will coordinate their behavior to increase the efficiency of their influence process.

There may also be a nesting of steps within different levels. The credit-agent-only version may be simplified by omitting any of the following elements: contracts, one or two of the credit agents, and chance cards which apply to time periods other than the one in which they are drawn. Or a game may begin with just two credit agents, which reduces the number of alternatives a consumer has to consider. In a second play all three credit agents would participate and would require the signing of contracts. The addition or deletion of various elements in the game results in a change of emphasis on the different instructional objectives. Therefore, in deciding which level to use or which steps within a level to omit, the instructor must also consider the impact the changes will have on what the game teaches.

Alternative Strategies

It is desirable to incorporate more than one possible course of action for each player in a social simulation game. This is generally realistic in that there are usually alternative strategies or sets of goal-oriented behaviors which may be followed in most social situations. The social phenomena being simulated determine the number and kind of strategies available to be incorporated in a game. Then operational and pedagogical considerations determine the strategies actually incorporated in the simulation. From an instructional standpoint, it is important to structure the simulation so as to afford players the opportunity to follow wrong strategies. Making errors is a highly effective way of learning. As Schild notes in an interesting discussion on the shaping of strategies, "The core of a game is to establish certain consequences (winning or losing) as contingent upon certain behavior (the play of the participant)." (Schild, 1967: 1).

What has become increasingly clear in education is that simply exposing students to correct solutions or decisions does not guarentee that those decisions or actions will be followed in a real-life context containing wrong decision possibilities. The player who has been exposed to a "wrong" strategy (and its consequences) will be better able to rule out that strategy when confronted with it later as a possible course of action. He still may not choose the best strategy, but he will at least be able to eliminate some poor strategies. It should be obvious that unless the simulation contains appropriate feedback mechanisms, the utility of having competing and differentially rewarding strategies will be largely lost.

A number of alternatives may be followed in Consumer, most of which are not very rewarding in terms of winning the game. First of all, a player is not under any circumstances required to borrow money. When faced with the need for funds to settle a negative chance card, he has the option of auctioning off some of his possessions to obtain the needed cash, even though this may not be wise. His monthly income is just sufficient over the period of the game to allow him to buy all items, particularly if he draws a "sale" chance card. In fact, there is no requirement that he buy any products. When borrowing money he is not required to shop around for the best rates or to evaluate the implications of borrowing on a six-month rather than a twelve-month basis. Nor is there any required buying sequence for those items he does purchase. However, because of the way the utility points and credit rates are structured, there is really one best course of action. The majority of adolescents and adults who play this game do not have insight into the best strategy at the outset and, for some, not even after one complete game session. Rather, their behaviors typically are governed by such extra-game predispositions as their attitudes toward the various financial institutions represented, their inclinations to defer gratification, or even how well they know each other. Occasionally a player will drop a wise buying strategy in order to initiate or follow the behavior of another player who he thinks may be wiser but who, in fact, is following an unwise buying policy.

In addition to those extra-game predispositions, there are other reasons why participants do not necessarily discern the best strategy in the game right off. Being unfamiliar with the social context of the simulation, a player may not realize that there is more than one possible course of action. Therefore, he may not look for alternatives, but simply choose the most salient solution. A consumer may not know that interest rates vary among credit agents and may therefore simply borrow from the most aggressive agent. When different courses of action are expected, they will not necessarily be equally obvious to all participants. Furthermore, even when different strategies are discernible as alternatives, it may be difficult for players to determine their probable consequences on an *a priori* basis. There is something to be said for making game strategies more obvious than they are in real life and for exaggerating somewhat their payoff differences.

An alternate approach is to allow for or facilitate the functioning of interpersonal processes whereby players exert pressures on each other to follow wrong strategies. (An example has already been mentioned with regard to imitative behavior in buying products.) Such pressures may be deliberately built into the game. The goals for players in different but interacting roles may motivate such behavior. For instance, the credit agent is motivated by his goal (to conclude as many transactions as he can) to induce consumers to borrow as frequently as possible and with as little thought as possible. Toward this end, credit agents in the game will sometimes suggest to their potential clients buying and borrowing strategies which work only to the credit agents' advantage. The absence of behavioral constraint rules which might curb this behavior is intentional. Our earlier example of the lack of prescribed do's and don't's with regard to the negotiating of contracts also bears upon this point.

TESTING THE GAME

Earlier discussion focused on the importance of feedback mechanisms in a game in order for participants to learn effectively from their experiences. Developing a social simulation is also an important learning experience for the designer, and the major feedback mechanism in this learning experience is the field testing of the game. The nature of the information provided the designer at this stage ranges from the theoretical soundness of the social model being used to the feasibility of various pieces of physical equipment. Since the main concern here is with the construction of educational rather than theoretical tools, we shall have to leave aside the very important problems involved in testing the basic theoretical model of the game and of using simulation games to develop social theory.

Consumer was tested among approximately twenty-five hundred persons prior to its first-edition printing. A number of factors influence the degree to which testing is undertaken. Generally, there is a positive relationship between the amount of testing required and the following factors:

1. The number of different roles in a game
2. The heterogeneity of the intended audience
3. The number of specific learning objectives
4. The complexity of the game model and role behaviors
5. The number of informal behaviors desired.

The remainder of this paper will discuss some of these factors.

Variety of Roles

The number of different roles and number of players in identical roles may influence the number of game sessions required. Given the optimal number of players in a game session, the larger the number of different roles, the fewer the number of testing experiences obtained for each role per session. In Consumer the suggested number of consumers is twelve and one player for each of the other positions (bank, department store, finance company, salesman, and coordinator). Thus, in one game session, information is obtained about one role (consumer) from twelve different players while there are the experiences of only one player as source of feedback on the problems related to each of the other roles. As a result, more frequent testing was necessary to accumulate the necessary experiences with these roles. The role of consumer became operational more quickly than did some of the other roles. This is not to say that changes related to the consumer role were not made after it was first considered operational. Because consumers interact with players in all other roles, changes in rules and equipment related to these other positions often required some adjustment in consumer rules and record sheets. The effect of these changes on consumers had to be assessed continuously.

The Audience

The testing and operationalizing of the role structure cannot be done without regard to the particular kinds of players who will be assuming these roles. Players who differ in age, level of education, learning abilities, and other socio-economic dimensions bring different predispositions to the game. Social simulation games are unlike conventional role-playing techniques in which the actor is supposed to empathize with the social and psychological set normally associated with a particular role. Simulation games present a structure of that particular role within which the player may act out behaviors associated with that role without having to adopt the emotional qualities of that role. Because players are bringing in their own social and psychological traits and are not asked to drop them for a different collection of traits, special attention must be given to the task of structuring the simulation and its constituent roles so that it is relevant and workable for a heterogeneous audience. This requires that the structure of the various roles and the game in general be meaningful to a variety of persons.[4]

An example will illustrate the problem of a heterogeneous audience. With regard to the adaptation of equipment, the use of dice as a means of introducing environmental responses into the game posed no problem among students from middle and upper class families. However, in testing the game among adolescents from economically depressed inner-city areas this aspect of the game was found particularly disruptive, especially among female players. It became evident that this was due to the use of dice which had an unacceptable gambling connotation among these players. The problem was overcome by substituting chance cards for dice.

Instructional Objectives

The most important consideration in the testing process and the one to which all other aspects of the game being evaluated should be subordinated is simply this: Is the game teaching what it is intended to teach? How much a player learns from a game is probably a function of several things:

1. The visibility of alternative strategies
2. The salience of the consequences of pursuing good and bad strategies
3. The importance the participant places on the consequences of his strategies
4. The extent to which a participant perceives himself as able to control the outcome of the game
5. The level of participant involvement

The decision as to which of these (or the many other considerations which could have been listed) should be manipulated to increase the instructional efficiency of the game must be based on feedback that the designer receives from the test sessions.

There are at least three basic sources of information available to the designer concerning the instructional effectiveness of the simulation.

[4] It might be added here that a simulated social structure capable of "accepting" varied social input (e.g., varied socio-economic player traits) is a fairly accurate and relatively high-order theoretical representation. The nature of the changes a designer must make, i.e., what specific formulations of a rule he must sacrifice as a new population is brought within the realm of the game, can provide considerable insight into the social mechanisms that differentiate that population from others with regard to the social phenomenon being simulated.

The first is the response provided by students. In the early stages of testing Consumer this came entirely from post-game discussions. Prior to each session players were told about the general teaching objectives of the simulations. In addition, they were told that their comments would be very helpful, and they were asked to make note of any changes they felt would help improve the game. At the conclusion of the game the different strategies and experiences of the players were discussed along with their suggestions. These discussions of strategies and game experiences provided good indications as to whether the game was functioning as intended. It would be difficult to over-estimate the value of the suggestions received from players in this way.

Using the *same* students for different testing sessions is recommended in the early testing stages: first, there are fewer start-up costs in introducing and explaining the game. Also, the helpfulness of the participants' advice increases. Furthermore, the designer is able to know the players better and to this extent gain some additional insight into less obvious obstacles in the game. The case of the dice is an example of this latter point.

As the game becomes more refined on the basis of the post-game discussion, it becomes useful to administer a written questionnaire among persons playing the game for the first or second time. A word of caution is in order here: There is evidence that not all learning in a game, and perhaps not even the most important learning, can be adequately gauged through the use of a written questionnaire (North Carolina Advancement School, 1968; Boocock *et al.*, 1967).

Another source of information is not solicited from players directly. It is generated during the course of a game session and is generally recorded by participants on their various playing forms. From these forms one can determine not only which activities were undertaken but also their sequence and frequency. In the Consumer game, without asking consumers, it is possible to determine, among other things, whether they purchased items in the most appropriate time period (or whether they were more likely to do so as the game progressed) and who they borrowed from.

One can also simply eavesdrop on conversations between players. This practice may provide information on procedural elements of the game not readily understood, and it may provide insight into whether the nature of the exchange relationships between players is conducive to learning. (e.g., Are consumers asking about interest rates and contract terminology?) The use of tape recorders would seem to be an effective way of collecting this information in lieu of or in addition to the designer's or game administrator's listening in. Although this device was not used in the testing of Consumer, it appears in retrospect that the testing phase would have moved faster had this been done.

The third source of information is provided by game administrators. The originator of a device can usually guarantee its success so long as he directs its use. It may be quite another story when someone to whom the device is new must take charge of its administration. Unless persons who are unfamiliar with a simulation game are able to understand it and administer it without difficulty, the game will realize little of potential value for lack of use. It is important, then, that feedback be received from the teacher or administrator about his experiences with the simulation. After the designer has gathered sufficient information from the first two sources and made the necessary adjustment, his efforts should be devoted toward having persons unfamiliar with the game use and evaluate it.

CONCLUSION

It has been said that art is reality seen through a temperament. In many ways this is also descriptive of simulation games. The developer starts with the raw material of an idea and out of it creates a social situation consistent with his world view. Unfortunately, little attention has been devoted in the past to the multifaceted technical aspects of building social simulation games. It was the intention of this paper to specify the various processes and criteria which constitute the technique of simulation game building. Hopefully, because of an increased awareness of these techniques, more people will become involved in the building of these new educational tools.

REFERENCES

Boocock, Sarane S., Erling O. Schild, and Clarice Stoll
1967 *Simulation games and control beliefs.* Center for Study of the Social Organization of Schools, The Johns Hopkins University: Baltimore, Maryland.

Caplovitz, David
1961 *The Poor Pay More.* New York: Free Press.

Homans, George C.
1950 *The Human Group.* New York: Harcourt, Brace and World.

Mors, Wallace P.
1965 *Consumer Credit and Finance Charges.* New York: National Bureau of Economic Research.

North Carolina Advancement School
1968 "Appendix." *Annual Report for 1968.*

Schild, Erling O.
1967 "The shaping of strategies." *American Behavioral Scientist,* 10, 3, 1–4.

Troostrup, Arch W.
1965 *Consumer Problems and Personal Finances,* (third edition). New York: McGraw-Hill.

MICHAEL INBAR

Chapter 9

Artificial Community Disasters[1]

The Disaster Game is an example of a simulation for which the model (that of "disaster behavior") was systematically abstracted from the literature before the design process began. The reader will be able to follow in some detail how the model was embedded into a simulation, and how problems of complexity and playability were and still are being tackled.

—THE EDITORS

[1] The author gratefully acknowledges the collaboration of Samuel Livingston in the preparation of the final version of this paper.

Artificial Community Disasters

The idea of a Disaster Game should probably be credited in the first place to Edgar J. Reeves, Jr., of the 4-H Clubs staff. His concern about training young people efficiently had led him to try some of the games developed for teaching purposes by James Coleman and others of the Hopkins group. The response that they had generated induced him to ask Coleman whether a special game could be devised for one of the teaching programs of the 4-H Clubs, and Coleman relayed the suggestion to the author, then a graduate student of his.

The problem was to enhance the interest of youngsters in a civil defense program which had been going on with meager success for years. Young people did not show evidence of reading the printed material which was given to them, their reaction to lectures was often more polite than interested, and they showed very little curiosity in the subject. Teaching by means of a simulation game seemed to be an ideal way to overcome the youngsters' indifference; indeed, as pointed out in Chapter 19, simulations are a powerful means to familiarize people with unusual situations and to bring hypothetical future situations into the present. This telescoping of time and space can cause the participants in a simulation game to involve themselves deeply in situations which otherwise remain as remote from their interest as from their personal experience.

I began by reading A. F. C. Wallace's *Human Behavior in Extreme Situations,* the first in a series of Disaster Studies published by the National Research Council. This introduction to the study of disasters immediately prompted several questions about the proposed simulation game.

> Should the simulation teach general principles or specific facts?
> Should it teach the players what behavior in a disaster *ought* to be, or what it *is?*
> Should it focus on the situation in the impact area or in the community as a whole?
> Should the players be confronted with the problems of public officials or only with the problems of private citizens?
> What kind of disaster should be simulated? Bombing (conventional or nuclear)? Natural catastrophes?
> Should the game start before the disaster, during, or after the impact of the disaster?

With these questions in mind, I began a selective study of the available scientific literature concerning disasters. My own inclinations as a sociologist led me to concentrate on the phenomenon of the behavior of people affected by disasters. (Had I been a physician, or an economist, or a civil engineer, my research would have concentrated on other aspects of disasters, and a very different simulation game would have resulted.) The limitations of the scientific literature I had available (see Inbar, 1969) forced me to concentrate my inquiry on disasters which:

1. Were caused by natural forces (e.g. flood, tornado, earthquake) rather than by a hostile enemy;
2. Occurred in the United States, and;
3. Destroyed only part of the community, leaving the rest intact and able to respond.

Because disasters occur suddenly and with little or no warning, studies of behavior in a disaster can be designed only after the disaster has occurred. As a result, most disaster studies are purely descriptive in character. And of course, Nature offers no guarantee that the communities which *are* struck by disasters are a representative sample of the communities which *could* be struck. Nevertheless, there are certain common characteristics of "disaster behavior" which can be abstracted with reasonable confidence from the available reports of localized natural disasters in the United States.

BUILDING THE MODEL [2]

Perhaps the best way to begin a description of "disaster behavior" is to specify what it is *not:*

1. There is very little panic (that is, nonadaptive behavior which is emotional, irrational, and highly active). Reactions of "daze" (lack of any response) are much more common. (See Ilke and Kincaid, n. d.: 7–8; Barton, 1962: 232; and Wallace, n. d.: 111–116.)
2. Traffic and communication jams, which usually accompany disasters, are caused mainly by people who were not in the impact area when the disaster struck. (See Fritz and Mathewson, 1957.)
3. Looting is rare, and when it occurs, it is almost always done by outsiders, not by the afflicted population who has the opportunity but lacks the motivation. (See Fritz and Mathewson, 1957.)

[2] For a more comprehensive report on the model of this simulation and for the complete bibliography, see Inbar (1969).

Artificial Community Disasters

It is now possible to turn profitably to the question of what "disaster behavior" *is*. First of all, it is a behavior which is temporally very limited. Usually rescue begins to arrive in a disaster area within minutes, and the primary impact is overcome at most in a matter of hours. (See Killian, n. d.: 5; Wallace, n. d.: 58; and Raker et al., n. d.: 22.) This is another important reason for limiting this description of "disaster behavior" to the culture and the types of catastrophe that were specified. Indeed it is not at all certain that the generalizations would hold in a society where help would be less lavish and/or rapid; by the same token, other types of disaster, e.g. atomic bombing, which might hinder rescue activities—by curtailing them or even by merely postponing them for a significant period of time—might have behavioral consequences for which too little evidence is yet available to permit tenable generalizations.

In the short time before outside help arrives, disaster behavior is characterized by a temporary breakdown of social organization. An explanation of this phenomenon is provided by A. H. Barton (1962: 223), who conceptualizes human behavior as being organized on three levels: individual, primary group, and community. Each level depends on the previous one, so that an individual who suffered a traumatism cannot perform properly as a member of his family or his community. In the same way, a man who is anxious about the fate of his family or whose help is requested by close friends does not turn to community tasks, even if, objectively, he, as well as the collectivity, would benefit much more from the performance of these tasks than from any other behavior. The disturbance of the two first levels (the individual and primary group levels) accounts for the disorganization, the amazement, "daze," etc. which are observed in disasters immediately after the impact. *It is only when the individual shock is overcome and when anxiety about loved ones is reduced that the way is open again to community-oriented behavior*. When this stage is reached, cooperation and help take on the form of an increasing collective and altruistic behavior, until the primary consequences of the catastrophe are overcome.

Much of the damage and loss of life in disasters results from what Wallace calls "secondary impact:"

The impact period is the time during which physical destruction is being accomplished by the impact agent. The destruction accomplished during the operation of this agent (whether it be tornado, flood water, hydrogen explosion, or whatever) is called the primary impact. The primary impact is *only* that damage inflicted during the action of the agent; the consequences of this primary impact are occasionally irreversible, unchangeable and final, but usually primary impact is followed by a *secondary impact*, which is susceptible to manipulation. . . . Let us take an example. The driving of a piece of glass into a man's arm, severing an artery, during the thirty seconds of the tornado's passage over an area, is primary impact. At the close of the brief impact period (i.e., when the tornado is past) the man is left with a cut arm, blood spurting out of it. The bleeding which follows, and which may, if unchecked, cost the man his life, is secondary impact. . . . What happens of a destructive nature during the operation of the disaster agent is primary impact; destruction which follows in time is secondary impact. (Wallace, n. d.: 9.)

Obviously, the faster the community can organize an effective rescue effort, the less the secondary impact of the disaster will be. In order for the rescue effort to be effective, certain key community agencies *must* perform their functions:

The department of public works, to clear the roads in order to facilitate both the approach of the rescuers and the evacuation of victims.
The gas, water and electricity companies, to take care of possible broken water mains, open circuits, etc.
The fire department, to fight blazes.
The police force and the civil defense, to preserve order, fight against the jams, ensure priorities (ambulances), etc.
The hospitals and red-cross network, to provide medical help and, if necessary, food and temporary shelters.
The transportation system: cars, ambulances, railroads, and airports.

For each of these agencies, the organizational problems involve both materials (tools, gasoline, etc.) and personnel.

To organize an effective rescue effort requires an effective communications system. The vital role that the telephone, radio, and television system can play in the transmission of information and help requests to the outside is only one aspect of the problem. The other aspect is the importance of establishing an effective communication network on the community level, i.e., between the rescue-agencies and the field. The lack of such a network has at least two major consequences. First, it makes for an inefficient demand and allocation of available rescues and efforts. Fire trucks may be sent where there are no fires, and ambulances may be sent where there are no casualties. Second, the lack of effective communications perpetuates the unstructured and ambiguous character of the situation, with the resulting spread of rumors and confusion. The public tends to react to the lack of clear-cut information by jamming both the roads and the telephone switchboards.

It should be apparent that the consequences of "disaster behavior" are most serious when the persons temporarily incapacitated by it are those responsible for operating key community agencies. Killian provides some illustrations:

——In Texas City the chief of police remained at his post from the moment of the first explosion until seventy-two hours later, never returning to his home during the entire period and playing a vital part in the reorganization of the community. He ascribed his ability to give undivided attention to his official duties to the fact that he knew that his family was safely out of town, visiting relatives, at the time of the explosion.
——One member of the volunteer fire department of a tornado town told of the thin margin by which his community escaped a disastrous fire following the "Twister:" 'I was at my house, right on the edge of where the storm passed, when it hit. Neither me nor my wife was hurt. The first thing I thought of was fires. I knew there'd be some, so I went to the fire station right away. On the way, I could see that there was a fire right in the middle of the wreakage—a butane tank had caught fire. I got out the truck, drove over there, and fought the fire by myself until the army got there to help me. All the rest of the firemen had relatives that were hurt, and they stayed with them. Naturally they looked after them. If it hadn't been that my wife was all right, this town probably would have burned up. It's hard to say, but I kind of believe I would have been looking after my family too.' (Killian, 1952: 309–314.)

The foregoing points led me to the following general model of the response of communities to disaster:

In a community disaster, the role conflicts experienced by people are likely to give rise to individualistically oriented behaviors. These, and the general lack of structure of the situation, lead to dysfunctional consequences: cooperation on the community level is lowered, rumors spread, and telephone switchboard and roads tend to get jammed. Consequently, some crucial agencies may not perform properly for a variable length of time. The more and the longer this holds true, the greater the probability of destructive secondary impact consequences. Once cooperation on the community level is resumed, however, it is likely to grow quickly and the essential functions tend to be given an increasing priority over others by all the individuals.

These were the basic processes I sought to reproduce by means of a simulation game.

BUILDING THE SIMULATION

To me, the most striking characteristics of disasters were the elements of surprise and uncertainty. I was especially struck by the resemblance of disasters to the game *Kriegspiel*, a variation of chess in which each player can see only his own pieces. This game is played on three boards; each player has a board showing his own pieces, and a third participant, the director, has a master board with both sets of pieces. Neither player is told the other player's moves; he is told only when one of his pieces has been taken and when his king is under attack. If he attempts to make an impossible or illegal move, he is told that his move cannot be made, but he is not told the reason.

It occurred to me that the techniques of *Kriegspiel* could be used to simulate certain aspects of a disaster; the reader will undoubtedly recognize their influence in the construction of the game, which is now briefly described.

The First Simulation

The first version of the game (1964) involved any number of players, from 6 to 16. It was played on a board reproducing schematically the map of a medium-sized town (or an area of a large town). The map showed the location of the important community agencies (police department, fire department, hospitals, etc.) and places where many people would be (residential areas, schools, shopping centers, etc.). These were spread over the map and were connected by a network of roads. The roads were marked off into spaces. To move from one road space to another required one "unit of energy." Each player was represented on the board by a pawn. The player also received a "role structure" card which specified his job, his location, and the locations of his relatives or friends in the community.

At the beginning of the game the players were told that a disaster had occurred somewhere in the town. (They were not told where.) They were also told that each player would receive "anxiety points" for each friend or relative listed on his role structure card, and would continue to accumulate anxiety points until he had verified that the person either was unaffected by the disaster or had been taken to a hospital. A player could acquire this information by listening to radio broadcasts, by placing telephone calls, by asking other players whose pawns were at the same location as his, or by moving to the location where the friend or relative was when the disaster struck. In the course of these actions, the players would discover that traffic jams and switchboard jams were the direct result of their behavior. Similarly, they faced the fact that the public agencies, whose services were necessary to rescue their loved ones, performed their functions only if the players in charge stayed on the job. For example, if the phone company or the police radio cars were not operated, the community would be without a communication network. In this case, the players had to remove their pawns from the board and were forbidden to talk with each other. Likewise, the radio would be silent if the announcer did not broadcast.

A printed decision form was filled out at each move by each player. The forms were handed over to the director of the game, who computed the results of the move after reproducing the decisions of the players on a second board out of their sight. The disaster area was indicated only on the director's board until all players were in a position to know the location and extent of the impact; it was then indicated on the players' board also. At this point, some players would be faced with the fact that they had relatives trapped in the diaster area. To evacuate them, they had to enter the impact area, and this required the intervention of the department of public works to clear the roads, the fire department to master the blaze, the police station to fight traffic jams, etc. These activities were expensive in terms of the units of energy that their performance required, and units of energy used were added to the players' anxiety scores. Each player had to keep his anxiety/energy score as low as possible, because the winner was elected by the group from among the three players with the lowest total of negative points (anxiety points + energy units used). A wise allocation of one's effort was, thus, an important strategy. Despite this strategic constraint, however, the players whose anxiety was high as long as their wounded relatives were not transported to a hospital had no choice and had to perform the community and rescue tasks on which their relatives' evacuation depended. Those with low anxiety scores, on the other hand, also had to take on social responsibilities in order to be highly regarded by their fellow players; otherwise they would not be elected as winner. Moreover, after the fifth move, the disaster area would spread, and in such a case any one of the players as well as the relatives could be wounded or killed. There was, therefore, a generalized interest to overcome the community disaster as quickly as possible without at the same time disregarding one's own anxieties. This double aim was expressed by the fact that in order to win, a player had to solve his own problems (i.e., become *eligible* by means of a low negative score) and had to be selected by the other players, who voted according to how well he helped solve the community problems.

The main problem with this version was that the director's job was all but impossible. In the shortest possible time (so as to minimize waiting time for the players), he had to:

Collect and read all the players' decision forms.
Determine which agencies were being operated. (Entry into

the disaster area was not permitted unless both the fire department and the public works department were being operated.)

Make the moves for all players on his own board and see what the actual result of each intended move would be. An attempt to move could be stopped by a traffic jam (more than two players on the same road space) or by the disaster area. However, traffic jams could occur only if the police department was not being operated on that turn.

Write on each decision form the actual result of each move.

Determine if any players had arrived at the same location and inform them that they could talk to each other.

Return the decision forms to the players.

In addition, if the phone company was being operated, he had to:

Count the number of phone calls attempted.

Spin a spinner for each call to determine whether it got through: the more calls, the lower the probability of each call's getting through.

For each successful call to a location outside the impact, inform the player making the call that the call had succeeded, and, if another player happened to beat the location to which the call was made, that the two could talk with each other.

On each round after the fifth round, he also had to roll a die. If the die showed a "one," he had to:

Extend the disaster area on his own board.

Announce to the players that the disaster had spread, and tell them in which half of town the spread had occurred. Each player then again began receiving anxiety points for all his friends or relatives in that half of town.

Inform any players caught by the spread of the disaster that they were dead and had to leave the game.

Inform any players on the edge of the new disaster area that they had to move away from the spreading disaster.

The Second Version

In an attempt to make the director's job more manageable, the game was revised so as to give to the players some of the tasks which had been done by the director. The director's board and the players' board were sandwiched into a single board, divided into thirty compartments, each with a lid. The lids were printed so as to reproduce the map of the territory they covered, while they concealed the tokens or markers in the compartment. Each player was permitted to look inside the compartments he passed through or completed a phone call to. He had a paper map on which to record whatever information he wished; this map and his role structure card were combined with his decision form onto a single sheet. Instead of handing in their decision forms to the director, the players came to the board in turn to make their own moves. Cards placed beside the board indicated whether the fire department and public works department were being operated, to allow entry into the impact area. The job of handling phone calls was given to the player operating the phone company. Finally, the maximum number of players was reduced from sixteen to twelve.

There were still serious problems with the game. The worst of these was tedium. Eleven players had to wait while each player made his move. Another problem was the complexity of the rules, which made it extremely difficult to learn to play. The scoring system took some getting used to, as did the restrictions on communication. The roles of the police, fire, and public works departments were also unclear to most of the players, and the possibility of a spreading disaster area added to the confusion. Clearly, further changes were necessary.

The Present Version

Once again, the game was revised. The maximum number of players was decreased to ten. The lids, which had been separate, were made into a single board (with flaps over each compartment), to allow the compartments to be revealed one at a time or all at once. The map was redrawn for greater clarity.

A more basic change was in the operation of the police, fire, and public works departments. Three new kinds of markers were introduced, representing traffic jams, fires, and roadblocks. These are placed by the administrator before the game begins—in the compartments below the lids, so that a player can not see the marker until he has reached the compartment containing it. No player may pass one of these markers, and each marker can be removed only by a player operating the corresponding agency (police department for traffic jams, fire department for fires, and public works department for roadblocks).

The rules for phone calls were simplified. Each player who wants to make a call submits a phone call slip for each call. The player operating the phone company then chooses three of these slips at random (two, if he is making a call himself) and throws the rest away. He then checks the three calls to see if the location called was in the disaster area. If so, he throws the slip away; if not, he gives the slip back to the player who made the call.

The problem of complexity was handled by dividing the game into four levels of increasing complexity. Each level is to be played only by a group that is already familiar with the preceding level. In the first level there are no roadblocks, only fires and traffic jams, and hence the public works department does not need to be operated. There is also no radio station, and the disaster does not spread.

Level II introduces the public works department and the radio station. It also introduces the possibility of the spread of the disaster.

In Level III, any community agency in the disaster area is destroyed and cannot operate for the rest of the game. However, the community may duplicate three of its agencies by building them in vacant areas on the map. Before the game starts, the players meet for ten minutes to decide which agencies to build and where to build them. Level III also introduces competition between communities, when two or more groups play at the same time. In this case, the communities must have the same set of rules and the same placement of disaster, fire, roadblock, and traffic jam markers. After a community overcomes the disaster and chooses a winner, all the players' scores are added together. The winning community is the one that overcomes its disaster with the lowest total.

Level IV—the most advanced level of the game—introduces a new set of roles. In the first three levels, the players are assigned roles which give them responsibility for the key community agencies. In Level IV, the roles are those of private citizens. No player can operate a community agency unless he is trained for the job. Before the game begins, each player has the option of training himself for two community tasks, or of building two shelters for his family members, or of training himself for one task and building one shelter. There are also three first-aid centers, which reduce anxiety for family members near them and which the community must decide where to build.

While this last version of the game has proved more playable than any previous version, it may still be improved. Even in its first level, it remains a complex game; players usually take at least a half hour to "catch on" to the basic structure. And because only one player plays at a time, there is still waiting time involved. A strict rule requiring every player to move immediately when it becomes his turn—or else lose the opportunity to act, while continuing to receive anxiety points—might be a solution.

Of course, the possibilities of modification are far from exhausted. Only limitations of time and money have prevented the construction of an electric version which would signal fires, traffic jams, roadblocks, and the impact area automatically, by means of a series of lights. And when a computer with an on-line display screen becomes available to the author, possibilities will grow tremendously. And so, as I continue to try to improve the playability of the game and to find out how well it fulfills its pedagogical purpose (Inbar, 1969; also 1970), the process of revision goes on with no end in view.

REFERENCES

Barton, Allen H.
1962 "The emergency social system." In Baker and Chapman's (eds.), *Man and Society in Disasters*. New York.

Fritz, Charles E. and J. H. Mathewson
1957 "Convergence behavior in disasters." *Disaster Study No. 9, Publication No. 476*. Washington, D. C.: National Academy of Science, National Research Council.

Ilke, F. C. and H. V. Kincaid
n. d. *Disaster Study No. 4, Publication No. 393*. Washington, D. C.: National Academy of Science, National Research Council.

Inbar, Michael
1969 "Development and educational use of simulations: An example 'The Community Response Game.'" *International Journal of Experimental Research in Education*, 6, 5–44.

Inbar, Michael
1970 "Participating in a simulation game." *Journal of Applied Behavioral Science*, 6, 2, 239–244.

Killian, L. M.
n. d. "A study of response to the Houston, Texas fireworks explosion." *Disaster Study No. 2, Publication No. 391*. Washington, D. C.: National Academy of Science, National Research Council.

Killian, L. M.
1952 "The significance of multiple-group membership in disaster." *American Journal of Sociology*, 57.

Raker et al.
n. d. "Emergency medical care in disasters." *Disaster Study No. 6, Publication No. 457*. Washington, D. C.: National Academy of Science, National Research Council.

Wallace, Anthony F. C.
n. d. "Tornado in Worcester." *Disaster Study No. 3, Publication No. 392*. Washington, D. C.: National Academy of Science, National Research Council.
n. d. "Human behavior in extreme situations." *Disaster Study No. 1, Publication No. 390*. Washington, D. C.: National Academy of Science, National Research Council.

JERRY L. FLETCHER,
DONALD A. KOELLER,
DAVID S. MARTIN

Chapter 10

The Caribou Hunting Games

The Caribou Hunting Games are among the most recent to be developed. Not surprisingly this is reflected in the systematically-planned design at all stages—a feature that few other games display. Based on their experiences the authors offer some general principles for designing educational simulations. The main focus of the report is the playability problem. Because the game was tested from the beginning in classrooms of young children (fifth graders), consideration was given to details which are often overlooked.

—The Editors

PART II. CASE STUDIES SECTION A. MAN SIMULATION

The Caribou Hunting Games

This chapter reveals the partly anecdotal and partly analytical history of the development of two specific educational games for the fifth grade. The story, however, should be relevant to anyone who plans to design classroom games and should help the reader avoid some of the traps into which we occasionally fell.

The hypothesized mechanism by which a player learns from a simulation game is well characterized as follows:

> Each simulation is built around a theoretical *model.* The model makes it possible for the simulation participants to encounter "reality;" they make decisions which are "fed into" the model, and the model produces "feedback" for the participants, outlining the consequences of their decisions. In each of several time periods, there are similar cycles of planning . . . deciding . . . putting the decisions into the model . . . receiving feedback from the model . . . and beginning a new cycle with planning, etc. (Western Behavioral Sciences Institute, 1965.)

Thus a simulation game is a context in which a student can translate his own ideas or his verbal learning into overt actions and find out the consequences. The player makes decisions which get fed into the simulation; the simulation produces feedback as to the consequences of this decision. Over several cycles, by making use of the feedback and trying again, the participants gradually learn the most effective actions.

The Caribou Hunting Games are, in design, very close to the requirements of this theoretical model. In these games, the players, in the role of Netsilik Eskimo hunters, attempt to maximize the number of caribou they catch, by manipulating the variables under their control. Regardless of the amount of knowledge they have, few adults and no fifth graders (judging from pilot tests of the game) recognize and carry out the maximizing strategy on the first attempt. Rather, they must play the game by some strategy and see what the outcome is. With the insight from this experience they then must adjust the strategy (or choose one) and see how many more caribou they catch. By constantly utilizing the feedback from each completed game, a player can gradually master the strategy the Netsilik use in catching caribou.

The Caribou Hunting games are somewhat unusual in that they are designed to be both true to the above theoretical model and an integral part of a larger curriculum unit. The games were designed to achieve certain specific objectives of the overall curriculum package. A description of the curriculum will clarify this relationship.

Education Development Center's elementary social studies curriculum, entitled "Man, a Course of Study," (Bruner, 1966: 73–101) is designed to provoke children to investigate the question, "What is human about human beings?" The first section of the curriculum is entitled "Perspectives on Man and Animals" and approaches the general objective of identifying what makes men human by considering behavioral and morphological differences and similarities between man and certain other animals: the salmon, herring gull, and baboon.

In the second section the children are confronted with a classic case of the interaction of man and animals through a detailed study of the traditional Netsilik Eskimo culture of the Pelly Bay region in the Northwest Territory of Canada. The section is centered on life in the hunting camps of the people: the "inland camp" of the summer and fall when fish and caribou are hunted; and the "sea ice camps" of the winter and spring when seal are hunted. Each unit concentrates on the interaction of such diverse factors as technology, world-view, social organization, and physical environment in the effort of the people to hunt the animals successfully. The Netsilik are completely dependent on these animals for their food, clothing, tools, heat and shelter.

In terms of the differences between man and other animals the task of catching caribou can be conceptualized as follows: the caribou has a number of physical advantages over man, such as greater speed on land and a much keener sense of smell. On the other hand, man has a number of advantages over caribou: he can see much more clearly; he can plan and make changes in his behavior; he can make and use tools; and, by division of labor, he can cooperate with other men to accomplish goals which one man alone could not achieve. Since every family of four needs at least thirty-five caribou skins every year in order to survive, the Netsilik Eskimo man must use whatever attributes he has to overcome his physical limitations and catch the needed caribou. It is because the Netsilik interaction with the caribou is such a pure illustration of the differences between man and other animals that it was chosen as one focus for the second section of the course.

The Eskimo kills caribou in two ways: by using the bow and arrow, a tool which can kill at a distance and thus overcome the speed and nullify the sensory advantages of the caribou; and by driving the herd into a narrow "crossing place" in a lake, where hunters in kayaks can overtake the swimming herd and spear the caribou. In the latter case three important tools are used: the kayak, the spear, and the "inukshuk." An inukshuk is a pile of stones (a cairn) which to a caribou probably looks like a man. These, properly placed, frighten the caribou (much as scarecrows frighten birds) and help drive them into the water.

Bow and arrow hunting is simpler in conception but does not yield many caribou. Even if the hunters do manage, without frightening the herd, to get close enough to shoot one, the herd will flee as soon as one

The Caribou Hunting Games

is killed. It is rare that a bow-and-arrow hunter has a chance to catch more than one in any herd. Although driving the herd into a lake (crossing-place hunting) is a more effective procedure, it requires considerably more planning and cooperation. Some hunters have to be concealed along with their kayaks near a crossing place, while others ("chasers" or "beaters") have to build inukshuks in strategic positions and then position themselves in just the right location so that by shouting and running toward the herd at the proper moment, they can drive it into the lake at the point where the hunters are waiting. There are two games in this section of the curriculum, one to simulate each of the kinds of hunting.

In the lessons leading up to the games the children study the attributes of men and caribou, study the tools available to man, and read an ethnographic account of the strategy of hunting with the bow and arrow. Then they play the Bow and Arrow Hunting Game. When they have finished playing several rounds of the game and have discussed the results, they see vivid films of an actual crossing-place hunt filmed in Pelly Bay. They draw pictures of this hunt, read about it, and even see a diagram of the strategy used in the film. At the end of these activities the children play the Crossing-Place Hunting Game.

Because the children are forced in the game to use ideas that they have already learned in a new and interrelated way, the designers coined the phrase "an integrative experience" to describe the role of the game experience in the curriculum unit. That is, the games should not add new knowledge so much as help solidify what is already "learned."

Originally there were four major objectives for the use of the Caribou Hunting Games in the curriculum:

1. To aid the student in distinguishing between the instinctual behavior of animals and the planning and decision-making processes of man.
3. To demonstrate how cultural adaptation had enhanced man's ability to survive and how this differs from morphological adaptation.
3. To illustrate the nature of Netsilik social organization. To show that cooperation is based on the need for survival rather than any high moral value attached to cooperation *per se*.
4. To familiarize students with the use of a symbol system of their own design and given them practice in manipulating it to communicate with other members of the class.

THE ORIGINAL VERSION

In this original form the games were played on a huge acetate-covered map, measuring nearly six feet by eight feet. This map was literally a reproduction to scale of the geographic details of an actual four-mile-square area of the Pelly Bay region of Canada. There were nine separate player roles in the game, and nine children were placed at various points around the huge map. Each child was given an Eskimo name and name-tag, and a one-paragraph description of his role in the hunting group, including his relationship to the other individuals played by the other students.

There were tokens representing each of the players and the caribou herd. The herd was moved by turning over cards in a deck, each of which had a prescribed move written on it (a certain number of squares marked on the board). By shuffling the cards the herd's exact path could be changed from game to game, although the deck was "stacked" to insure a general southerly movement to simulate the Fall migration. Players could move two spaces on one move and one on the next, simulating the ability to both run and walk; players had to choose the correct tool to use to kill the caribou; wind direction could change during the game according to a mounted spinning arrow; and once the Eskimo player tokens were separated by more than a few spaces, the players around the game board were not permitted to talk to each other, to simulate the inability to communicate at a distance. Instead, they were supposed to communicate by hand signals.

The early attempts to play this version of the game with fifth-graders were utter failures. (It had been designed by a commercial company with seemingly little experience in designing classroom devices.) The children could not pronounce their Eskimo names. Several of them could not read their profile cards, much less understand what they were supposed to do if they were told that they had a certain relationship (nephew, wife, father) to some other player in the game. The map was so large that there was no place to put it in a classroom; if placed atop seven desks, it still hung over the sides. It was so wide that many of the children could not reach the plastic tokens which represented their place on the map. In trying to reach the tokens, children often bunched up the map with their bodies, scattering the plastic tokens. The tokens all looked alike and many players forgot which were theirs. The tokens were too big to fit more than one on a square, and there was no rule governing what was supposed to happen if two players were on the same square. There were little lakes all over the map, and the important one at the bottom, where the caribou were supposed to be directed, became lost in the process. No one could keep track of which turn he could run (i.e., move two spaces) and which he could only walk. Certainly the teacher could not keep track of all nine of the players. The limitations on conversations across the gameboard effectively dampened motivation and strategy planning of any sort. However, when this restriction was removed, there still were too many children separated by too much distance for any group planning. At best, two or three children who were clustered at one end discussed strategies—who ought to do what—but usually in such a way that other children could not hear them. Many important rules did not exist; the hunter who caught the most caribou was the "winner," but the rules provided no way to catch more than one. It was not clear whether players could walk across the small lakes or whether they needed kayaks. And finally, there was only one gameboard for an entire class; the remaining eighteen students were supposed to sit quietly and watch the other nine play the game. Needless to say, they did not. (Fletcher, 1966.)

This early disaster drove us back to our learning objectives for the game, as, more than likely, many of the practical problems were the result of attempting to achieve conflicting objectives. While the objectives were not well-stated, several things became obvious in comparing the outcome of the field trials with the objectives.

Using hand signals across a few feet inside a classroom was too artificial. Not only did the students not develop a symbol system to communicate across the board, but the attempt to achieve this objective severely inhibited strategy discussion and planning. Attempting to simulate too much of the actual situation had caused the mechanism of the game to break down.

Knowledge of the social organization of the Netsilik could be achieved in the game only by memorizing the information on the role description cards which the students were supposed to read. Yet this knowledge was not related to anything in the game. There was no way in which a player was supposed to play differently because somebody else was his father or brother, and there was no pay-off in the game which would induce a player to learn the material.

Although the demonstration of cultural and morphological adaptation was a stated objective, it was not a part of the game. The behavior of both the men and the caribou was bound by the rules of the game. Changes in such behavior to simulate adaptation would involve changes in the basic rules of the game, and no such changes were permissible. A player could not try out various kinds of cultural or morphological adaptation and receive feedback from the system as to which was best.

The only objective which was even potentially in the game was the difference between instinctual behavior of animals and planning and decision-making by man; while the herd followed a predetermined program, the men could decide to change their direction at any time. But even in this dimension there was so little planning among the children and so many obstacles to such behavior that it could hardly have been expected that the game would teach this difference.

REVISION AND REVISION

After these early trials, the contract with the commercial game designing company was terminated, and the notion of using games in the curriculum was nearly dropped. However, the decision was made to redesign the games completely and try again. Eskimo names, profile cards, and the explicit playing of roles were eliminated. The map was reduced to the size of a desk top and mounted so it would not wrinkle. All the lakes except the one at the bottom were eliminated. Tokens were redesigned to look like inukshuks, beaters, and caribou. Movement was standardized: men moved one space per turn on land and two in kayaks; caribou moved two on land and one in water; a frightened herd fled three spaces. Each board had only three players: two were supposed to plan and discuss together as hunters; the third moved the herd. The herd was moved by a twelve-sided die marked with various compass directions, but men could move in any direction they wished. Wind direction was kept constant. Strategy considerations were now the only dimensions of the games: for Bow and Arrow Hunting, the proper starting places and the coordination of hunter movement; for Crossing-Place Hunting, the proper placement of inukshuks and beaters to drive the caribou into the water and the selection of the crossing place at which to put the kayaks and hunters. In Crossing-Place Hunting provision was made for determining how many caribou were killed by numbering the dots in the crossing place. The more toward the middle of the crossing place the kayaks intercepted the herd, the larger the number of caribou that were "killed." A rule was added which prevented the herd from entering the water at any place xcept a crossing place. If the die directed the herd into the water at some other place, the herd was to move along the edge of the lake until it either came to a crossing place or was directed by the die to move away from the water. Painted caribou tracks indicated the direction of the herd movement along the lake shore.[1]

[1] Professor Richard Rosenbloom of the Harvard Business School was at this time working for Education Development Center and contributed substantially to the first revision.

The Caribou Hunting Games

The physical apparatus for the first revision of the games was a peg board painted in various colors.[2] The men and the caribou were represented by different colored pegs, and an inukshuk was made by piling three pegs on top of one another. This version was pilot-tested and at least was more playable, but there were still difficulties. Pegs were often moved inaccurately. Once a peg was moved it was hard to remember exactly where it had been, in case corrections were needed. The sense of smell of the caribou remained a part of the game, largely to justify the existence of wind direction as a factor, but with the pegs it was difficult to determine when the caribou were frightened by smell. Also, the lake shore was parallel to the bottom of the board. The herd migrated in a south*west*erly direction; the beaters had the task of diverting the herd to the south to get it into a crossing place. This confused the children, who had learned that the herd migrated south. In addition, a cost-analysis determined that a peg board was much too expensive for large scale production and sale.

So the games were redesigned again. This time the board had a thick cardboard backing with a styrofoam interior that would hold pins. Beaters and hunters were signified by pins with a red flag on top; caribou by pins with a yellow flag. In one variation there was even a printed figure on each flag to show what the token represented. Inukshuks were made of three beads through which a pin could be stuck, and inukshuks could be built at the rate of one bead per turn. The lake was redrawn and placed diagonally across the southeast corner of the board. Now the herd migrated directly south, though still governed by the twelve-sided die. Footprints again directed the herd's movement along the lake shore.

At about this point it became apparent that the games we were developing had a very rapid cycle, so that one team could play the games a number of times in one or two class periods. The notion of recording the moves in one play of a game so they could be used for planning for a subsequent play and for later discussion began to seem vitally important. Then students could make deliberate use of the feedback from one play of a game to do better in the next. Consequently, in the pin-board version four students were placed at a board. One was the record keeper, recording on a smaller map-like version of the gameboard exactly where each person and the herd moved. This feature necessitated a coordinate system (letters on the horizontal, numbers on the vertical)

[2] Michael Sand of Cambridge, Massachusetts, was the artist/designer for the Caribou Game apparatus. He managed to maintain the artistic quality of the materials, while keeping costs low, and contributed innumerable other ideas throughout the development of the games.

which was added to the edge of the gameboard and the record sheet.

An eight-classroom test of the pinboard version of the game uncovered serious problems. The little plastic balls which were to be skewered by a pin to make an inukshuk kept getting loose, falling on the floor, and rolling everywhere. The board material was difficult to penetrate with a pin. The colored flags fell off the pins. Some children delighted in jabbing each other with the pins! A plastic overlay scent indicator, to indicate when a herd was frightened by human scent, had been developed because children had continually misunderstood this rule, but it could not be used with pins sticking out of the board. The role of record keeper was boring as well as extremely difficult, since the children could not accurately transfer the location of Eskimo and caribou moves to the small record sheet.

The next version used a gameboard made of a pad of throw-away paper sheets on which children marked their moves with felt-tip pens, using different colors to distinguish the hunters or beaters from the caribou and a symbol to represent an inukshuk. Since this method provided an automatic record of actions during a game, the fourth player at a gameboard could be eliminated. The twelve-sided die had proved too expensive to produce, and it was replaced with two six-sided dice.

Still, pilot tests uncovered more problems. The relative rate of movement between man and caribou had to be adjusted. The proper starting point for the herd had to be determined. The best distance for the herd to "flee" was changed. A rule was adopted to permit players to place their inukshuks *before* the game began, rather than having to build them during the game in order to simulate more closely advance planning. Finally the game was ready.

In the Spring of 1968 the games were tested in over twenty classes, with systematic observation, interviewing, and pre- and post-tests. It was concluded that the game activities were both workable and educationally valuable. There was clear evidence that the students learned a great deal from playing the games and that what they learned fit the objectives for the course (Fletcher, 1969).

Some problems remained. The rules on the direction of flight of a frightened herd turned out to be too complicated. The analysis of the used game sheets identified numerous cases of students mis-using the rules. Since both games were played on the same gamesheet, children often asked about those portions of the game map that pertained only to the Crossing-Place game while they were being introduced to the Bow and Arrow version. The use of a film strip to present the rules made it difficult to introduce the games to a small group within the classroom. The film strip also made it difficult to go back over the basic rules if students were unsure, and the mimeographed rule sheets stating the rules verbally were of little or no help to fifth graders. There was also some concern that the expense involved if the teacher was liberal in the number of game maps used. Still, the games had functioned quite effectively in their existing condition and there was disagreement on the need for and the wisdom of further revision.

The impetus for yet another revision came from some very disappointing experiences in an inner-city school. The games were unplayable, apparently because of the complex nature of some of the rules and because of the long time involved in the initial "rule session." It seemed that for the games to be usable everywhere, they should be even simpler for their first playing, with complications to be introduced through instructions to the teacher if the students had no trouble with the initial version.

A new version was then planned that would use inexpensive 8½" x 11" ditto maps, one style for each game, simplify the more complex rules, and introduce a separate rule booklet for each student with a diagram illustrating each rule. Each of these changes was pilot-tested in both suburban and city schools.

The use of separate maps for each version of the game eliminated all of the problems previously encountered when children would ask about those portions of the map that pertained only to the Crossing-Place game when they were learning Bow and Arrow, making it much easier to introduce the first game and then to follow the logical sequence of the whole unit. The smaller maps were easy to handle, shortened the game time, and created no special problems (although they were less attractive, due to their small size and inexpensive design). But the cost had been reduced; teachers would not hesitate to let the children play as long as more maps could be run off on the ditto.

The use of a smaller map suggested the first simplification in the rules. The rule that determined when contact was made with the herd, both for frightening or for killing, was changed from being on the dot "adjacent" to the herd to being on the same dot. This eliminated the need for clarifying the meaning of the word "adjacent" and reduced the number of possible contact situations from over forty to thirteen. It was then possible to group these and illustrate the direction of flight for each possible condition of contact. Furthermore, the new rule limited the directions of flight to either East or West (not all eight compass points as before). This was much simpler and also reduced the chance that the herd would retrace its path on the next move. The use of the rule regarding wind direction and the ability of the caribou to smell the hunter was dropped from the basic game entirely and added to a brief list of suggested optional variations.

The rules were placed on two 8½″ x 11″ manila cards, one for each game. They were grouped both according to the logical sequence of play and in columns appropriate to each of the players. The text was kept at an absolute minimum, and each group of rules had an example drawn out on a small section of the game map. The students' attentiveness to the initial presentation was not as complete as it had been with the film strip, probably in part due to the fact that each child could be involved with any of the rules at any time, rather than just the one being presented on the screen. But if a teacher quickly covered the basic rules, relying on the reference value of the rule sheet, the game could get underway in half the time previously required. Student use of the new rule sheet during the game play has been high; and the new form provides the opportunity for teachers to deal with the more complicated rules in small groups as the problems are encountered, rather than having to deal with all contingencies at the outset.

The final version involves two pads of highly stylized printed paper sheets, three crayons of two different colors (one color for caribou, one for hunters), and a pair of dice. Each game is played by three children. In Bow and Arrow Hunting two play the hunters while the third rolls the dice, moves the herd, and acts as referee. In Crossing-Place Hunting two children play the two beaters while the herd is on land, then switch and play hunters in kayaks after the herd enters the water. Again, the third child moves the herd and referees. After each cycle of each game the children rotate roles. The games are played on similar, but not identical game sheets, and many of the rules are the same for each. The more complex Crossing-Place game simply involves the addition of rules to handle kayaks, inukshuks, and herd behavior in or near the water.

The game is designed so that there is one best strategy, which is directly analogous to the one the Netsilik use, and the payoffs in the game are roughly proportional to the quality of the strategy the players use. In an effort to teach or integrate knowledge of the "pattern" of the Netsilik interaction with their environment, it was assumed that the most effective approach was to demonstrate that, given the contingencies of their environment, the pattern the Netsilik use works best. In spite of the fact that the children have seen that strategy on paper and film before ever playing the games, it is interesting that almost all children have to "rediscover" that strategy after some trial and error within the operational framework of the game situation.

The Caribou Hunting Games

ADMINISTRATIVE PROBLEMS

The problem of training teachers to use the Caribou Games was multidimensional. For many teachers the Caribou Games were the first exposure to *any* classroom game. The initial reaction was anxiety—anxiety at having to help children use a piece of material which had rather complex procedures. We found this was best relieved by involving the teachers in playing the games. Once they had mastered the games at the adult level and discussed the issues raised by the games on that level, their anxiety subsided.

A second dimension of the teacher-training problem was the teacher's feeling that somehow the unified authority of the classroom would no longer be in his hands. This feeling seemed rooted in the unusual noise level of children participating actively in the games, often for an hour at a time and the fact that children were working in small groups in interaction with *each other* rather than interacting with and through the *teacher*. This problem was best overcome when teachers saw the enthusiasm and involvement of children playing the games in a classroom. Virtually all liked what they saw.

A third problem was procedural. For the first time in many classrooms the teacher had to consider moving classroom furniture somewhat radically. He had to consider optimum combinations of pupils—should children be grouped by sex, by emotional stability, by intelligence, by achievement in reading, by friendships, at random, by their own choice, or some other way? We tried to gather some data to aid the teacher in making this decision, but to determine optimal groupings for the games remains a long-range research question.

A final dimension of the teacher-training problem involved the best way to capitalize on the game experience. As with many classroom games, children playing these games tend to become involved in the games *per se*. The teacher must see to it that the game experience generalizes to other aspects of the course. He must be capable of making creative use of the increased imagery and associated experiences of the games while remaining faithful to the general framework of the course of study. We were able to provide questions and guidelines for a follow-up discussion, but what seemed to be the best technique—moving from playing group to playing group seeking particular events which could be used to make the follow-up relevant to the game experiences of the children—could not be written into a lesson plan. At the very least, we are convinced that for teachers to use games effectively, there must be simultaneous teacher in-service workshops or seminars, particularly for those who are using games for the first time.

A GENERAL VIEW

The development and testing of the Caribou Games took more than two years, numerous classroom tests both large and small, and a substantial portion of the time of four people: two teachers on the staff, an evaluator, and a designer. Many other people were involved from time to time. The overall trend was clearly one of increasing simplification. Every time a difficulty was uncovered, some way was found to eliminate the problem, usually by removing some features from the games.

On the basis of our experience with the Caribou Hunting Games, we wish to suggest the following principles for designing educational simulation games.

1. A game must be designed so that learning how to play (the rules, the varibles, the permissible actions) is fast and simple. Then the players can concentrate on playing better.
2. A game must be designed so that the actions of a previously completed game are recorded and available for study. This record becomes the feedback for correcting and improving subsequent play.
3. The particular causal relationships between a strategy and an outcome must be clearly identifiable, so the player can determine what aspect of a particular strategy was inadequate.
4. The degree of success in a game (the feedback) must be directly related to the quality of the strategy employed.
5. A game must be designed so that any individual can play the game numerous times. Only then can he gradually improve his play. Whatever the time constraints of the normal use of the game, it must be possible to play the game several times within that time constraint.
6. A game must be designed to encourage players to experiment actively with different strategies. It must discourage players from sticking with the same strategy play after play.

7. A game must be designed so that every player can play every different role several times to gain the insights of that role. In order to do this, the number of different roles must be kept to a minimum.

The course makes ample use of other media: films, filmstrips, records, and sort-cards. Yet as a medium for instruction the games have several unique properties. They are able to engage students directly in an interactive process in such a way that the students have some control over the outcome of the process. No matter how exciting or realistic the films, records, or filmstrips are, they remain essentially things which students observe. While they can be stopped or started, while students can vicariously participate in the action by identifying with the actors, while children can *discuss* the nature of the medium (why the photographer chose this camera angle, why this time of day) the children cannot actively take part in an control the action. They cannot (at least the way the course is designed) try making their own version of a film and see which created the more powerful image—their own or the one they were given. For all their power, the other media remain essentially linear in their action, and the action remains outside the control of the students.

In games children are part of an on-going process, what they do affects the outcome of the game, and they can directly experiment with nature of the medium by changing the strategies they use or the rules of the game to see which approach works best. The essence of the games' contribution to the curriculum is that for the first time the children have to take the factors they have studied independently, as static entities, and deal with them as parts of a process. They must simultaneously manipulate and coordinate the variables, over a period of time and under the tension and excitement of the game, to "catch the caribou."

REFERENCES

BRUNER, JEROME
1966 *Toward a Theory of Instruction.* Cambridge, Mass.: Belknap.

FLETCHER, JERRY L.
1966 *Report of the Classroom Trials of Caribou Hunting and Bushmen Exploring and Gathering.* Cambridge, Mass.: Education Development Center.
1969 "The effects of two elementary school social studies games: An experimental field study." Unpublished Ed.D. Harvard Graduate School of Education.

WESTERN BEHAVIORAL SCIENCES INSTITUTE
1965 *Napoli.* La Jolla, Calif.: Western Behavioral Sciences Institute.

SARANE S. BOOCOCK

Chapter 11

The Life Career Game

Rather than being built around a process (e.g., bargaining, communication, coalition formation), Life Career is an example of a game built around an environment. Boocock was required to reduce into manageable form great quantities of statistical data descriptive of the educational environment, the labor market, and the family-leisure activities of Americans. The result is characteristic of training games, where individual decision-making is more important than social interaction.

—THE EDITORS

The Life Career Game

The idea for the Life Career game grew out of some research I had done on the value systems and aspirations of adolescent girls, as part of a larger study of adolescent value systems and reference groups, carried out at Rutgers University under the general direction of Matilda W. Riley. In the process of collecting data for my Master's thesis, I interviewed a number of high school girls and their parents. While the girls claimed to be doing a lot of planning for their futures, about all they were really planning for was their weddings. Most could not project themselves beyond the day they landed a husband, or at most beyond the birth of "lots of kids."

When I went to Johns Hopkins University in 1962, I joined a small group of social scientists, headed by James Coleman, who had just been awarded a grant by the Carnegie Corporation to explore the use of simulation gaming as a teaching tool at the secondary level. During the development and testing of an election game I was introduced to the construction of probability models of social processes as well as to the enormous promise of gaming as a motivating and training device.

During this period I also engaged in informal conversations with students who participated in the election game and with the wives and girl friends of graduate students in my department on the topic of self-image and perceptions of the future. My earlier impression that girls simply do not consider the full range of alternatives open to them nor make decisions about their own lives in any organized way was reinforced.[1] The combination of the exciting experience I was having with the first Hopkins simulation game and the need I perceived for some kind of training that would force girls to think about themselves and their lives in a more direct, realistic way led to the idea of developing a game about career planning. My original purpose was to give the individual girl experience in making the kinds of decisions about marriage,

[1] It was further reinforced in the first field tests of *Life Career*. A common response of the volunteer players to the general goal of the game, which required them to plan the lives of fictitious women up to the age of forty or fifty, was that they could not conceive of ever being that old themselves.

That this tendency of American women to wear blinders with regard to their own futures is becoming costly to us as a nation is documented in the report of the Kennedy Commission on the Status of Women (1963). The critical shortages in nursing, teaching, social work and other fields traditionally staffed mainly by women; the declining ratio of women receiving B.A.'s and graduate degrees; the increasing number of girls dropping out of high school because of pregnancy; the shocking number of women whose training does not allow them to establish and maintain minimal standards of housekeeping and child care—these are just a few of the results of our lack of concern and planning in the past. Among their recommendations, the Commission called for a drastic increase in counseling facilities and for new methods of counseling which would help women to evaluate the alternatives open to them and to make intelligent decisions about them.

children, education, and jobs that typical American women must face throughout their lives, thereby enabling her to make satisfying choices and to avoid errors in judgment that would be costly in later life. In particular, I wanted the game to provide (1) a general feeling for what her future life would be like, including some sense of the pattern of a

	Model	Game	Field Testing	Research on Player Reactions
1962-1963	Review of Literature Reanalysis of Available Data on Social Mobility Formulation of Model	First Version	—	Unstructured interviews and essays Development of structured questionnaire
1963-1964	Revision of Model in Types and Extent of Decisions	First quantity production (with 4-H)	Three types: college, high school, 4-H groups	
1964-1965		Revised version production (Hopkins group)	Test groups varying in: size, ability, motivation	Analysis of Data Publication of papers and reports on data analysis
1965-1966			Test by groups outside of Hopkins project Extensive tests in ghetto Jr. and Sr. high schools	
1966-1967	—	First commercial game produced		Controlled experiment in three high schools

Figure 1

Chronology of the Development of *Life Career*

woman's life cycle; (2) accurate information about the career alternatives or opportunities available; and (3) practice in decision making.

While my original purpose was a limited and practical one, I became increasingly intrigued with the potentialities of simulation as a sociological research technique. In the process of designing the game, I learned a great deal about theory construction and the interaction between theory and empirical data, as well as about the specifics of occupations and the factors contributing to satisfying family life and leisure. I think it is fair to say that if one can construct a workable game about some social situation or process, one has understood the crucial features of its structure and operation.

Figure 1 gives an overview of my activities in connection with Life Career. As the figure shows, the general sequence began with work on the basic model, from which the game was then built. After some preliminary field testing, which led to further changes in both model and game, I began to collect data on its effects as a learning device. In the following sections, I shall take up these four kinds of activities in order, describing what I did over the full period of the project. It is important to keep in mind what Figure 1 only suggests—that the work did not flow smoothly from one area of activity to another, but moved back and forth as problems, research opportunities, and occasional brainstorms arose, and that I was often working in two or more areas simultaneously.

THE GAME MODEL

I began work in 1962 with only the most general notion of what the game would be like—I envisioned players "walking through" a designated span of years in the future as decision-makers for a fictitious person (who would be presented to them in the form of a "profile" or case history) making multiple decisions for this person, and receiving feedback on their decision-making at regular intervals. My first task was to select the major decision-making areas and to specify not only the choices that were to be made within each area, but also the factors which affected an individual's range of choices and the way in which different individual choices were related to each other. A major part of the first year was spent in a search of the literature, in particular for empirical studies on the career-related alternatives open to and the actual choices made by different types of individuals in our society. On the basis of this research I postulated four general decisions that must be made repeatedly by most American women. The sequence of events in a given decision period or round of the game, including the major deci-

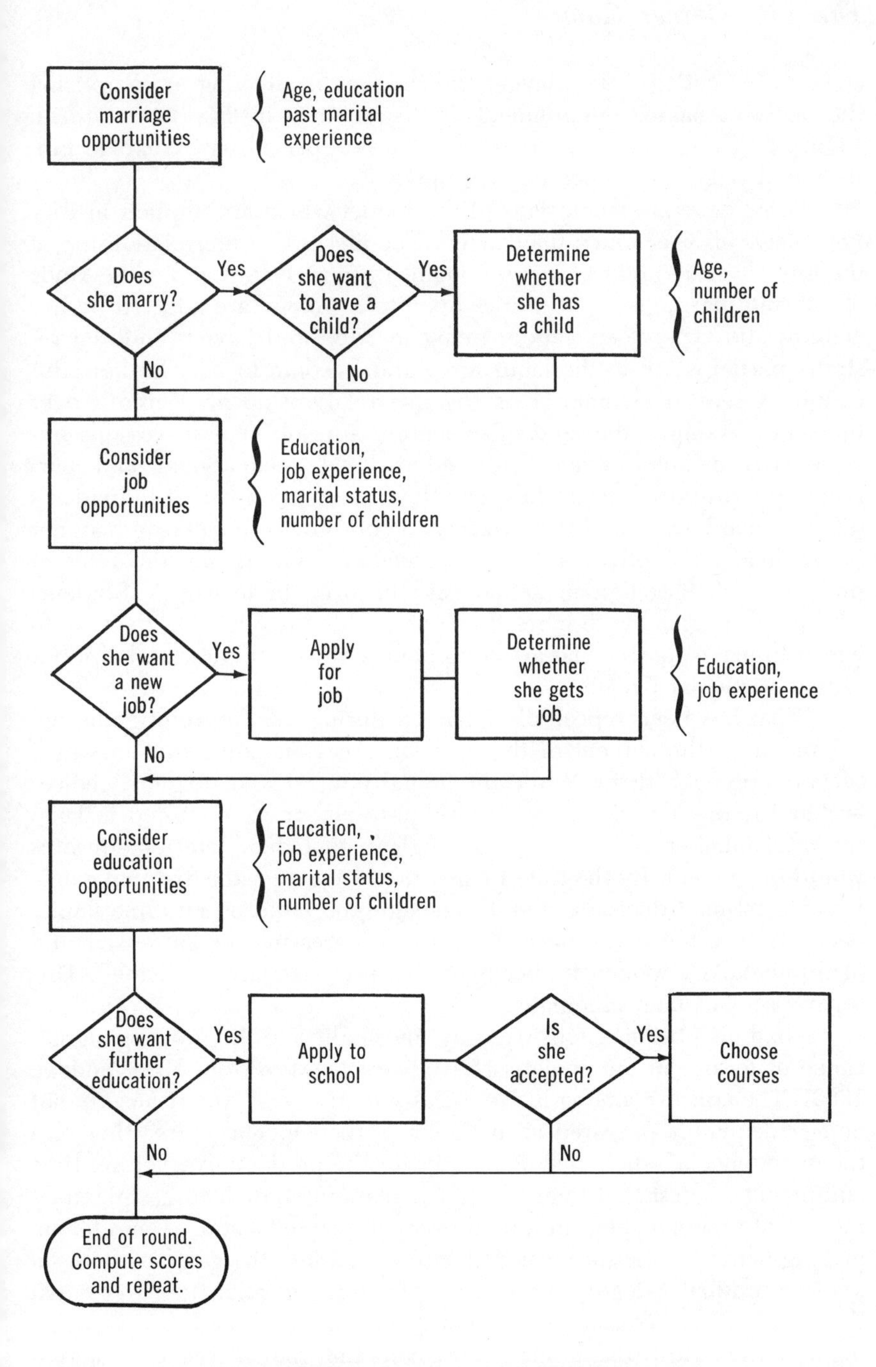

Figure 2: Sequence of game decisions

sions to be made by the players and the factors affecting or comprising the decision-making environment, is diagrammed in flow-chart form in Figure 2. The general pattern of the decision period has remained fundamentally the same since the beginning.

Three general assumptions of the model which are implicit in Figure 2 have also remained unchanged. The first is the interrelationship of the four decision areas at any one point in time. For example, the kinds of job and marriage opportunities open to a woman are affected by her amount and type of education; being married and having children restricts participation in the labor force and freedom to seek further education. A second assumption is the interrelationship of decisions over time. For example, the kind of education and job experiences one obtains early in one's career affects educational, occupational, and marriage opportunities later in life. The third assumption is that individuals differ in many ways and that what is a good life for one person may not be as good for another. The Life Career kit contains several different profiles, each based upon actual case histories of teenagers. Students who play the game with more than one profile discover that the way to win is to make choices that are congruent with the interests and abilities of that particular person.

What has been repeatedly changed during the course of game development is the content of the decision areas and the order in which players approach them. While the actual number and range of choices within any one decision area can be quite elaborate, I wanted to keep the total number of areas small enough so that their interrelationships would be evident. By the time I came to put together the first real game, I had combined decisions about marriage and children into one family decision area, but had broken down the job area into its impressive and instrumental components: "occupation" and "standard of living." This separation was later eliminated.

I had also become sensitized by my reading to the growing significance of leisure in our society. (Larrabee and Meyerson, 1958; Smigel, 1963). The concern among many social scientists that Americans are not being adequately prepared to make use of their increased free time and the emergence of whole new industries for the production of leisure time equipment suggest that total life career planning now includes planning the use of time not spent in formal occupational, educational, and homemaking activities. Leisure was first introduced into the game model as a kind of residual category, termed simply "fun and relaxation"; personal development was considered to be a result only of educational or training activities. However, leisure now covers the whole spectrum of activities from unorganized relaxation to hobbies, clubs, and other activities that may require substantial investments of time and effort and which may contribute as much to a person's self-development as formal education. In fact, in the game as in real life, excessive amounts of unorganized free time may detract from one's total satisfaction in the leisure area because of the boredom that great amounts of such time may produce.

Once I had named, if only temporarily, the general components of the career decision-making model, I needed to specify the actual alternatives open in each area, that is, to describe the decision-making environment. For this task I needed statistical data from which I could compute the game parameters, in the form of probabilities of various opportunities and events for the profile persons whose lives were to be planned by the players. Since a basic assumption of the game model was interrelationship among decision areas, I needed not only statistics on the distributions of individuals in various educational, occupational, and marital and other family status categories, but also data which, with multivariate analysis, would show the contingencies which affected or altered these distributions. For example, I needed to know not only the proportions of individuals who were married at various ages, but also the extent to which marriage opportunities are limited by educational and occupational background. I used a number of available data sources, including Bureau of Labor Statistics bulletins and reports, as well as the projected demographic model of U.S. households produced via computer simulation by Orcutt *et al.* (1961). I also re-analyzed some survey data myself, including the original data from Havemann and West's study of U.S. college graduates (1952), in order to examine the interaction of various background and experiential factors and their effects upon subsequent career choices.

It should be noted, however, that the final game model was not the product of a complete multivariate analysis of a single representative sample. Rather, it was a synthesis of several empirical studies using different kinds of samples and data gathering techniques. There was thus a fair amount of deduction and pure conjecture on my part.

The objective structure of the decision-making environment was, however, only part of what I wanted to show; I also wanted to include some of its subjective features. By showing the rewards and punishments that were likely to result from a given set of choices, I hoped to get the players to think about the larger question of their life satisfactions. For this I needed attitudinal data, so during the first year I searched for studies of how people felt about their jobs, their marriages, and their life styles in general. One such study is Blood and Wolfe's *Husbands and Wives in America: Dynamics of Married Life* (1960), a survey of a sample of Detroit families in which responses to a number of questions on satisfaction with marriage and family life were cross-tabulated with such characteristics as education, occupation, and length of marriage. While good studies of this sort are few, I was able to piece together enough data to construct a scoring system for the game.

THE GAME

Once I had gotten into the review of literature and analysis of empirical data, I began to work on the game itself. Given the basic dimensions and structure of the model, the following kinds of materials were needed:

> profiles or case histories of the persons for whom career decisions are to be made by a team of three players;
> forms on which players can record all of their decisions;
> materials for informing the players about the educational, occupational and marriage opportunities that are available for their profile person;
> procedures for providing feedback to the players on how well their profile person is doing;
> instructions for playing and calculating results.

Another basic decision in making the transition from a model to a playable game was to specify the intervals of play, translating the real-life time into game time. This was not an easy decision; originally I thought simulation of 25 years was necessary to demonstrate substantially the pattern of a life career, but for practical purposes I wanted a game that could be played in five or six hours without monotonous repetition. The first game was broken by rounds into the following: age levels: 16, 17, 18, 19, 21, 23, 27, 31. Two additional four-year rounds were optional. What I found out in the first field tests was that changing the number of years in decision periods presented serious problems to players and scorers. The players were continually confused as to the age of their person and the number of years they had to be planning for, and certain real-life possibilities were very difficult to handle in the later rounds (e.g., how could a person switch jobs in the middle of round 7 or 8? If a divorce occurred at the beginning or middle of these rounds, how could the person compensate by seeking new education, job, or marriage opportunities?). Because I was never able to solve the host of practical problems of this sort, I eventually made all of the rounds equivalent to one year. While I sacrificed giving the players a sense of a relatively wide span of a total life career, by moving the start of the game to the profile person's junior year in high school, I was able to include within eight to ten single-year rounds the decisions in each area that were most relevant to high school players. Of course, with college players, the game could begin even later in the profile person's life and could thus get further into his later life with the same number of game rounds.

The profiles never presented any serious problems. While I was continually polishing up the wording of the profiles and adding new ones, I never made any basic changes in their style, length, or structure, The game also works well when teachers or students write profiles themselves, and the Administrator's Manual for the present game includes a short section of hints on how to write new profiles.

The other materials have been repeatedly revised and redesigned. Looking back at the earliest version of the game, it seems remarkable that the players got through even the introductory instructions with any energy or motivation left to play the game! The first "simplified" version of Life Career employed a notebook containing a 22-page Administrator's Handbook. Even though by this time I had succeeded in eliminating the use of wearisome log tables for computing the probabilities of various events, the scoring process alone still involved sixteen steps. There were 12 pages of players' rules, a set of person and school profiles, an Education Record form, a supply of Decision Forms and a Life History Form (one for each round), and a supply of Application Forms. This version also included reference materials on jobs and schools.

In general the process of game development consisted of continuous efforts to cut down on the number and/or complexity of the decisions the players had to make within a round of the game, and to make the playing equipment more attractive, and either to make the materials self-explanatory (via the use of colors, physical analogues, etc.) or to clarify the written instructions. One major simplification of the first sort was the elimination of goal-setting in the basic game. Originally, in addition to the series of decisions about their person's education, occupation, family life and use of free time, players also set general "life goals" for their person, indicating the relative importance of the major decision areas. They received additional satisfaction points for reaching their goals. While general, long-term goals are certainly an important part of career planning, including them in the game for beginning players made the amount of reading and the length of pre-play preparation too long for the non-motivated and academically-weak students we were most anxious to reach. My compromise was to make goal-setting an optional part of the game, recommended for very bright or motivated students or for those who had already learned how to play the game without these decisions.

The Life Career Game

As with the other game materials, my concern in writing the players' rules and administrator's instruction was to communicate precisely—but at the same time leave the game open-ended enough to allow for the interests and learning styles of different kinds of players and for variations of the basic game. An important thing that I learned from my field testing of the game was that for players in general—but particularly for players with low motivation or verbal skills—it was important to get into actual play of the game as soon as possible. Rules that were erroneously or not fully understood could be corrected in the course of play; in fact, even the slowest students were able to correct many of their misunderstandings themselves as they got into the game and got a feel for what "made sense" in the sequence of play.

In the current version of the full rules are printed in a separate booklet, which may be given to bright students at the beginning but may be held back for other players until they have gone far enough into the game to want this additional information. It may also be communicated orally for players who are very weak readers.

One part of the game in which I have been continuously searching for a better design is the simulation of the labor and school market. My research and reading indicated that one obstacle to good career decision-making is that most young people's knowledge of educational and occupational opportunities is limited to the experiences of their own families and friends, a limitation that becomes very serious in an age of rapid technological change. Therefore, I wanted the game to communicate to students something of the full range of jobs and schools available in the United States. Because our labor market and educational institutions are themselves complex and changing, I felt that it was important for students to become familiar with general *types* of jobs and schools and to know *how* to obtain more detailed factual information about specific jobs and schools when they need it. (Most factual information which is accurate today would in any case be obsolete by the time the players were ready for post-high school education and jobs.) I began by including already available reference materials as a part of the game—the Science Research Associates *Handbook of Job Facts,* the Labor Department's *Occupational Outlook Handbook,* college catalogs—and having players make choices for their profile person from these. I soon learned that the expense and effort of acquiring an adequate reference library just to play the game would discourage many teachers and group leaders from using it, and I gradually incorporated the factual information needed to make game decisions into the game package. The present game has a Job and School Catalog which contains all this information.

Because I wanted to simulate at least part of the real-life experience of getting a job or getting into college, I included as one of the steps in the game the filling out of application forms. These forms are a composite of a number of real-life forms on file in the counselor's office of a local high school.

A major design development was the use of spinners to simulate the combined effects of chance and planning in being accepted by schools, getting jobs, and meeting potential marriage partners. For example, the job spinner is a circle divided into wedges of different sizes, labelled as follows:

Yes, you got the job
Yes, if there are 500,000 or more workers in the field
Yes, if your last 2 years' grade average was B or better
Yes, if there is a growing demand in the field
Yes, if 75 percent or more of the workers in the field are of the same sex as you
Yes, if you have held a job before
No, you didn't get the job

By using the spinner, players learn that while there is an element of chance or luck in getting a job (simulated by the act of spinning itself) they can also control their luck to some degree by their individual efforts, by matching the job to the profile person's individual characteristics, and by taking into account conditions of the labor market. The spinner had the advantage not only of eliminating tedious mathematical calculations but also of making the operation of this part of the model visual; simply by fooling around with the spinners, students can learn something about the labor market and about the way in which probability models work.

FIELD TESTING

Let me note the outstanding conclusions based upon my experience. First, I found it profitable to try the game on college students first, even though they were older and more experienced than the type of student for which the game was intended. They were able to go through long plays of the game—up to forty simulated years of age—and could articulate well inaccuracies in the model, as well as spell out obscurities in the rules.

Once the game reached a more playable and accurate shape it was given testing in normal classroom situations and in 4-H club meetings. There were two features to this stage of the testing. First, I became less a direct participant and generally limited my involvement to the training of game administrators. Second, my test samples became larger as the game development progressed. The college group consisted of twelve students who met weekly for a semester. Then I went into one high school, playing at first with small groups of students, and then having teachers use the game in their classrooms. The culmination of the field testing was a youth convention at which 50 teenage delegates administered and scored the game for 650 of their fellow delegates. This test was also notable because it was the first one at which no one connected with the original development of the game was present.

Eventually my observations, along with the data I was collecting provided a number of clues about the kinds of students who were likely to gain the most from the game. First, the lower age limit appears to be eighth grade. While younger children played the game with enthusiasm, there was evidence that the experience may have left misleading impressions. Second, the game appears to have special value for adolescents from culturally-deprived groups. For them, the simulated environment supplies a kind of experience lacking in their own lives, a chance to have control over their actions (Boocock and Coleman, 1966).

One memorable experience from the testing has had a deep influence upon my thinking about the education of deprived children, as well as the design and presentation of instructional games. One group, consisting of youngsters who were considered all but uneducable by most of their teachers, taught themselves to play the game in one afternoon with no assistance other than a very inadequate set of rules (seven pages long, hastily typed, with a large amount of crossed-out words, misspellings, etc.)! The first half hour, during which these students struggled to work with the awkward, unattractive materials, was painful to observe, but within two hours, all were playing with some degree of facility, had corrected most of their own initial mistakes, and, most important, had for the first time shaken off the passivity, aloofness, and faint hostility that had characterized this group. From that afternoon, I began to look at games in a different way; specifically, I saw that the maximum learning from a game may result when the player has to put something of his own ideas and effort into it. (Application of this general principle to teaching with games at the college and university level is discussed in Boocock, 1970.) [2]

EVALUATION OF THE EFFECTS OF THE GAME

Once I had worked out the major procedural problems with my first test groups, I began to collect data from the players, first from group

[2] Other groups performed field-testing independently. See, for example, Farran (1968), Varenhorst (1968).

discussions at the end of playing sessions and later from short written essays. This first data collection was largely impressionistic, my objective being to get the players' perceptions of their experiences in the game. The following excerpts from essays written by the girls in my test group at Nova High School, while of a subjective, testimonial character, did indicate to me that at least some players were seeing the purpose and principle of the game as I intended:

> Most students would have had impractical views of their future lives before they played this game, just as I did. After playing the game they would learn that a twenty-four hour day is not long enough to allow a girl to hold a job, be a wife, raise a family and get an education. Something must be left out.
>
> I think many girls would be happy to learn of all the things they can do besides being wives and mothers. Many girls who might have been resigned to being a housewife could see that if a girl in the game could get a successful job, so could they.
>
> A woman can have a successful life without going to college, and the same goes for a man. As long as I can remember, it has been drilled into me that anyone who doesn't go to college is a moron.

From the clues obtained from these early essays and from my own formulations of what could be learned from the game, I began to write more structured questions. After pre-testing a questionnaire consisting mainly of multiple choice questions, a revised version was administered to all participants, before and after a large game session. The design of this experiment, the kinds of questions asked, and the empirical results have been discussed elsewhere (Boocock, 1966; Boocock and Coleman, 1966; Boocock, 1968). To summarize the major findings, there was evidence of factual learning: Players did better than a control group in producing correct information in response to open-ended questions. Play of the game also produced attitudinal changes such as increased confidence in their own capacities for handling such situations.

These data, while generally supportive of the educational value of the game, were far from conclusive. The next major research, in 1967, was designed to specify more precisely the kinds of learning that the game produced and the conditions (including the kinds of students) under which it was most effective. In particular, we wanted to measure the effects of games upon students' self-confidence, their sense of control of their environment and destiny [3] (Boocock, Schild, and Stoll, 1967). The major significance of this experiment was that it pointed to ways to use the game more effectively.

[3] An attitudinal dimension which had recently been shown by Coleman *et al.* (1966) to be related both to students' individual characteristics and academic achievement.

CONCLUSIONS

Almost by definition, a game on career decision-making requires mechanisms for constant re-examination and revision. The factual information (such as job salaries and demand for different types of jobs) needs to be constantly updated. However, we have tried to emphasize in the administrator's manual that the information in the School and Job Catalog is not even *currently* exact for all parts of the United States and have included suggestions for having students check this information against local reference as a part of the game experience. Also, I continue to find new studies or data which suggest modification in other parts of the model. For example, information being collected by John Robinson at the University of Michigan on how women spend their time indicates less time on child care and even more time for leisure activities (especially television watching) than I have allocated; also that college graduates spend *more* time on housekeeping than less-educated women do.

Field testing and our growing familarity with new kinds of materials and gadgetry continue to suggest better ways to design and use the game. In the area of research, the number of relatively sophisticated evaluation studies in process or recently completed are adding to our understanding of the kinds of learning that can be produced by Life Career and the conditions under which it is most effective. What has still received insufficient research attention is the problem of validating the game model. Vern Bengston and I are attempting to obtain validity estimates for the game model (by comparing game decisions and scores with responses to questionnaire items and other data on subject-players).

Thus, this paper can best be seen as a progress report rather than a final report. Indeed it seems to be one of the characteristics of games research and development that one is continuously manipulating and changing things, shifting the parameters, introducing new components, trying the game in new settings. Because a social simulation is a device especially relevant to the study of dynamic situations, the technique does not lend itself to the creation of finished products.

REFERENCES

BLOOD, ROBERT AND D. M. WOLFE
1960 *Husbands and Wives in America.* New York: Free Press of Glencoe.

BOOCOCK, SARANE, S.
1966 "The effects of games with simulated environments upon student learn-

ing." Baltimore, Md.: The Johns Hopkins University, Department of Social Relations, unpublished doctoral dissertation.

1968 "An experimental study of the learning effects of two games with simulated environments." In Sarane S. Boocock and E. O. Schild (eds.), *Simulation Games in Learning.* Beverly Hills: Sage Publications.

1970 "Using simulation games in college courses." *Simulation and Games,* 1, 67–79.

Boocock, Sarane S. and James S. Coleman

1966 "Games with simulated environments in learning." *Sociology of Education,* 39 (Summer), 215–236.

Boocock, Sarane S., E. O. Schild, and Clarice Stoll

1967 *Simulation games and control beliefs.* Baltimore, Md.: The Johns Hopkins University, Center for the Study of Social Organization of Schools.

Brunner E. and S. Wayland

1961 "Occupation and education." In A. H. Halsey, *et al.* (eds.), *Education, Economy and Society.* New York: Free Press.

Coleman, James S., Ernest Q. Campbell, *et al.*

1966 *Equality of Educational Opportunity.* Washington D. C.: U. S. Government Printing Office.

Farran, Dale C.

1968 "Competition and learning for underachievers." In Sarane S. Boocock and E. O. Schild (eds.), *Simulation Games in Learning.* Beverly Hills: Sage Publications.

Havemann, E. and P. S. West

1952 *They Went to College.* New York: Harcourt Brace

Larrabee, E. and R. Meyerson (eds.)

1958 *Mass Leisure.* Glencoe: Free Press.

Learning Institute of North Carolina

1968 Final Report on the North Carolina Advancement school 1964–1967: Appendix L. Academic Games and Educational Simulations. Durham, N. C.: Learning Institute of North Carolina.

Orcutt, Guy H., *et al.*

1961 *Microanalysis of Socio-Economic Systems: A Simulation Study.* New York: Harper Brothers.

President's Commission on the Status of Women

1963 *American Women.* Washington, D. C.: U. S. Government Printing Office.

Science Research Associates

1963 *Handbook of Job Facts.* Chicago: Science Research Associates.

Smigel, E. O. (ed.)

1963 *Work and Leisure: A Contemporary Social Problem.* New Haven: College and University Press.

The Life Career Game

U. S. Department of Labor
1964 *Occupational Outlook Handbook*. Washington, D. C.: Government Printing Office.

Varenhorst, Barbara A.
1968 "The Life Career game: Practice in decision-making." In Sarane S. Boocock and E. O. Schild (eds.), *Simulation Games in Learning*. Beverly Hills: Sage Publications.

Section **B** **MACHINE AND MAN-MACHINE SIMULATIONS**

JEANNE E.
AND
JOHN T. GULLAHORN

Chapter **12**

A Non-Random Walk in the Odyssey of a Computer Model[1]

Homans' parsimonious theory of elementary social behavior has tempted mathematicians to give it formal expression. This paper discusses an avatar of the theory in simulation form. The translation has given rise to a slightly different theory on which the Gullahorns have been working for a decade. The journal of the development of HOMUNCULUS reports the reasons which led to various changes and evaluates the fruitfulness of the endeavor.

—The Editors

[1] Preparation of this chapter was facilitated by National Science Foundation Grant No. GS 1822, PHS Research Grant No. MJ 14582-01 from the National Institute of Mental Health, and Michigan State University. Other sources of support for the research reported here were NSF Grant No. GS 781, a National Science Foundation Senior Postdoctoral fellowship, System Development Corporation, and the Michigan State University Computer Institute for Social Science Research and Department of Psychology.

A Non-Random Walk in the Odyssey

After repeated experiences, we are convinced that most crucial happenings in our lives stem not from deliberate, long-range planning, but rather from an exploratory "look-ahead" at the probable consequences of pursuing exciting chance occurrences. Actually, these "chance" events are not fortuitous, since in terms of the communications we selectively expose ourselves to, they have a relatively high probability. The initial follow-up of an idea seems to be a function of our preparatory set of whimsy. Such was the case history of our early involvement in computer modelling. Of course, a fatalist might claim that we were destined to progress to computers because a desk calculator had been the eliciting stimulus for our acquaintance. (John had a calculator in his Harvard office at the time Jeanne was taking statistics.) But to this interpretation we would counter that the very development of our relationship resulted from the process mentioned before.

What stimulus conditions enhanced the attractiveness of computer modelling? Perhaps because of their association with rewarding interaction, computing machines had become secondary reinforcers for us. In addition, Michigan State University's first computer, MISTIC, had been a great boon in completing statistical analyses of our survey data; furthermore, it had proved fun to use, especially in the early open-shop days of the computer center. Aside from these positive past experiences, we were further set to note developments in computer applications in social science because of a relative satiation with the field and survey studies we had been conducting. The familiar shortcomings of correlational versus experimental research were bugging us; however, some ideas we were hatching concerning theory development and testing were not completely amenable to laboratory analysis.

Under similar conditions, some social scientists turn to mathematical modelling. Despite encouragement and proselytizing by such friends as Frank Restle, our brief foray in this direction proved non-reinforcing. The logic of mathematics and the well-defined methods of symbol manipulation were attractive for investigating the dynamics of a formalization. However, we were uncomfortable with the translation process—perhaps because of a lack of "mathematical sophistication"—and we balked at the apparently necessary oversimplification of our verbal formulations. Though we had not yet verbalized our need, we were looking for a method of expressing and manipulating propositions that would prove more tractable and more readily translatable so that we could remain closer conceptually to the phenomenal processes we were investigating.

Such was our state when, in preparing lecture material for his small groups course, John read Fred Bales' review chapter on small group theory and research (1959) in which Bales suggested that the next advances would come not from further laboratory experimentation but from computer simulation of group processes. Intrigued by this speculation, we began searching for information concerning simulation and were particularly gratified by a Social Science Research Council's *Items* report on a RAND workshop on simulation (Simon and Newell, 1958). The report captured the excitement generated by Simon and Newell and described some of the imaginative applications undertaken by Hovland and others. Simulation sounded like what we were looking for; so we wrote to Simon asking how we could learn to program in a list-processing language. (The machine language we had learned for MISTIC was not useful for simulating complex cognitive and social processes.) Since we had no teaching or research commitments for August, 1960, we were able to accept Simon's generous offer of tutorial assistance and office space at Carnegie Tech so that we could learn Information Processing Language, Version V (see Newell, 1961). This investment of time gave us a head start on a forthcoming grant from the Social Science Research Council to develop skill in computer simulation under the guidance of Feigenbaum and Feldman at Berkeley. The period at Berkeley and the ensuing summer at System Development Corporation—an opportunity resulting from a complex network of contacts—enabled us to make considerable progress in programming HOMUNCULUS, our model of elementary social behavior.

HOMUNCULUS

Since detailed presentations of our computer model appear elsewhere (Gullahorn and Gullahorn, 1963, 1964, 1965a; Loehlin, 1968), in this account we shall only briefly describe the overall processing and focus instead on some of the problems we encountered in simulating social behavior. Perhaps our first consideration should be, why HOMUNCULUS? At this time it is difficult to recapture (or rationalize) the elements in our decision to begin with a complex, theoretical-construct model. The choice of Homans' social exchange theory is easy to explain: Homans had been John's adviser at Harvard, and we both considered Homans' *Social Behavior* a seminal contribution. But why didn't we start with a limited portion of Homans' theory and explore in depth just one or two propositions instead of incorporating all five propositions at once? In part, our strategy reflected the reckless optimism characteristic of new converts—an enthusiasm that was consonant with the *Zeitgeist*. At that time computer modellers were extrapolating far beyond actual achievements: Simon forecast that psychological theories soon would be expressed in program format; he further predicted that by 1967 the world's champion chess player would be a computer. Simon's charisma and the promise of such early simulations as the Newell, Shaw, and Simon General Problem Solver and the Feigenbaum and Simon Elementary Perceiver and Memorizer encouraged our headlong plunge into the full set of Homans' propositions.

Before describing some of our experiences in programming, let us make a few comments about Homans' system (1961). Like other social exchange theories, it envisages humans as exchanging behavior as well as commodities. In face-to-face interaction, each person's rewards and costs tend to come from the behavior of others. Thus, an individual's responses depend on the quality and quantity of the reward and punishment that his actions elicit. The core of Homans' theory lies in five propositions derived from experimental psychology and classical economics. They include consideration of stimulus generalization, response generalization, recency and frequency of reward, value of reward, deprivation and satiation, and distributive justice (the norms requiring that a person's rewards should be proportional to his costs and his profits proportional to his investments).

Our early work in programming Homans' theory proved difficult, but self-reinforcing. Never before had we been able to formalize verbal theory in such a way that our imagery represented such a literal, albeit more precise, translation. Even as we flow-charted the routines representing Homans' propositions, we discovered that the discipline of deciding how to program a computer to simulate social behavior gave us a different perspective in our thinking about how humans react in social contexts. This new frame of reference forced us to specify explicitly our conception of a person as an information-processing system.

In order to behave according to the principles set forth in Homans' explanatory propositions, our programmed model of a person had to be able to receive, recognize, store in memory, and compare and contrast stimuli; he had to be able to emit activities, differentiate reward and punishment, associate a stimulus situation with a response and associate a response with a reinforcement. Moreover, on the basis of past experience, he had to be able to predict the expected consequences of each contemplated activity. Representing such a complex organism in a computer model was facilitated by the fact that many of the necessary information-processing functions were analogous to the digital computer's symbol-manipulating capacities; furthermore, programming in a list-processing language meant that simulated individuals could be represented by hierarchies of lists whose memory structures could be searched readily and modified easily. As programmed, an individual's list structure specifies his identity, abilities, relative and absolute positions in various social groups, as well as elements of his past history and resulting values and needs. It also includes his image lists of his membership and other reference groups, his image lists of other group members, and his memory lists of past interactions with different individuals, including information on activities exchanged, the value of social reward received, etc. Each individual's list structure thus is unique.

In operationalizing Homans' propositions we designed the routines to be constant for all simulated persons, since Homans assumes these propositions apply generally to all humans, regardless of their cultural backgrounds or institutional relationships. Flexibility and individuality in the model derive from the fact that the information retrieved from a participant's list structure determines whether certain subroutines will be executed and what their outputs will be in specific contexts.

Since decision-making is the main operation of our programmed representation of Homans' theory, the processing emphasizes information retrieval and judgment as a simulated individual evaluates prospective actions at successively finer levels of detail and finally estimates the relative rewards and costs of surviving alternatives. Along with this hierarchy of decision-making routines, various subroutines update each person's relative state of deprivation or satiation with respect to available social rewards on the basis of their recency and frequency. Still other subroutines evaluate emotional reactions and store or emit anger or guilt responses according to considerations involving distributive justice.

Our first social scenario was a civil service office described by Peter Blau (1955). In the simulation, two employees (Ted and George) of equal rank but unequal competence begin interacting when Ted emits a symbol representing a request for assistance from his co-worker, George. In evaluating this input, George first consults his reference group lists to determine whether the input is appropriate in terms of office norms. If it is, he considers whether the general stimulus situation has proved rewarding in the past and, if so, whether his responses to such an input have been rewarded previously by Ted, the person currently introducing the stimulus situation.

This two-step processing—involving a global response to the general stimulus situation followed by assessment in terms of the specific stimulus agent—was not specified by Homans' first proposition concerning stimulus and response and generalization.

> If in the recent past the occurrence of a particular stimulus-situation has been the occasion on which a man's activity has been rewarded, then the more similar the present stimulus-situation is to the past one, the more likely he is to emit the activity, or some similar activity, now (1961, p. 53).

In trying to program this proposition, however, we found that the apparent clarity and precision of the verbalization actually masked certain ambiguities. In terms of the social exchange we are considering, does a "particular stimulus situation" include every request for help one has received, or is it limited to requests from the same person for assistance on the same problem within the same social context? We finally concluded that the processing sequence described above was a reasonable way to set this proposition in motion.

In the program the subroutines evaluating the stimulus agent locate George's image list of office colleagues, find the sublist describing Ted, determine whether Ted has emitted the present stimulus to George previously and, if so, whether Ted has generally rewarded George's responses to such requests. If it is thus determined that Ted has reinforced George in such contexts previously, then George retrieves up to three activities from a memory list of responses that Ted has rewarded. In the remainder of the program George processes information regarding the relative frequency with which Ted has rewarded past responses (Homans' second proposition), and the value of Ted's rewards in terms of subjective attractiveness and in terms of George's current state of relative deprivation or satiation (Homans' third and fourth propositions). George then compares the overall expected reward from his contemplated response to Ted with the anticipated reward from continuing with his own work, and he computes what Homans terms the "psychic profit"—the reward of an activity less its cost.

Having selected what he expects to be a socially profitable activity, George emits that response to Ted. At this point the program cycles, and George's response becomes a stimulus to Ted, who must select an appropriate and profitable reaction to George. At the end of each interaction sequence Ted and George update their image lists of each other.

The exchanges generated in one early run of the model can be summarized as follows:

Ted: Asks for help
George: Gives help
Ted: Gives social approval
Ted: Asks for help
George: Gives Help
Ted: Asks for help
George: Refers to another worker
Ted: Gives social approval
George: Gives reassurance, exits

Perhaps such an interaction sequence plausibly reproduces some of the interpersonal behavior characteristic of office settings; however, stated in such a limited activity vocabulary, it appears to simulate the theater of the absurd—particularly the opening scenes of Pinter's *The Birthday Party*.

Trying to make program provision for an extensive repertoire of qualitatively different activities proved extremely difficult, especially when we expanded our model to include three simulated individuals. Initially we programmed each person with a limited repertoire of characteristics and allowed him to develop others on the basis of experiences. After a hundred interactions, therefore, there could be a fivefold increase in each participant's memory structure—say from 200 to 1,000 computer words. Even for the dyads, tracing such sprouting trees proved unwieldy, and with the triads we found our own information-processing capacities severely taxed. Furthermore, despite the efficiencies of a list-processing language, storage problems began to threaten.

Finally, we abandoned our attempt at more detailed verisimilitude and shifted to a more generalized level of describing activities by grouping responses into broad conceptual classes. Of the available category systems for coding small group interaction, we considered Bales' comprehensive system (1950) best suited to our needs; therefore, we modified our program so that instead of exchanging individual acts, simulated individuals exchanged categories of interpersonal behaviors (e.g., gave or requested information; agreed or dissented with opinions; expressed group solidarity or antagonism, etc.).

While incorporating Bales' category system made the computer-generated social exchanges more abstract, this modification facilitated other program changes that provided a better simulation of group interaction. Instead of "starting" the model with a particular stimulus agent, we supplied each simulated person with a new motive—a need for social interaction. A master executive routine checked each person's list structure to determine whether his need to act was above his preset threshold value. If so, control was turned over to this simulated individual; if not, each participant's need for interaction was incremented on the basis of his need for social interaction and his energy level. The program cycled (thus there was silence in the group) until some member passed the threshold level. When a simulated individual acted, his need for participation diminished while that of his "listeners" increased so that interruptions could occur.

Making program provision for interruptions was another important innovation in our model. Heretofore, a simulated person always could "single-mindedly" chug through the necessary processing to select his action—the others remained "quiet." In the new version of the model, a programmed person could keep in available memory at least two types of activities he might wish to emit: a normally-selected response that could be thwarted by someone else's interruption, and an anger response that could be suppressed because of threatening circumstances. If he had been interrupted, his need to participate increased, which then increased the probability of his interrupting. His intention to act persisted over several cycles, so that if he assumed control during that period he would emit the thwarted activity; otherwise, he "forgot" it.

With this modified version of HOMUNCULUS, we explored conditions influencing whether triads maintained relatively equal interaction among participants or devolved into a dyad with an isolate. Most frequently, with groups of three unacquainted persons, initial episodes of friendly exchanges between two participants resulted in information being stored on their image lists showing that interaction with each other would probably bring social profit. Such data increased the probability of further interaction between this pair; so that they received little information for developing image lists of the third group member—in spite of his interruptions. Over time, therefore, the triad devolved into a friendly pair and an isolate. These findings indicate that our formalization of Homans' social reinforcement theory is sufficient to produce and explain coalition formation in a triad of unacquainted individuals, and more complicated mechanisms need not necessarily be invoked to account for this classical group phenomenon. This demonstration thus illustrates one of the principal merits of simulation: the results are generated by the explicitly programmed processes and involve no extraneous, implicit assumptions.

Before describing the subsequent paths we followed in our simulation odyssey, perhaps we should disclose the content of our acronym, HOMUNCULUS. The name is obviously related to that of its intellectual father—Homans. Furthermore, in the historical context of psychological homunculus-type theories, the name also serves as a sobering reminder of possible pitfalls in constructing our *homo ex machina.* But we said the name is also an acronym, and here is what it represents: *Ho*mans' *O*rganismic *M*achine *U*niverse *N*arrating *U*tterances *L*isting *U*niversal *S*erendipity.

VALIDATION CONSIDERATIONS

Having demonstrated that it was feasible to express a complex social theory as a computer model and then to generate data following exclusively from the programmed formulation, we next focused on validation issues. Actually, because of our latent Rube Goldberg-type tendencies, we regretted the high cost of forgoing the rewards from further tinkering with the total HOMUNCULUS program. Observing the consequences of various modifications on the model's behavior and outputs was a tempting possibility: the computer is indeed a seduction machine. But unlike mathematicians—who apparently reinforce explorations of formal models for their own sake, without reference to "reality"—behavioral scientists are socialized to feel guilty when they neglect to establish firm linkages between their models and the empirical world. Thus our internalized self-reinforcement "routines" as well as the reinforcement contingencies to be expected from our professional reference groups (and fund-granting foundations) deterred us from the path of intellectual dalliance and steered us toward efforts at more stringent validation.

As noted in our previous discussion, the reasonable behavior generated by HOMUNCULUS suggests that the program provides a sufficient explanation of elementary social behavior. The results of the triad simulations further reinforce this belief. But such a plausability test is weak, often leading one to conclude his model is valid when actually it is not. Still, as Polya has remarked, "plausible grounds are important. . . . In dealing with the observable reality, we can never arrive at any demonstrative truth, we have always to rely on some plausible ground" (1954, p. 199).

The complexity of HOMUNCULUS precluded our attempting to validate it in its entirety. With the full program, the demonstration of coalition formation in a triad seemed to be as far as we could go. We therefore decided to concentrate on small segments of the model, beginning with the routines concerning the effects of value, cost, and profit on social behavior. To test this portion of the program we decided to simulate situations in which humans produced quantitative data that could be compared with similar quantitative output from runs of the abridged model. In order to have as much of the original data as possible and to be familiar with background information, we selected a questionnaire situation from John's previous research on role conflict among labor union members.

THE ROLE CONFLICT SIMULATIONS

Some significant changes had to be introduced in the model as a consequence of the problem chosen. Compared with HOMUNCULUS, the role conflict investigation appears static and situationally dependent. Only the decision-making processes, and not those for learning and modification of list structures, were relevant to the abridged social exchange model simulating role conflict resolution. Furthermore, the new model shifted context from face-to-face interaction to the sort of symbolic social interaction a given person engages in while completing a questionnaire concerning responses to various reference group pressures.

Because our new model was situationally-dependent, we had to spend more time developing a symbolic representation of the experimental situation. The task was analogous to that confronting modellers who simulate human chess playing: they must represent the chess board, the pieces, and the operating rules concerning legal moves. All of this is a separate problem from programming hypotheses concerning human strategies in playing. Therefore, in simulating the behavior of labor union members participating in our survey, we had to develop a computer representation of the questionnaire items and of the administration of the questionnaire. Then we proceeded to write routines specifying the information processing that culminated in the selection of one of the questionnaire response options.

In the first role conflict situation simulated, each respondent was asked to choose between two valued positions (an important office in a company-sponsored employees' club or a union chief stewardship) or to retain both positions under the condition that he really did not have time to fulfill obligations to both roles. Pressures from three relevant reference groups were introduced and systematically varied, favoring first one position, then the other. To explain the original questionnaire findings, we had proposed alternative hypotheses, but with the available data we had been unable to choose among these formulations. By modularizing the role conflict simulation program so that alternative decision-making routines could be incorporated in different computer runs, we were able to generate data resulting from each hypothesized decision strategy and to compare each output with the answers of the actual respondents.

Since details of the role conflict program appear elsewhere (1965b, 1969), we shall only summarize some features of the decision-making routines. One of our hypotheses concerning role conflict resolution treated the decision confronting the respondent as essentially a binary choice, with the option of retaining both positions a choice by default, selected only when the profit level from the other alternatives proved "unacceptable."

In the program, each respondent's list structure contained information supposedly distilled from his past experience regarding the positions in question as well as the reference groups pressuring him. (Actually, these parameters were generated at random for each respondent, with a mean and range corresponding to these statistics from the distribution of survey responses to certain items.) A simulated respondent thus had personal values attached to each position as well as a value for each reference group, representing the expected social approval that would be accorded for conformity with its desires. In estimating the total reward value of each position, therefore, the respondent summed its personal value and the total value of the anticipated rewards from the reference group(s) favoring the role.

At this point we could have programmed a simple social profit decision rule involving the selection of the alternative with the higher reward value, and a random choice or a decision to retain both positions in case of a tie. We rejected this possibility because we assumed that a social profit must have some minimum level of acceptability before an individual would conclude that the expected rewards from one position sufficiently exceeded the expected costs in terms of the forgone rewards from the relinquished alternative. Operationalizing this reasonable-sounding conception of "minimum level of acceptability" of profit proved difficult. Finally, we decided that, while such a level would vary among individuals, at the minimum the profit from a decision such as that posed here should exceed the cost of the choice.

In the program, therefore, a simulated respondent calculated the expected profit (or loss) from each decision by subtracting the total reward value of one position from the total reward value of the other. When the profit associated with selecting one position exceeded the cost of relinquishing the other, then he chose that position. When the expected profit from either decision did not exceed the cost involved in the choice, then the respondent decided by default to select the option of retaining both positions.

While the decision-by-default hypothesis processed reward expectations for only two of the response alternatives, the other role conflict resolution hypotheses we programmed included an estimate of the reward value of retaining both roles in the profit comparisons. Lacking questionnaire data for directly generating reward values for this response option, we estimated such values for each simulated respondent on the basis of his values for the competing roles (since we regarded the decision to retain both roles a function of the conflict).

The description of the role dilemma specifically warns the respondent that he really hasn't time to do both jobs well. In reacting to the questionnaire situation, at one extreme a respondent might conclude that fractionating his time would cost so much in time and effort and lead to such dissatisfaction from relevant reference groups that he would get no reward from attempting to keep both positions. At the other extreme a respondent might decide that he is the unusual sort of person who actually can organize his life so as to realize the full rewards of both positions. To represent this range of possible definitions of the situation, we programmed a random number generator that output a value for the option of retaining both positions based on a range between zero and the sum of a simulated respondent's total reward values for both positions.

With total reward values thus available for all three possible responses to the role conflict situation, we then programmed two alternative hypotheses concerning the resolution of the dilemma. One of these incorporated a straightforward optimizing strategy in which the simulated respondent simply selected the decision with the highest value. The other hypothesis involved minimaxing postdecision regret by considering additional potential rewards that Homans claims are operative in conformity conflict situations (1961, pp. 93–99).

One of these rewards, consonance, results from the affirmation of an individual's personal preference by relevant reference groups. In the program a consonance increment was added to the total value of a decision when the simulated respondent's personal preference for that decision was in harmony with the overall reference groups' pressures. In considering how to represent such a consonance increment, we hypothesized that an individual's reluctance to select the role he and his reference groups preferred depended on the value of the less desired role, inasmuch as post-decision regret or dissonance varied directly with this value. In our operationalization, therefore, the maximum value of the consonance increment increased as the cost of the foregone alternative increased.

When others oppose an individual's preference, then another reward—personal integrity—becomes relevant. In the computer model, integrity increments based on the value of an individual's preferred decision were added to the total value of that decision when most of the reference group pressure was aligned against him.

As mentioned previously, our role conflict simulation model was so modularized that in successive runs the same respondents could use each of the decision-making strategies in resolving the role dilemmas presented in the programmed questionnaire. By comparing the "answers" of the simulated respondents with those of the labor union members originally surveyed, we were able to evaluate the explanatory power of each of our three hypotheses concerning role conflict resolution. In this situation, the social profit strategy incorporating reward values for consonance and integrity produced data that did not differ significantly from the item responses of the original union members.

This statistical validation of one of our social profit hypotheses was highly reinforcing. We went on to test the generality of this formulation in simulations of other role conflict situations. In addition, we tested other hypotheses concerning decision-making in role conflict resolution, including a "satisficing" as opposed to an optimizing strategy.

After these explorations, we came to another branching point in our simulation odyssey. The simulations with the abridged model had demonstrated the utility of operationalizing different hypotheses so that the output they generated could be evaluated against human data. But reinforcing as this hypothesis-testing capability was, still we felt that we were not fully exploiting the unique advantages of computer modelling. The role conflict simulations neglected the computer model's capacity to simulate learning by modifying list structures on the basis of experience. While we did not want to relinquish the increased rigor and control that had been achieved in the role conflict simulations, we wanted to reincorporate the dynamic potentialities uniquely afforded by a computer modelling approach. To do this we decided to return to simulations involving face-to-face interaction.

THE OPINION ANCHORAGE SIMULATION

On the basis of our previous experience in tracing individual changes, we decided to limit our new small group simulations to interactions among triads. We finally chose Gerard's investigation of opinion anchorage in small groups (1954), since his data had proved so amenable to reinterpretation in terms of Homans' hypotheses concerning consonance and integrity—reward values whose importance had been confirmed in our role conflict simulations. In Gerard's study subjects first read a case concerning a union-management dispute and predicted the outcome on a seven-point scale. Gerard then selected subjects for three-man discussion groups, varying the degree of agreement on the predictions. He also manipulated cohesiveness through instructions to the subjects.

Our first simulation runs of this experiment involved the following independent variables: level of liking among members, amount of disagreement among opinions, and degree of confidence of each simulated person in his opinion. Since the full Bales' category system actually proved unwieldy, we limited communication exchanges to the following: gives opinion, agrees, disagrees, shows solidarity, shows antagonism, emits neutral communication.

During simulated interaction, a recipient's liking for another member was increased over time by expressions of solidarity, or agreement, or of opinion that was identical to the recipient's. Conversely, his liking for another was decreased by expressions of antagonism, disagreement, and dissenting opinion. The recipient's confidence in his own opinion was increased by another's agreement and by a member's stating an opinion that was consonant with his own; his confidence was decreased by another's disagreement or statement of a dissenting opinion. A simulated individual also increased his own confidence whenever he stated his own opinion—a programmed provision suggested by other studies on the consequences of public commitment. The impact of the communications on the third member, if he was a witness instead of a joint recipient, was similar but more complex. Both liking and confidence were manipulated by counters and sub-counters in the computer representation of each group member. Parameters for initial values and rates of change could be set empirically or according to certain assumptions (including random assignment).

In assigning subjects to experimental groups, Gerard considered only the average disagreement among opinions and neglected considerations concerning relative positions along the seven-point continuum as well as degree of confidence in opinions. Reasoning from social exchange theory, we predicted that a subject's confidence would vary directly with the extremity of his stated position. Since Gerard had lost his original data we could not check this prediction against his findings; however, other studies we uncovered tended to support our expectation. Since opinion distribution conceivably could affect the experimental findings, we decided to test the sensitivity of the simulation model to different patterns of opinion distributions along the seven-point scale. These sensitivity runs confirmed our prediction. In fact, holding all other parts of the model constant and varying only the initial distribution of opinion, we were able to reproduce Gerard's findings concerning change of opinion toward agreement with another group member.

Our computer-generated data thus enhanced the credibility of a rival hypothesis concerning some of Gerard's findings. Lacking the original data, however, we could not check on the opinion distributions actually represented in the experimental groups. Before going on with the simulations, therefore, we decided to replicate Gerard's study, controlling this time, however, for initial opinion distribution.

The laboratory replication experience is a story in itself. One problem we encountered, for example, involved the case discussion material. While the labor-management dispute Gerard used in his original study apparently involved the interest of college students of the 1950's, it proved non-salient to our population of subjects. Finally, after much experimentation with different topics, we developed discussion material concerning the use and legality of marijuana.

Data from this study currently are being analyzed. On the basis of our experience in simulating small group interaction, we conclude that it is best to select a study one has done himself in order to be more certain of having available the data needed for parameter setting in the computer model as well as for checking against computer output. Indeed, working back and forth between the modelling and the laboratory seems to be a good strategy: in programming one quickly uncovers gaps in theory and in empirical findings that suggest new studies; and the experimental situations themselves suggest manipulations that might be worthwhile to test at least in simulation before implementing them in the laboratory.

CONCLUDING REMARKS

At this point in our simulation odyssey, having encountered smooth roads and blind alleys, we are perhaps a bit wiser (more experienced, anyway) happier, and sadder. Computer simulation is not the brave new world heralded by its advance press notices. It is a challenging, rewarding, frustrating, and time-consuming approach. Some of the rewards and costs depend on exogenous factors—the cooperativeness of the computer center one is dependent upon, and the willingness of system engineers not to tinker with the machine when their efforts to save nanoseconds clobber the interpreter for one's simulation language. On the basis of some non-reinforcing experiences in utilizing programmers, we conclude that the bulk of simulation programming is a do-it-yourself operation. Communicating some of the imagery of social science theory to individuals with engineering or mathematical backgrounds is difficult, and all too often the elegant programming devices they incorporate actually introduce nontenable assumptions into the system.

What does one get out of simulation? Something certainly different from the input—whether it is "more" or "less" depends in part on individual cost-benefit analyses. Among the continued attractions for us is the capability of actualizing a theory's dynamic processes—and concurrently getting a more precise and more tractable representation of the verbal propositions as a result of the discipline imposed by the programming procedure. Running information-processing models on a computer creates pseudo-worlds operating completely in accord with the theories operationalized in the programs. One thus can explore the dynamic implications of the theories, and also get some of the reinforcement for creative expression afforded the social cosmologist. At a more rigorous level, programming specific hypotheses that generate data for comparison with human output provides opportunity for assessing the relationship between one's formalization and actual social behavior. Coupled with empirical investigation, computer simulation is a useful tool for developing and verifying social theory. And so our travels with HOMUNCULUS continue.

REFERENCES

BALES, R. FREED
1950 *Interaction Process Analysis*. Cambridge, Mass.: Addison-Wesley.
1959 "Small-group theory and research." In R. Merton, L. Broom, and L. Cottrell, Jr. (eds.), *Sociology Today*. New York: Basic Books.

BLAU, PETER M.
1955 *The Dynamics of Bureaucracy*. Chicago: University of Chicago Press.

GERARD, HAROLD B.
1954 "The anchorage of opinions in face-to-face groups." *Human Relations*, 7, 313–325.

GULLAHORN, JOHN T. AND JEANNE E. GULLAHORN
1963 "A computer model of elementary social behavior." In E. Feigenbaum and J. Feldman (eds.), *Computers and Thought*. New York: McGraw-Hill.
1964 "Computer simulation of human interaction in small groups." American Federation of Information Processing Societies Conference Proceedings, Spring Joint Computer Conference. Baltimore: Spartan Books.
1965a "The computer as a tool for theory development." In D. Hymes (ed.), *The Use of Computers in Anthropology*. The Hague, Netherlands; Mouton and Company.
1965b "Some computer applications in social science." *American Sociological Review*, 30, 353–365.
1969 "Computer simulation of role conflict resolution." In W. Starbuck and J. Dutton (eds.), *Computer Simulation in Human Behavior*. New York: Wiley.
Forthcoming *Explorations in Computer Simulation*. New York: The Free Press.

HOMANS, GEORGE C.
1961 *Social Behavior: Its Elementary Forms*. New York: Harcourt, Brace and World.

LOEHLIN, JOHN C.
1961 *Computer Models of Personality*. New York: Random House.

NEWELL, ALLEN (ed.)
1961 *Information Processing Language—V. Manual*. Englewood Cliffs, N. J.: Prentice-Hall.

POLYA, G.
1954 *Induction and Analogy in Mathematics*. Princeton, New Jersey: Princeton University Press.

SIMON H. AND A. NEWELL
1958 "Simulation of cognitive processes: A report on the summer research training institute, 1958." *Social Science Research Council Items*, 12, 37–40.

ROBERT B. SMITH

Chapter **13**

Developing Computer Simulations From Modules[1]

The author describes a computer simulation of military authority and recruit behavior, using survey data as a criterion of validity. The case study highlights the way empirical data and the model interplay in the process of developing the theory that the final simulation represents. Smith utilizes and details the modular approach of simulation design.

—THE EDITORS

[1] Preparation of this chapter was facilitated by grants from the Academic Senate of the University of California, Santa Barbara; and from the Inter-University Seminar for Armed Forces and Society. Other sources of support for the research reported here were a PHS fellowship (1Fl MH-22, 188-01) from the National Institute of Mental Health, numerous grants-in-aid for research from the Department of Sociology, Columbia University, and grants of free computer time from the Department of Social Relations, Johns Hopkins University.

Developing Computer Simulations From Modules

Each Mars-bound vehicle would be assembled in earth orbit. Its rocket portion would probably consist of three nuclear-powered stages mounted side by side. The outer two would be fired to send the center stage and the manned spacecraft on their way to Mars.

The two outer stages, having separated, would then fire rocket blasts in the reverse direction so that they would return to earth for re-use.

Once in orbit around Mars, the spaceship would detach the landing craft to send three men to the surface for a possible month of exploration before returning to their orbiting main ship.

—Thomas O. Paine

Simulations are usually created to model a specific substantive process. As many chapters of this volume testify, simulation designers usually start with a rough sketch and then improvise as they go along. The assumptions are modified by trial and error until the simulation is satisfactory. This "one shot" approach probably limits the complexity of the models. But even so, the usual simulation requires two unusual resources: highly skilled designers and permissive deadlines.

McPhee (1963: 1–23) has suggested an alternative "modular" approach. He advocates synthesizing complex models from simple standard components.[2] In addition to enabling the model maker to synthesize complex models, the modular approach would reduce the skills required and would save time.

My colleagues and I used the modular approach to develop a computer model that simulates soldiers' rates of discipline and disobedience. This model is comprised of component processes originally developed by McPhee, et al., to simulate voting (McPhee, 1961; McPhee and Smith, 1962; McPhee and Ferguson, 1962; McPhee, et al., 1963).

MCPHEE'S MODULES FOR COMPUTER SIMULATIONS

Three basic modules comprise the voting model and the related models to be described here. These are (1) the stimulation process, (2) the influence process, and (3) the learning process. The usual linkages are diagrammed in Figure 1. At the beginning of a simulation run, sub-

[2] The modular approach has also been advocated, either explicitly or implicitly, by other social scientists for game simulations (Coleman, 1967) and for computer simulations (Abelson, 1968: 290; Coombs, et al., 1968; and Smith, 1969).

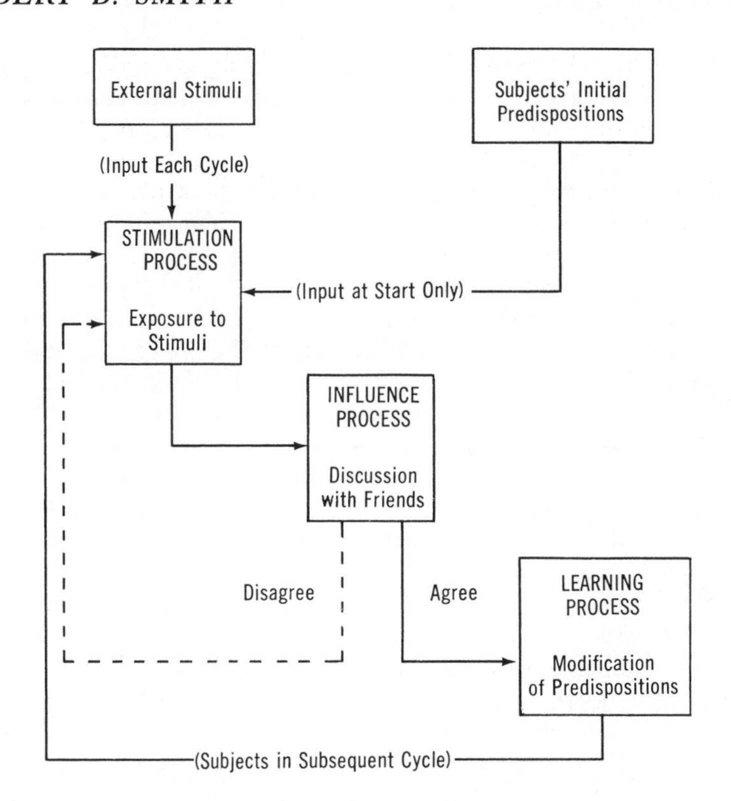

Figure 1: Linkages between the modules*
*Modified from McPhee and Smith (1962:129)

jects with initial values of predispositions are read in. These scores can be hypothetical or correspond to those of actual survey respondents.

In the stimulation process the subjects are exposed to distributions of stimuli that represent perceptual dispersions (McPhee, 1961: 186), or "climates." Lazarsfeld's stimulus-organism-response mechanism is the core of this process (Berelson, et al., 1954: 277–279). This mechanism combines a perceptual *stimulus* drawn at random from a distribution with a subject's attitudinal *predisposition;* the combination results in a *reaction potential.* If the reaction potential is greater than a specified threshold value, then the simulated subject makes a tentative decision about his *behavioral response;* he tentatively chooses one alternative rather than another. Aggregate rates of intended behavior are derived by simply counting the individual choices.[3]

[3] In the voting model (McPhee and Smith, 1962) the distributions of stimuli represent campaign appeals; the predispositions are party loyalties to the Democrats

The influence process takes as input the subjects with the intentions they have formed during the stimulation process. It produces as output subjects with firm convictions (McPhee, et al., 1963: 79–82). This is accomplished by testing each subject's intention against social influence. In this process a subject may or may not talk about his intention with a friend. Conversation will take place between a pair only if their average reaction potential score is higher than a threshold value. This can happen if one of two situations occurs: either both of the scores are larger than the threshold value, or one score is sufficiently larger than the threshold to make up for the other's deficit. If there is no conversation, then no pressure to change will be exerted; the individual choices remain unchanged. But if a conversation does take place, then there will be either disagreement (pressure to change) or agreement (social support). If there is disagreement, then both the subject and his discussion partner will be re-exposed to the stimulation process to form new choices. But if there is agreement, then the social support will maintain the original choices. After all of the subjects have been processed, their final choices are counted as behavior. The program then switches to the learning module.

The learning process modifies the attitudinal predispositions on the basis of current behavior (McPhee and Smith, 1962: 139–145). Each subject has a past history of choices which are an intrinsic part of the predisposition. These past histories are weighted tallies of the number of times the subject has emitted the various choices of interest. In most instances the tallies are weighted by the amount of reaction potential in excess of the threshold. But when the behavioral alternative chosen is not behaving (e.g. not voting), the weight is the amount of reaction potential below the threshold. At the beginning of this process the past histories are multiplied by a forgetting parameter (say 85) which reduces the influence of past behavior on current disposition. Then the current choice plus the weighting is added to the appropriate tally of past choices. Finally, a new score for the predisposition is calculated using the following general formula:

$$\text{Predisposition score for a choice alternative} = \frac{\text{Weighted tally of past choices of the alternative}}{\text{Sum of weighted tallies of past choices of all alternatives}}$$

and Republicans; Democrat, non-voting, and Republican interests are reaction potentials; and a Democrat, non-vote, or Republican choice is the intention. In a residential mobility model (Smith, 1969) the stimuli are complaints about the neighborhood, the predisposition is prejudice, the reaction potential is anxiety about moving, and a decision to move or to stay is the intention.

After new predisposition scores are calculated for each subject, the program returns to the first module to begin a new cycle.

SURVEY RESEARCH AND COMPUTER SIMULATIONS

The social mechanism and social processes portrayed by these modules should not be applied to explain individual behavior. The modules were originally designed to order findings from Berelson's inventory of findings from the panel studies of voting (Berelson, et al., 1954: 327–345) and to study variations in *aggregate* rates of voting. The general theory is too simplified to be an adequate theory of individual behavior. However, the modules can be used to order other survey findings and to study variations in other aggregate rates of behavior. It soon became apparent to me while reading *The Effects of Leadership*, Selvin's (1960) excellent survey of the causes of variation in recruits' rates of non-duty behavior, that McPhee's modules were isomorphic to this data.

Summary of Selvin's Survey

In this survey Selvin related differences in leadership climates (perceptual stimuli) to differences in rates of non-duty behavior (responses). Three status characteristics (indicative of a predisposition)—age, marital status, and education—intervened.

The recruits were asked to describe the behavior of their leadership cadre (their commanding officer, their executive officer, their platoon officer, and their sergeants). Selvin aggregated these ratings of the individual officers to obtain average ratings for the occupants of each leadership position in each company. Then he pooled this data to describe all of the leaders in the army camp. By factor analysis he found two dimensions of perceived leadership: a positive dimension indicated by recruits' perceptions that their leaders emphasized goals (they created confidence, fighting spirit, etc.); and a tyrannical and vacillating dimension indicated by perceptions of interpersonal barriers toward reaching the goals (they treated the recruits like dirt, they punished at every opportunity, they induced fear, etc.). Selvin created a typology of four leadership climates from these dimensions. Because of incomplete data he analyzed the effects of only three—the "arbitrary," "persuasive," and "weak."

In the arbitrary climate the leadership cadre does not behave in a positive manner; they are tyrannical and vacillating, as Selvin states (1960: 45):

> In the *Arbitrary Climate* . . . the leaders do not evoke the confidence of the trainees; they are perceived as aloof, punitive, inconsistent, and untrustworthy.

Of the three climates the arbitrary probably generates the highest level of anxiety. The trainees live in virtually constant fear of punishment, not so much because of what they have done or not done, but rather because of the essentially capricious non-rational behavior of the leaders.

The persuasive climate is the exact opposite; the leaders are positive, and they do not behave in a tyrannical and vacillating manner (Selvin, 1960: 45):

Persuasive Climate. This climate comes closest to what is generally regarded as "ideal" leadership. The trainees have confidence in their leaders and would follow them in combat; and the leaders give their men strong support. The leaders are not coercive nor punitive; they do not play favorites; and they keep their promises.

In the weak (lassez-faire) climate the leaders are not positive, and they do not behave in a tyrannical and vacillating manner. Selvin's definition follows (1960: 45):

Weak Climate. Compared with the persuasive and arbitrary climates, the weak climate, as the name implies, has virtually no effective leadership. These trainees are neither inspired by leaders they like nor driven by leaders they fear; in effect, the leaders do not lead . . . such leaders are merely organizers.

The weak climate engenders rates of intensive non-duty behavior intermediate between those of the arbitrary and those of the persuasive.

Selvin (1960: 59–65) explained these differences in rates by postulating the intervening variable of tension. The different climates create different levels of tension which the recruits release in non-duty behavior. Because they independently contribute to tension, the three status characteristics (age, marital status, and education) also mediate the influence of leadership climates on non-duty behavior. The younger, married, and uneducated categories seemed to predispose the recruits to intensive non-duty activities (Selvin, 1960: 91–109).

Selvin also factor-analyzed the recruits' reports of their non-duty behavior (1960: 242–257). He found five factors that are similar to Merton's (1957: 140) five adaptations to anomie. He labelled these factors *Aggressive Activity* (drinking, drunkenness, and fighting), *Institutional Activity* (eating between meals, mass entertainment, and going to chapel), *Socio-Sexual Activity* (primarily intercourse with prostitutes), *Company-Area Activity* (reading, voluntary athletics, and bull sessions), and *Dependent Activity* (seeing the chaplain, going on sick call, and going AWOL). The amount of variation explained by the factors and the factor loadings of the items was very small. Selvin could not make use of the factors in his analysis. Instead, he analyzed the effects of leadership climate and intervening variables on rates of each individual behavior.

SIMULATION MODELS OF LEADERSHIP EFFECTS

There are three computer simulation models based on *The Effects of Leadership* and subsequent research. The first is a simple mapping of Selvin's findings onto the stimulation module with an added non-duty behavior process. The second model is more complex; the social influence and learning modules are added, and the variables are reconceptualized in the anomie-deviant behavior tradition. The third is an empirically grounded and more parsimonious version of the second.

Figure 2 Stress Distributions (Hypothetical Data)

Arbitrary		*Weak*		*Persuasive*	
*Interval**	*Stress*	*Interval*	*Stress*	*Interval*	*Stress*
$0 \leq X \leq 1$	1	$00 \leq X \leq 9$	1	$0 \leq X \leq 13$	1
$2 \leq X \leq 5$	2	$10 \leq X \leq 19$	2	$14 \leq X \leq 26$	2
$6 \leq X \leq 11$	3	$20 \leq X \leq 29$	3	$27 \leq X \leq 38$	3
$12 \leq X \leq 19$	4	$30 \leq X \leq 39$	4	$39 \leq X \leq 49$	4
$20 \leq X \leq 29$	5	$40 \leq X \leq 49$	5	$50 \leq X \leq 59$	5
$30 \leq X \leq 39$	6	$50 \leq X \leq 59$	6	$60 \leq X \leq 69$	6
$40 \leq X \leq 51$	7	$60 \leq X \leq 69$	7	$70 \leq X \leq 78$	7
$52 \leq X \leq 65$	8	$70 \leq X \leq 79$	8	$79 \leq X \leq 86$	8
$66 \leq X \leq 81$	9	$80 \leq X \leq 89$	9	$87 \leq X \leq 93$	9
$82 \leq X \leq 99$	10	$90 \leq X \leq 99$	10	$94 \leq X \leq 99$	10

*** The random number x = 12 would result in a stress score of 4 when drawn in the arbitrary; a score of 2 in the weak; and a score of 1 in the persuasive.**

Selvin's findings call for a model comprised of a stimulation process, in which the recruits are exposed to the leadership climate of their company, and a non-duty behavior subprocess, in which the resulting tensions are released. Exposure to leadership is stimulated by a random draw of a stress symbol (the stimulus) from the probability distribution representing the recruit's leadership climate. Figure 2 presents hypothetical distributions for each climate. The arbitrary climate is portrayed by a distribution biased toward high stress; the persuasive, by one toward low stress; and the weak, by an unbiased distribution.

Anxiety scores (representing predispositions) are related to the subjects' background characteristics by a simple additive formula. Starting from a base of zero, each subject receives three points if he is below the median age, three points if he is married, and three points if he has less than a high school education. His anxiety score is the sum of these points and can be 0, 3, 6, or 9.

This anxiety score is then added to the subject's stress level (which has been selected by the random process previously described). From this sum the threshold value of ten is subtracted; the difference represents the subject's excess tension. The amount of excess tension determines the subject's behavioral response, according to the following function:

If the subject's excess tension is:	His behavioral response is:
0 or less	institutional activity
1, 2, or 3	company-area activity
4 or 5	socio-sexual activity
6 or 7	aggressive activity
8 or 9	dependent activity

Table 1 presents actual outputs of non-duty behavior for different leadership climates and anxiety levels for a one iteration-simulation run using these parameter values. As expected, intensive non-duty behavior is associated with the arbitrary climate and high anxiety.

Table 1 Non-Duty Activity by Leadership Climate and Anxiety

	Leadership Climates								
	ARBITRARY			***PERSUASIVE***			***WEAK***		
Anxiety Groupings	***High***	***Med.***	***Low***	***High***	***Med.***	***Low***	***High***	***Med.***	***Low***
Non-Duty Activities	%	%	%	%	%	%	%	%	%
Dependent	**29**	—	—	**15**	—	—	**12**	—	—
Aggressive	**23**	—	—	**23**	—	—	**21**	—	—
Socio-Sexual	**15**	**50**	—	**16**	**29**	—	**13**	**19**	—
Company-Area	**25**	**21**	**52**	**15**	**25**	**35**	**21**	**33**	**25**
Institutional	**8**	**29**	**48**	**31**	**46**	**65**	**33**	**48**	**75**
Total Number	**(48)**	**(48)**	**(48)**	**(48)**	**(48)**	**(48)**	**(48)**	**(48)**	**(48)**

The construction of theoretical simulation models can not be justified unless they are useful. Usefulness is usually gauged by gains in substantive knowledge derived from the model, but other criteria such as educational uses are also important. The simple model above has only two uses: (1) it concisely organizes Selvin's findings, and (2) it makes explicit the model of the actor Selvin used to organize his survey findings.

The potential usefulness of this theory was increased by reconceptualizing the variables and by adding other modules. The leadership climates were reconceptualized as situations of anomie; the non-duty behaviors, as Merton's individual adaptations (1957: 140). This generalization of the model enables it to be applied to other substantive problems besides behavior in basic training. It thus becomes more useful because it organizes more data. The addition of the social influence and the learning modules enables it to be used to study change over time in anxiety and in on-duty participation in basic training. Since the design of the influence module enables the experimenter to vary sociometric structure, the model can be easily applied to study the effects of differences in peer cohesion on these variables and on non-duty behavior. This added deductive power obviously increases the utility of the model. Moreover, the added complexity points out gaps in empirical evidence, thereby guiding empirical research. With these benefits in mind I elaborated on the simple model. Next, I will describe how this was done.

RECONCEPTUALIZATIONS

The reconceptualization of the variables was facilitated by simplifying the substantive problem to a dyadic relationship between a gruff sergeant and an inexperienced recruit who converse with each other about goals and means in basic training.

The leadership climates were reconceptualized using the following heuristics. I thought of the sergeant constantly yelling: "Be a good infantryman! Be a good infantryman! Be a good infantryman!" This is the major goal of basic training; to transform raw recruits into combat-ready infantrymen. The naive recruit responds by asking how to reach this goal. The sergeant gruffly replies: "Accept the regimen of basic training! Accept the regimen of basic training! Accept the regimen of basic training!" This is the institutional means: conformity to the training program imposed by the Army.

The sensitizing observations are as follows. Some sergeants emphasize both goals and means—they yell: "Be a good infantryman! Accept the regimen of basic training!" This takes place in the persuasive climate which approximates Merton's (1957: 134) integrated society. But others emphasize only the means—these sergeants yell: "I don't care if you are a good infantryman, but accept the regimen of basic training." This is common in the arbitrary climate which is similar to Merton's (1957: 134) tradition-bound society. Other sergeants emphasize neither goals nor means—they softly whisper: "Be a good infantryman; accept the regimen of basic training." This takes place in the weak climate which approximates an anarchic society. These reconceptualizations are summarized in Figure 3.

As noted above, the most important goal of basic training is to be a good infantryman. This goal makes sense when on-duty behavior is con-

Figure 3 Reconceptualization of Climates

Leadership Climate	*Relationship Between Goals and Means*	*Type of Society*
Persuasive	Appropriate emphasis on both the cultural goal and institutional means	Integrated
Weak	Weak emphasis on both the cultural goal and on institutional means	Anarchic
Arbitrary	Weak emphasis on cultural goal, but heavy emphasis on institutional means	Tradition-Bound

sidered, but what about non-duty activities? Think of the naive recruit walking over to his sergeant and asking: "What shall I do when I am off duty?" The sergeant replies: "Participate in those non-duty activities that will help you to perform better when on duty." In essence this means to be a good infantryman. The recruit next asks: "What recreational facilities should I use?" The sergeant walks over to the recruit, pats him on the back, winks his eye, and says, "Use the recreational facilities the army provides." The recruit salutes and leaves the barracks.

This vignette suggests that the cultural goal for non-duty behavior is "participate in those non-duty activities that help on-duty performance." The norm governing institutional means is "use the facilities the army provides." The cross-tabulation of these goals and means defines different individual adaptations to anomie, which the paradigm of Figure 4 summarizes.

The above reconceptualizations transformed the very restricted model of behavior in basic training into a more useful general theory of anomie and individual adaptation. In this model anomie and individual adaptation are linked by the stimulation, influence, and learning modules. Each recruit is assigned to a company of soldiers; he belongs to one of eight subgroupings defined by his age, marital status, and education; and he is tied into a sociometric network with other recruits.

Stimulation Module

The initial exposure to the climate of anomie takes place during the stimulation process. Each recruit in turn draws a two-digit random num-

Figure 4 Non-Duty Behavior and Modes of Individual Adaptation

Selvin's Factors	*Merton's Adaptations*[a]	*Army Goals*	*Institutional Means*
Institutional Activities	Conformity	+	+
Company-Area Activities	Innovation	+	−
Socio-Sexual Activities	Ritualism	−	+
Aggressive Activities	Rebellion	±	±
Dependent Activities	Retreatism	−	−

[a] (+) signifies "acceptance," (−) signifies "rejection," and (±) signifies "rejection of prevailing values and substitution of new values"

ber. As in the simple model, the random number and the intervals control the selection of the stress symbol. The value of stress is added to the recruit's anxiety value to produce a value of tension. If tension is below a specified threshold, the recruit chooses to participate in basic training. If it is above, he chooses nonparticipation. (These behaviors are discussed in detail below.) Intended participation rates for companies are derived by counting the individual decisions.

Influence Module

In this process each recruit has an opportunity to discuss his Army experiences with other recruits. Conversations take place between dyads; a pair of recruits will talk about Army life, verbalizing their complaints if the average of their combined tensions exceeds the threshold. If a conversation takes place, there will be a disagreement if only one recruit has chosen to participate in basic training. When this happens both are re-exposed to their own company's anomie climate. They draw new stress symbols, which create new tension levels and new decisions about participation. But if both agree, then they are not re-exposed to the climates. If a pair has insufficient pressures to communicate, then they will not talk and no social influence is exerted. After all of the potential conversations specified by the sociometric structure have taken place, the recruits' final choices are counted as behavior.

Non-duty Behavior and Learning Module

In this process the recruits' excess tensions are released in non-duty behavior, and their anxiety scores are modified to reflect current behavior. As in the simple model, the amount of excess tension and the hypothetical cutting points control the adaptation to anomie. For example, if a recruit has no excess tension, then he will adapt by Conformity; if his excess tension is very high, he will adapt by Retreatism. After tension is released in non-duty activities, anxiety is modified. First the effect of past history on current anxiety is reduced by the forgetting parameter. Then a new anxiety score is calculated, weighted by current tension. If excess tension is positive, then anxiety will be increased. If not, it will be decreased. After all of the recruits have been processed the program iterates to the simulation module, thereby beginning a new cycle. The programmed model readily simulates the effects of climates of anomie on recruits' behavior (see Table 2); the stressful tradition-bound (arbitrary) society creates high tension and high rates of non-participation. The influence module changes the participation decisions of deviating recruits. Those with high tension adapt by the more intensive non-duty activities. The learning module changes anxiety as a function of excess

Table 2 Consequences of Anomie * (One Iteration)

Consequences	Tradition-Bound (Arbitrary)	Anarchic (Weak)	Integrated (Persuasive)
Average Stress			
During Stimulation	6	5	4
During Influence	7	5	5
Average Tension			
After Stimulation	12	11	9
After Influence	12	10	10
Percent Not Participating			
After Stimulation	64%	52%	46%
After Influence	74%	58%	54%
Individual Adaptations			
Retreatism	11%	2%	3%
Rebellion	6	10	6
Ritualism	19	14	15
Innovation	38	32	30
Conformity	26	42	46
Average Anxiety			
Initially	5	5	5
At End	5	5	5

* The hypothetical data and cutting points of Figures 2, 3, and 4 were used. There were 96 recruits in each climate.

tension. The model is reasonably parsimonious; there are eight parameters (one for each of the two climate dimensions, one for anxiety, one for the forgetting parameter, and four for non-duty activities). But is the model empirically true?

Secondary Analysis of Selvin's Survey

Figure 5 diagrams the propositions of the system of variables. Even though this system formalizes findings from a completed exploratory survey, most of the propositions are empirically unsupported. The relationships between stress and anomie are of primary importance, but neither variable has been measured directly. The concepts *participation* and *non-participation* need clarification and measurement. The relationships between background characteristics, anxiety, and participation rates need documentation. There is very little empirical evidence in support of the influence and learning modules. The five factors of non-duty activity explain very little of the total variation of these rates, thus casting doubt on the non-duty behavior subprocess. Moreover, the causal effects of the variables are unquantified. I reanalyzed the data of *The Effects of Leadership* in order to correct these deficiencies in evidence that were created by constructing the simulation models. First, I tried to corroborate the mechanism of the model; then, the social processes. This was a lengthy, involved procedure, and I shall illustrate merely one small portion of it.

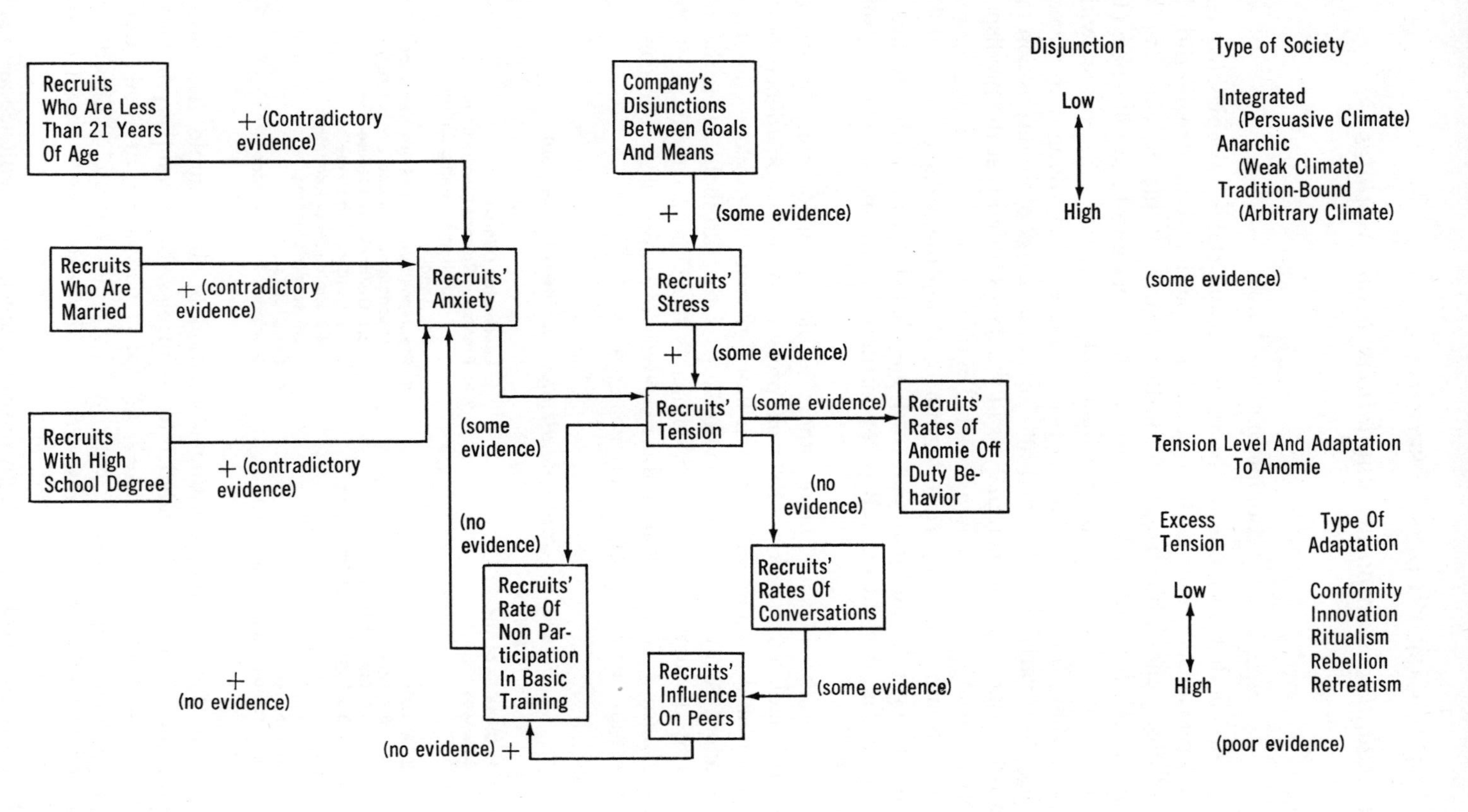

Figure 5: The propositions of the system

Completing the Model

Recall that only one of the three original status variables (education) previously presumed to be a factor in participation actually did affect discipline-disobedience. In further search of the Selvin data, I uncovered three additional status variables that also have influence: (1) home near to army camp (less than 350 miles away); (2) contact with home; and (3) heavy smoking (a pack or more daily). Along with education, these variables combined into an *ad hoc* index of predisposition toward deviance. In further analysis of the data I found that the predisposition toward deviance is associated with low scores on a legitimacy index (Smith, 1967: 36). Here legitimacy means the capacity of the military to engender and maintain the belief that the Army authority structure, codes of conduct, and other institutions are appropriate (Lipset, 1960: 77).

These findings and many others enabled the model's mechanism to be reformulated as follows. External pressure toward disobedience, domination, and anomic combine with low legitimacy to produce complaincts about Army life. If complaints surpass the threshold, then the recruit is disobedient. Figure 6 compares the conceptualization of the mechanism before and after the reanalysis of survey data. The conceptualization has been completely changed.

Figure 6 Conceptualization of the Mechanism

Before	After
1. Climates of Anomie	1. Leadership Climates
2. Stress	2. Pressures Toward Disobedience
	2.1 Domination-Manipulation
	2.2 Anomie
3. Anxiety	3. Predisposition Toward Disobedience (Associated with Low Legitimacy)
3.1 Age	3.1 Distance from Home
3.2 Marital Status	3.2 Contact with Home
3.3 High School Education	3.3 High School Education
	3.4 Heavy-Smoking
4. Tension	4. Complaints
5. Participation-Non Participation	5. Discipline-Disobedience

The logic of the resulting simulation is quite simple. The army basic training camp is divided into companies. Each company has one of the three leadership climates; arbitrary, persuasive, or weak. Each type of leadership climate is portrayed by a different probability distribution of pressures toward disobedience; the scale ranges from 1 to 10. The prevalence of domination and anomie in each climate determines the pressure distributions: high pressures toward disobedience are most

Definitions:

Variable	Definition	Range
PRESUR	= Pressures Toward Disobedience	$1 \leqslant \text{PRESUR} \leqslant 10$
BEHAVE	= Behavior	Disobedience = 1; Disciplined = 0
CMPLNTS	= Complaints	$1 \leqslant \text{CMPLNTS} \leqslant 19$
ILLEGIT	= Illegitimacy of Authority	$1 \leqslant \text{ILLEGIT} \leqslant 9$
GROUPING	= Recruit's Grouping Number	$1 \leqslant \text{GROUPING} \leqslant 16$
DSOBDNT	= Past History of Disobedience	
DISIPLND	= Past History of Discipline	
IDEN	= Recruit's Identification	
COMRAD	= Friend's Identification	
FORGET	= Forgetting Parameter	FORGET = .85

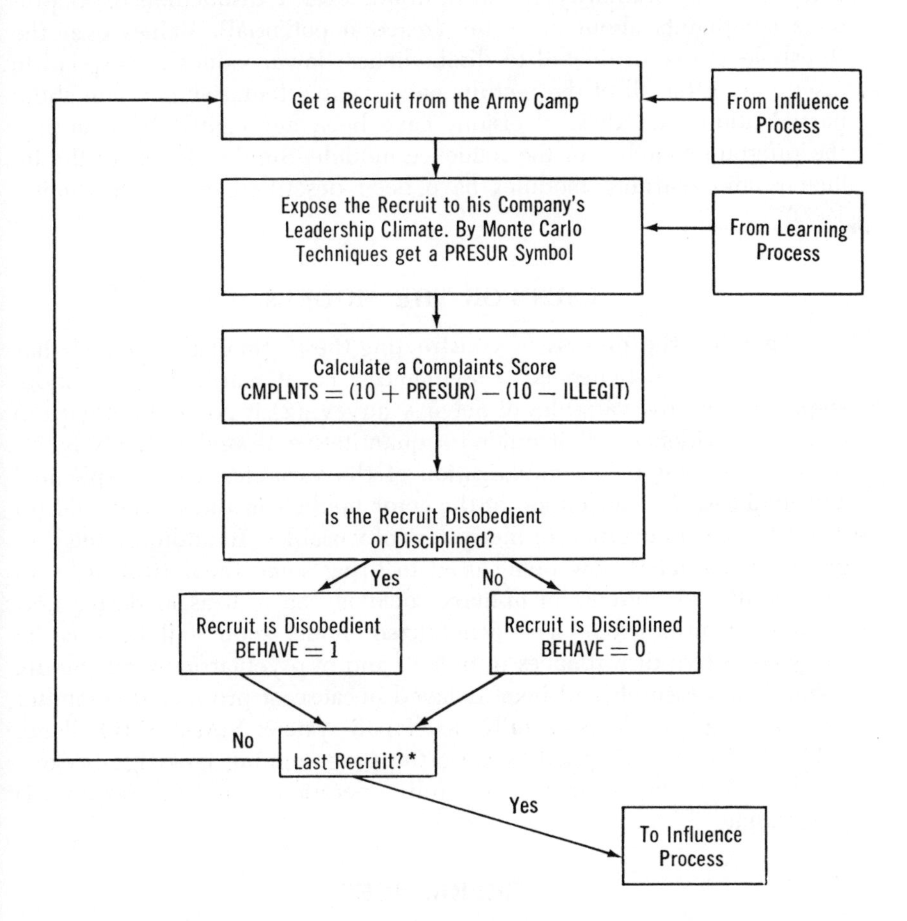

* Switch set to Yes when recruit enters from Influence Process.

Figure 7: The stimulation module

probable in the arbitrary climate; less probable in the persuasive; and least probable in the weak. The model is comprised of the three standard modules. One iteration is coordinated to a week of basic training.

The stimulation process, which is diagrammed in Figure 7, takes as input pressure distributions for each company, and recruits who are to be exposed to these climates. It produces as output recruits who intend to behave with discipline or with disobedience. This is accomplished by the following mechanism. Pressures toward disobedience from a leadership climate (the stimulus) are combined with attitudes about the legitimacy of Army authority (predisposition toward disobedience) to produce complaints about army life (reaction potential). Values over the threshold are co-ordinated to disobedience; lower values correspond to discipline. After all of the recruits have made a tentative decision about participation, and these decisions have been aggregated by counting, the program switches to the influence module. Similar details of the influence and learning modules have been described elsewhere (Smith, 1969).

USES FOR THE MODELS

Thus far, the process of constructing these stimulation models has produced several beneficial consequences: (1) it clarified the relationships between the variables of Selvin's survey; (2) it pointed out gaps in empirical evidence; (3) it guided a quantitative secondary analysis; (4) it forced a total reconceptualization of the variables; (5) it explicated and modified the conception of the actor implicit in the survey; and (6) it led to a generalization of the system of variables. In addition, the programmed model is now being used to bring some theoretical order to some scattered findings in military sociology as well as to derive new findings (Smith, 1969). The generalized model soon will be used to study collective disturbances in prisons and in psychiatric wards (Smith, 1969). This research had been delayed because of protracted computer programming problems—a fully developed system, SIM-A (Milholland, 1966), had to be scrapped because the programming language became obsolete. A second system is now fully operational, and the research is progressing.

REFERENCES

ABELSON, ROBERT P.
1968 "Simulation of social behavior." In Gardner Lindzey and Elliot Aronson (eds.), *The Handbook of Social Psychology* (second edition). Reading, Massachusetts: Addison-Wesley.

ROBERT B. SMITH

BERELSON, BERNARD, PAUL F. LAZARSFELD,
AND WILLIAM N. MCPHEE
1954 *Voting*. Chicago: University of Chicago Press.

COOMBS, STEVEN L., MICHAEL FRIED,
AND STEWART H. RABINOVITZ
1968 "An approach to election simulations through modular systems." In William D. Coplin (ed.), *Simulation in the Study of Politics*. Chicago: Markham Publishing Company.

LIPSET, SEYMOUR MARTIN
1960 *Political Man*. Garden City, New York: Doubleday & Company.

MCPHEE, WILLIAM N.
1961 "Note on a campaign simulator." *Public Opinion Quarterly*, 25, 184–193.
1963 *Formal Theories of Mass Behavior*. New York: Free Press.

MCPHEE, WILLIAM N. AND JACK FERGUSON
1962 "Political immunization." In William N. McPhee and W. A. Glaser (eds.), *Public Opinion and Congressional Elections*. New York: Free Press.

MCPHEE, WILLIAM N., AND ROBERT B. SMITH
1962 "A model for analyzing voting systems." In William N. McPhee and W. A. Glaser (eds), *Public Opinion and Congressional Elections*. New York: Free Press.

MCPHEE, WILLIAM N., ROBERT B. SMITH,
AND JACK FERGUSON
1963 "A theory of informal social influence." In William N. McPhee, *Formal Theories of Mass Behavior*. New York: Free Press.

MERTON, ROBERT K.
1957 *Social Theory and Social Structure*. Glencoe: Free Press.

MILHOLLAND, HARRY
1966 *A Description of the SIM-A System*. New York: Free Press.

SELVIN, HANAN C.
1960 *The Effects of Leadership*. Glencoe: Free Press.

SMITH, ROBERT B.
1967 "Examples of the interplay between survey research and computer simulations." Baltimore: Johns Hopkins University, mimeo.
1969 "Simulation models for accounting schemes." *American Behavioral Scientist* XII (July–August).

JIMMER M. LEONARD

Chapter **14**

Toy Store: A Computer-Based Educational Game

The Toy Store game conveys basic economic principles to elementary school students. An important design originality is that the needs of the target population were surveyed before the simulation was crystallized. The report makes most clear how pedagogical requirements influence the choice of parameter values beyond theoretical justifications.

—The Editors

Toy Store: A Computer-Based Educational Game

In mid-1962, work was begun on a project designed to explore one aspect of the possible use of computers in simulation. Specifically, three computer-based games were developed for the purpose of instructing sixth-graders in the field of economics. By the summer of 1965, two of the three games had been developed, and programming of these games had already begun. This paper describes the process involved in the construction of the third game in the series: selection of the environment to be simulated, design of a game model, preparation of a script, programming and revision.

Each of the games developed during the course of the project was to make use of simulated social and economic environment. The player, assuming a role as an actor in the environment, gains insight into the nature of the environment by making decisions and then noting, in simulated future time, the direct, indirect, and long-range consequences of these decisions. Primarily, these decisions require the allocation of available resources in such a way as to minimize costs and maximize rewards, in an effort to attain certain prescribed goals. As a player progresses in a game he discerns, on the basis of his experiences in the role, the relationships among the variables operating in the simulated environment. This understanding of relationships allows him to allocate his resources and meet the problems that arise in a more economically rational manner. Thus, he learns about the environment through trial and error, detecting its principles and structures himself.

Certain constraints were placed upon the design of the third game by the funding arrangements of the project and the predisposition of the projected director. The more important constraints and limitations are listed below:

1. The game was to be designed to be played by an "average" sixth-grader.
2. The game was to teach basic economic terms, concepts, and principles.
3. The game was to be of sufficient complexity to warrant its delivery through use of high-speed electronic data-processing equipment.
4. From a technical standpoint, the game was to be programmed for the special purpose IBM 7090 system, utilizing a Time-Sharing Monitor located at IBM in Yorktown Heights, N. Y. Delivery would be made via telephone lines and DATAPHONE to a single IBM Model 1050 Terminal with a slide projector that could

select any one of eighty slides in a tray under computer control.[1]

5. Only one student was to play the game at any given time. Thus, he would not be competing or cooperating with other players, but would simply be competing as an individual against an environment simulated by means of a computer-controlled typewriter-terminal and associated audio-visual devices. (This last constraint was attributable in part to the nature of the proposal submitted to the U. S. Office of Education and in part to the technical limitations imposed by the data-processing system to be used.)

SELECTION OF THE ENVIRONMENT TO BE SIMULATED

The two games developed earlier under Project 2841—the Sumerian Game and the Sierra Leone Game—emphasized the global aspects of an economic system.[2] In both of these games, the player is confronted with problems that affect the economy of a nation. The course of the nation depends upon the decisions made by the player. Although the economic principles and concepts taught in the Sumerian and Sierra Leone games are applicable to situations on a smaller scale than that of a national economy, I believed that the third game should be based upon a simulated environment closer to the individual level. One purpose of this decision was to determine whether concepts taught at such a level could be generalized to higher levels of abstraction.

During the period in which the game was devised, a great deal of interest and enthusiasm was being shown at The Johns Hopkins University over results obtained through the use of educational games designed to teach players how to solve very real and immediate practical problems. On this basis, I first thought that a "family finance" game would be a suitable vehicle to meet the requirements set for the construction of the game. It was with this intention that a series of depth-interviews were conducted in June of 1965 with approximately twenty-five students attending grades five through eight. The purpose of these interviews was

[1] The final version of the game was well suited to be used on a sophisticated system such as the IBM 7090, since it requires approximately 100,000 positions of core storage. Only a relatively small fraction of memory was used for text and messages.

[2] The Sumerian Game was designed by Mabel Addis; the Sierra Leone Development Game, by Walter Goodman. For research on these games, see Wing (1969); Leonard and Wing (1967); Wing (1967).

to determine the level of knowledge possessed by students in that age group concerning the manner in which family income is derived and allocated. The outcome of the interviews was hardly that originally anticipated. In probing to determine these students' awareness of opportunities and pitfalls for consumers in purchasing goods, one feature became glaringly apparent: *the students knew almost nothing about the basic operation of retail sales establishments.* Furthermore, the misconceptions they held were extreme! The most widespread misconception was that if a store sells merchandise for $1.00 to a customer, the store has, in effect, made a "profit" of $1.00. The students gave no consideration whatsoever to the fact that the store had to purchase the merchandise in order to make it available to sell to consumers; nor did they consider the overhead costs necessary for the operation of the store. The students also possessed little knowledge concerning the economics of the production of goods. They were aware of labor costs, but not of the costs of raw materials and equipment. On the basis of these interview results, I decided to construct a two-part game. In the first segment, the player would enter the area of manufacturing and make decisions affecting the production and sale of a consumer product. Only the first segment of the game is discussed here.

The next decision concerned the level of complexity to be reached in each of the two game segments. The retail store portion is relatively simple for an average sixth-grader and the probability of losing (i.e., going bankrupt) is small in this first game segment. Economic terms are introduced primarily "in context;" the player is expected to decipher and absorb their meaning through the context in which they would be presented. For a "slower" player (one who has attempted playing the game and has done poorly, or one whose teacher feels he needs special assistance) a special computer-controlled introduction is available to present definitions of important terms, in a format similar to conventional programmed instruction. In this optional introduction, terms such as "profit," "loss," "expenses," and "sales" are explained with the aid of visual displays, and the student is given an opportunity to review any terms not initially understood.

Another decision concerned the products to be sold and manufactured. I felt that the products sold should have some inherent appeal to a sixth-grader and that players of either sex should be able to accept the simulated role. Interviews with sixth-graders were used to obtain suggestions for the type of retail store to utilize in the simulation. During these interviews it became apparent that students chose their own "favorite" stores not necessarily on the basis of the items that were sold there, but rather on the basis of the store's location, the fact that they would meet their friends there, or their favorable disposition toward the owner and/or employees. Therefore, we asked the students, in effect, to "write a letter to Santa Claus" requesting approximately ten items. On the basis of these lists a composite store was designed. A toy store meets the necessary qualifications for the environment to be simulated; however, for students at this grade level, the store must also sell more sophisticated items, such as transistor radios, sporting goods (sleds, skis, archery equipment), and musical instruments. The player is cast into the role of the owner of such a toy store for the first segment of the game.

THE GAME MODEL AND THE GAME SCRIPT

The distinction between a game *script* and a game *model* is of fundamental importance for examining the construction of computer-based games. The *model* provides a skeleton, a mathematical framework upon which various substantive materials may be attached in the form of a *script*. However, the model also lays the groundwork and provides the rules for the attachments, and insures that the flesh and substance of the game belongs where it is placed.

For example, a script for a monthly report to the player in the Toy Store game would resemble the sample monthly reports appearing in Figure 1, except that it would contain no numerical values. The IBM 1050 terminal on which the game was used is rather slow, with a printing rate of approximately 15 characters per second and a line-feed/carriage-return delay of approximately one second. In revising the game, it was found that much time could be saved, without any loss of significant information, by revising the format of the monthly report to that shown in Figure 2. The process of designing a suitable format for a monthly report could be considered "script-writing," while determination of the figures that would appear in the report (representing mathematical variables) could be designated as "model-building."

The necessity of devising a working model before progressing too far in the design of a game cannot be overemphasized, particularly in the construction of a computer-based game. Sometimes a script is written with little concern given to the underlying model that will govern the consequences of the decisions made by a player. When an attempt is then made to fashion this script into a game, the result is likely to resemble an exercise in computer-controlled programmed instruction, with numbers appearing occasionally—numbers that might as well be random digits, as far as the student at the typewriter terminal is concerned.

Actual construction of the model consumed several weeks, during which alternate models were tested, using adults and fifth-through-

Toy Store: A Computer-Based Educational Game

Figure 1 Original Monthly Report Format

FEBRUARY 28, 1969

SALES *LAST* MONTH: $1317.
SALES *THIS* MONTH: $1317.

EXPENSES THIS MONTH: $ 165.

COST OF GOODS SOLD THIS MONTH $ 790.

PROFIT (SALES—EXPENSES—COST OF GOODS SOLD) $362.

CURRENT SAVINGS:
YOU HAVE $1317. IN YOUR CASH REGISTER FROM THIS MONTH'S SALES

MONTHLY EXPENSES, $165. HAVE BEEN PAID
$1152. REMAINS IN YOUR CASH REGISTER AFTER PAYING EXPENSES

THIS MONEY AND YOUR SAVINGS MAY BE DISTRIBUTED BETWEEN:
YOUR SALARY
MERCHANDISE TO REPLACE THAT SOLD
SAVINGS (MONEY SET ASIDE FOR FUTURE USE)

LAST MONTH'S SALARY: $200.
THIS AMOUNT WAS ADEQUATE

WHAT SALARY DO YOU WISH AS A REWARD FOR YOUR WORK THIS MONTH?

210.

$942. STILL REMAINS FROM MONTHLY SALES
CURRENT SAVINGS: $301.

TOTAL AMOUNT AVAILABLE TO SPEND $1243.

MERCHANDISE AT BEGINNING OF MONTH: $6004.
MERCHANDISE SOLD DURING MONTH: $ 790.
MERCHANDISE REMAINING ON SHELVES: $5214.

ANY MONEY NOT SPENT FOR REPLACING GOODS SOLD CAN BE SET ASIDE FOR FUTURE USE

HOW MUCH OF THE MONEY AVAILABLE WILL YOU SPEND FOR REPLACING THE TOYS SOLD?

800.

MONEY REMAINING FROM MONTH'S $142. THIS MONEY WILL BE ADDED TO SAVINGS.
CURRENT SAVINGS: $443.

* * *

MARCH 31, 1969

eighth graders as subjects and a desk calculator for computations. The results of these paper-and-pencil runs were graphed and analyzed. Through this process a basic model was devised that did not undergo any significant modification until the game was programmed and tested with students at computer-controlled typewriter terminals.

The model is *not* intended to reflect precisely the performance or

Figure 2 Revised Monthly Report Format

FEBRUARY 28, 1969

SALES _LAST_ MONTH: $1317.
SALES _THIS_ MONTH: $1317.

TOTAL EXPENSES THIS MONTH ($165.) HAVE BEEN PAID

COST OF GOODS SOLD THIS MONTH: $790.

PROFIT (SALES—EXPENSES—COST OF GOODS SOLD) $362.

MONEY AVAILABLE TO SPEND = SAVINGS ($301.) + MONEY REMAINING FROM SALES ($1152.) = $1453.

LAST MONTH'S SALARY, $200., WAS ADEQUATE
WHAT AMOUNT DO YOU WANT AS A REWARD FOR YOUR WORK THIS MONTH?

210.

MERCHANDISE AT BEGINNING OF MONTH: $6004.
MERCHANDISE SOLD DURING MONTH: $ 790.
MERCHANDISE REMAINING ON SHELVES: $5214.

ANY MONEY NOT SPENT FOR REPLACING GOODS SOLD WILL BE ADDED TO SAVINGS.
HOW MUCH OF THE REMAINING MONEY AVAILABLE (1243.) WILL YOU SPEND FOR REPLACING THE TOYS SOLD?

800.

NEW AMOUNT IN SAVINGS: $443.

* * *

MARCH 31, 1969

characteristics of an average toy store. For example, the monthly sales of the store are initially set at 20 percent of the capital investment in the store; in a real-life situation, this figure would probably average closer to 5 percent. However, this discrepancy and others are unimportant because the purpose of the game is *not* to teach an individual how to operate a toy store or any other type of store. Instead, the commercial environment is intended to serve as a vehicle for teaching more basic economic terms, concepts, and relationships.

Both the Sumerian Game and the Sierra Leone Game utilize progress reports that appear at fixed points in time. This seemed to be a satisfactory way in which to indicate to the player the results of previous decisions and to elicit a new set of decisions. Accordingly, I chose to divide the Toy Store Game into periods, each representing one month of simulated future time. At the end of each month, the player receives a report advising him of his sales, expenses, profit or loss, and other factors that could be of concern to him. The player then allocates his resources and makes certain decisions in an attempt to increase the net worth and monthly profit of his store or factory. On the basis of the inputs from the player and the characteristics of the model stored in the computer, a report for the next month is then printed.

The game itself ends when a player's net worth exceeds a predetermined value. When that point is reached, the player is presented with a final report containing statistical information on his progress throughout the game, along with appropriate laudatory comments. The overall goal of the game is to progress from beginning to end in the shortest amount of simulated future time, through avoidance of losses and prudent reinvestment of profits, so as to increase monthly profit figures. Increases in monthly sales do not always represent increases in profits. Thus, a player who reaches the end of the game successfully by the year 1980 in simulated future time has performed better than a player finishing in 1985. However, the amount of *real* time consumed in playing the game is not to be used in judging the performance of a player.

THE GENERAL MODEL FOR THE TOY STORE GAME

The underlying axiom of the retail model is that store sales each month remain constant until some action is taken by the player to increase monthly sales, assuming enough merchandise or stock is maintained to support such a sales level. A player can increase the sales of his store by obtaining a larger share of the market in the area, by expanding the market area covered, or by stimulating the overall demand for the merchandise he sells. Any attempts to increase sales necessitate the expenditure of resources, either in the form of outright purchases or by agreement to bear increased monthly expenses in the future.[3]

I decided that an average player's monthly sales would be allocated in the following manner:

Cost of goods sold:	60%	of sales
Expenses:	20	of sales
Profit:		
Compensation to owner:[4]	10	of sales
Available for reinvestment:	10	of sales

Of these proportions, only the cost of goods sold is actually fixed. The remainder varies with a player's decisions and on his luck. However, the model is constructed so that the monthly expenses for an average player would tend to be approximately 20 percent of sales, and certain constraints are placed upon the amount of compensation the store owner can receive. These constraints tend to leave approximately 10 percent of sales income available to be reinvested in the store.

The initial conditions facing a player under the model are the following:

Assets:	Merchandise on shelves	=	$4,000
	Equipment	=	1,000
	Savings	=	50

[3] A design-center built into the model is that the *average* period required for doubling store assets will be approximately thirty-six months in simulated future time. This figure was chosen in order to have the entire game take approximately fifteen hours of real time to complete, with the toy store portion representing 80% of the game, or about twelve hours. Assuming that the player would have to double his net worth four times to complete the toy store segment of the game, each doubling would have to take three hours. If each monthly report would require five minutes of real time to complete, then the three hours of real time for each doubling of assets would represent thirty-six months of simulated time. Although the assumptions concerning the time required to complete monthly reports proved to be inaccurate, they served as an important benchmark in the construction of the model. (The average length of time necessary for a monthly report proved to be approximately four minutes.)

[4] This profit figure would not conform to the way in which profit is defined by many economists, for it includes the value added to the store by the owner's own work during the month. However, for the sake of simplification, it was felt that the most readily understandable representation that could be given to profit would be that of: Sales (Cost of goods sold + Expenses).

Toy Store: A Computer-Based Educational Game

Monthly Sales: [5]

Cost of goods sold	=	600
Expenses	=	100
Profit	=	300

After the printing of the initial sales report, the player must allocate his resources (sales income plus savings) between replacement of goods sold and compensation for his own work in the store. The amount he owes for expenses ($100) is automatically deducted from the sales receipts before allocation of resources takes place. Thus, he may spend up to $950 for merchandise and his own compensation. Any more money remaining becomes the new amount of the player's savings.[6] This pattern of resource allocation is followed in each monthly report.

Replacement of Merchandise Sold;
Potential Sales vs. Actual Sales

As was noted earlier, sales will tend to remain constant unless some decision is made by the player which will change the monthly sales figure. Initially, the potential sales level and actual sales level are identical: $1000 per month. Through means of various subroutines that are introduced during the game (e.g., adoption of newspaper advertising), the player has an opportunity to increase the *potential* sales figure. Once increased, this potential level is maintained until it is again augmented through some action on the part of the player. Whether or not the *actual* monthly sales equal the potential sales level depends upon whether the player has maintained enough merchandise on his shelves. Therefore, when an increase in the potential sales level occurs, the actual sales will not increase unless there is sufficient merchandise on hand.

Originally I decided that not more than 25 percent of a player's merchandise could be sold in any single game month. (This proportion is consistent with other characteristics of the model.) The result was the following formula:

$$\text{If MM} \geqslant 4\text{ SP},\quad \text{SS} + \text{SP}$$
$$\text{If MM} \leqslant 4\text{ SP},\quad \text{SS} + \tfrac{1}{4}\text{MM}$$

[5] Initially, profit is a higher proportion of sales income and expenses are a lower proportion than that specified by the general model. As the game progresses, these proportions tend to approach the 20% figures specified. Although profit is initially high, money available for reinvestment tends to remain at 10% of sales revenue, on the average, throughout the game.

[6] This is the case only in the simplest monthly report. In some of the reports, the player may also allocate funds to the purchase of new equipment, or to the purchase of *new kinds* of merchandise. Under these circumstances, money remaining after the player has made (or declined to make) these purchases is automatically transferred to savings.

where MM is the value of the merchandise on hand at the beginning of the month, SP is the player's potential sales level, and SS is the amount of actual sales during the month. Note that if a player has not maintained an adequate merchandise level, his actual sales will be *less* than his potential sales level.

During pencil-and-paper trials, player would often allow their merchandise levels drop slightly below the initial level of $4,000, and they seemed unable to comprehend the reasons for subsequent decreases in sales. For this reason I modified the formula to permit a player to let his merchandise level fall as much as 10 percent below the initial level without experiencing a drop in sales. The revised formula is as follows:

$$\text{If MM} \quad 3.6\ \text{SP}, \quad \text{SS} + \text{SP}$$

$$\text{If MM} \quad 3.6\ \text{SP}, \quad \text{SS} + \frac{1}{3.6}\ \text{MM}$$

Therefore, under the revised formula a player's merchandise level can drop as low as $3600 without causing a decrease in sales. An additional consequence of the revised formula is that it permits a player to sell 1/3.6 or 28 percent of his merchandise each month instead of only 25 percent.

In a revised version of the game, a special chart is printed for players who suffer sales losses for three consecutive months due to inadequate merchandise levels for the last "good" month followed by figure for the next three. A message accompanying this chart states: "Perhaps it will be helpful if you study this chart."

One important characteristic to note is that, given the necessity of paying monthly expenses and withdrawing a minimum amount of compensation ("salary") from monthly sales income, it is possible for a player to reach a point from which recovery is impossible if he allows his merchandise level (and his savings) to drop too far. At merchandise levels below $2700, the amount remaining from sales after deducting expenses and salary does not allow the replacement of goods sold, and the player's inventory and sales level will shrink until he is forced into bankruptcy, which is reached when he cannot pay both his expenses and a minimum salary.

This problem was not anticipated, and was noted only after several players went through the agonizingly slow process of inventory depletion until their sales decreased to a level sufficient to trigger the entrance of the "bankruptcy/end-of-game" subroutine. A test was introduced in revised versions of the game to determine, after the printing of each monthly report, if the player cannot possibly succeed in the game. If a negative indication is given to this test, the game ends.

Toy Store: A Computer-Based Educational Game

A "rational" player might be expected merely to replace the goods sold each month. However, a player's best strategy is to spend slightly more than that amount on replacement of merchandise, so that his merchandise level is always adequate to allow him to take advantage of any increases that occur in his potential sales level.

Salary Calculations

The minimum salary that a player may take from store sales income in a given month is a function of the monthly profit of the store. Initially, the minimum compensation a player may choose is $200, which represents 66 percent of monthly profit. However, the minimum acceptable salary tends to approach 50 percent of profit as the game progresses. If a player selects a salary figure below the minimum amount allowed, the following message is printed: "That is not enough to provide food, clothing, shelter and other needs for yourself and your family. Try again."

Periodically, the model calls for an increase in the minimum acceptable salary figure. The rationale behind this figure is that personal and family pressures will generally lead the owner of a commercial establishment to increase his own compensation when the firm's profits rise. Furthermore, once a new minimum salary requirement has been set, this minimum figure will persist even though profits may decline. This requirement is based upon the assumed difficulty in reverting to a lower standard of living after an individual has become accustomed to a higher one.

The criterion for augmenting the minimum salary level is that whenever 50 percent of monthly profit exceeds the minimum salary by $100, the minimum salary is incremented by $100. Therefore, when profits climb from the initial $300 level to $600 per month, the minimum acceptable salary is increased from $200 to a level of $300. Similarly, when profits reach the $800 level the minimum monthly salary climbs to $400. In revised versions, $10 is subtracted from the minimum salary figure after its calculation, so that an "even-hundreds" response cannot be considered a "correct" answer. Whenever an increase in the minimum salary is appropriate, a message is printed stating: "From now on, you will need a larger salary in order to satisfy the needs (food, clothing, shelter) and wants of yourself and your family." [7]

[7] Although the 50 percent figure applies to the stabilizing points at which the revisions are triggered (i.e., profits of $600, $800, etc.), players tend to allocate slightly more money to salary than the minimum amount required. Thus, salaries *average* approximately 50 percent of profit throughout the various ranges of profit between the revision points ($600–$800, $800–$1000, etc.). If profit is approximately 20 percent of monthly sales, which is the average level expected under the terms of the model, then the amount spent for the store owner's salary will consume approximately 10 percent of sales income.

It should be noted that a player derives no advantage from taking a high salary for himself, considering the goals of the game. During the printing of each annual report, two lines are devoted to salary: the *average* monthly compensation derived by the player during the play of the game to date and the *total* amount received. Other than receiving self-satisfaction from seeing large amounts on these lines, a player cognizant of game goals and strategy has no reason for selecting salaries larger than the required minimum, once that figure has been identified. Selection of a larger amount only limits the financial resources available for reinvestment and thus extends the game in simulated future time.

Expenses

Initially, fixed monthly expenses amount to $100 or 10 percent of sales income. These initial expenses are *unavoidable* and absolutely necessary for maintaining the store in business. This unavoidable component of monthly expenses, which includes rent and electricity, must be distinguished from the other component, expenses of a *promotional* nature, which includes various forms of advertising. Promotional expenses are incurred voluntarily by the player in an effort to increase monthly sales. The unavoidable expenses must be met merely to maintain the store's position in the market-place; in most cases, the player is simply informed of the increase in expenses and is given no opportunity to decide whether or not he wants such an increase to occur. However, in many cases the previous decisions of a player are likely to determine whether or not these additional expenses will be introduced.

The 1:10 ratio between unavoidable expenses and monthly sales is intended to be maintained throughout the game. Therefore, additional expenses are periodically introduced to the player in the form of tax increases and similar expenses. On the average, the unavoidable component of monthly expenses consumes 10 percent of sales income during the game. Once an increase in monthly expenses occurs, the new expense level is maintained until the next increase takes place. During the first twelve game months, the player is faced with a yes-or-no question concerning whether he wants to pay his expenses. During the course of these twelve monthly reports, virtually all players answer "no" once. This leads to increased costs due to legal action undertaken by creditors. After the first game-year, expense payments are fully automatic; the amount is deducted from sales income before the player has an opportunity to allocate his financial resources.

As may be noted, the average proportion of monthly sales allocated to unavoidable expenses is 10 percent, while monthly expenses under the general model are expected to average 20 percent of sales. This 10 percent difference is to be filled by the other component of expenses—

those of a promotional nature. The manner in which these expense increases are incurred leads directly to discussion of another facet of the model: how sales increases occur.

Increases in Monthly Sales

There are three ways in which a player may increase his monthly sales:

1. He may purchase new kinds of merchandise never before carried in the store.
2. He may purchase new equipment which might conceivably increase sales; this would include items such as air-conditioning equipment and better display devices.
3. He may undertake the burden of paying additional monthly (promotional) expenses for various forms of advertising.

Purchase of *new* kinds of merchandise (not to be confused with replacement of merchandise sold) and purchase of new equipment are both capital expenditures. These expenditures are made utilizing funds remaining from sales revenue after deducting expenses, salary, and replacement of merchandise sold; this amount, available for reinvestment under the general model, can average 10 percent of sales revenue. The promotional expenses require no capital in the form of savings; they require only the willingness of the player to increase his fixed expenses for the remainder of this segment of the game. (Under certain circumstances, expenses contracted previously can be eliminated. For example, acceptance of television advertising allows the player to cancel radio advertising agreements made with the same broadcasting station.)

SUBROUTINES FOR THE TOY STORE GAME

The introduction of new opportunities or expenses to the player is accomplished through the use of self-contained subroutines, which must appear in a specific order, so as to avoid confusion and provide logical transitions. Therefore, I had to construct a pattern for the introduction of the subroutines and calculate the amount of money that would be associated with each subroutine. The general pattern for the introduction of subroutines and the specific dollar amount involved are highly interdependent. The pattern divides the game into four *phases*. In going through a phase, a player can double both his assets and his monthly sales figures. The same pattern for introduction of subroutines is maintained in all phases but the dollar amounts involved in each phase are twice as large as those in the previous phase.

Because the order of presentation of these subroutines is completely deterministic, I decided to construct other subroutines to be introduced on a pseudo-random basis. Their introduction is not completely random, since none of these routines appear during the first game-year of play, so as to avoid confusing the player during his initial exploration of the simulated environment. Furthermore, these routines do not appear during game months in which a player receives one of the ordered subroutines or learns the short-term results of decisions made under one of those routines. Thus, the "random" events are most likely to appear while a player is building up savings or merchandise to meet applicable levels for introduction of one of the ordered subroutines.

In all, six types of subroutines were constructed, each presenting the player with a different type of expense or opportunity, according to the constraints imposed by the general model.

Expenditures for New Kinds of Merchandise

Three types of new kinds of merchandise are offered to a player to be stocked in his store: winter (e.g., skis), summer (e.g., baseball equipment), and year-round (e.g., phonograph records). The kinds of merchandise available for purchase are about evenly divided between these three types. Although the sales increases obtained through purchase of new kinds of goods to sell should average 20 percent of the amount spent for this merchandise, the actual sales increase for any single deci-

Figure 3 Actual Sales Increases Resulting from Expenditures for New Kinds of Merchandise

Type of Merchandise and Season Purchased	Amount Purchased	Increase in Potential Sales	Diagnostic Message to Player (abbreviated)
Winter item bought in winter or	$E \leq 1/3\ (C)$	$.3 \times E$	"Should have bought more; item is in season."
Summer item bought in summer	$E > 1/3\ (C)$	$.3 \times E$	"Good decision; item is in season."
Winter item bought in summer or	$E \leq 1/3\ (C)$	$.3 \times E$	"Good decision; should not spend too much for off-season items."
Summer item bought in winter	$E > 1/3\ (C)$	$.3 \times 1/3\ (C)$	"Spent too much; item is not in season."
Year-round item	$E \leq 1/3\ (C)$	$.2 \times E$	"Should have bought more; item sells in any season."
	$E > 1/3\ (C)$	$.2 \times E$	"Good decision; item sells in any season."

C = the maximum amount of money a player could spend for new merchandise
E = the amount of money actually spent by the player for new kinds of merchandise

sion depends upon the type of merchandise for sale, the amount bought, and the game month during which it is purchased. October 1st through March 1st is assumed to be winter season. In practice, retailers would undoubtedly place orders for seasonal items many months before these items would be displayed and available for sale. However, it seemed that no useful purpose could be served by trying to introduce such details of commercial practice into the game. Unfortunately, a player who is somehow aware of the real-life circumstances surrounding stocking of merchandise by a store will tend to respond with an answer that is "wrong" in the game, but actually correct when placed in a realistic context.

As can be seen from Figure 3, if seasonal items are purchased during the appropriate season the sales increase is 30 percent of the amount of merchandise purchased. If these items are purchased at an inappropriate time, the maximum sales increase that can occur is only 10 percent of the maximum amount that can be spent for new merchandise. The increase in sales level following purchase of year-round items is 20 percent of the value of the purchase.[8] Thus, the expected value of the sales increment from, purchase of new kinds of merchandise is 20 percent of the maximum allowable expenditure.

Expenditures for New Equipment

The subroutines in which they player is provided with an opportunity to purchase new equipment in an effort to increase sales do not follow any general pattern. The average increase in monthly sales for these subroutines is designed to be 20 percent of the amount of the capital expenditure.

In the case of some of these expenditures (e.g., an outdoor sign, new lighting fixtures, or shelving, and display cases), the sales increase is simply .1, .2, or .3 times the amount spent, with the multiplier selected with equal probability for all three values through use of a random number generator.[9] Therefore, purchase of the equipment is always beneficial to the player, although the degree of benefit depends entirely on chance factors.

Many of the new equipment subroutines were designed individually and bear little resemblance to one another. In one, the player is offered

[8] It is assumed that the three types of merchandise appear in a manner that is effectively random and that there is an equal probability of these new merchandise subroutines occurring during either the summer or winter season.

[9] The "random numbers" are calculated by the power-residue method. When the game was first programmed, a new random number was calculated only when needed. Unfortunately, this meant that *every player had the same sequence of random numbers.* This problem was circumvented by having new random numbers continually calculated during every period in which a player is responding to a question. Since response times differ widely, the numbers take on random characteristics.

the opportunity, and is in fact encouraged, to purchase ten shopping carts each month for a three- or four-month period during the game. The cost is $400 for each set of ten carts. The return, in terms of increased monthly sales, is $200 for the first set of ten carts, $100 for the second set, $20 for the third set, and nothing for the fourth set. A player who makes these purchases thus experiences one facet of the principle of diminishing returns. In another subroutine of this type, the player may purchase a delivery truck for the sum of $1600. If he buys the truck, his monthly sales increase by $320, which means that his monthly profit is increased by $128. However, a player purchasing the truck soon learns that his monthly expenses have increased by $200, due to the need to provide gas, oil, and maintenance for the truck. Thus, although sales will increase if the truck is bought, profit will decline. This feature is intended to show the interdependence between the various factors operating in the simulated economic environment.

Permanent Promotional Expenses

Sixteen times during the game the player must decide whether to increase his fixed monthly expense level in an attempt to increase the potential monthly sales level. In these promotional expense subroutines, the player is also often asked to choose the amount of the increase in expenses, within boundaries specified by the model. Most of the routines offer various forms of advertising (newspaper, radio, television, and others) to the player. In some of these, the *sales* increase is simply 4, 5, or 6 times the increase in the expense level. This amounts to an increase in monthly *profits* equal to 60 percent, 100 percent, or 140 percent of the amount of the expense increase. In other subroutines, the rates of sales increase are fixed. For example, near the beginning of the game the player is offered a chance to install a telephone for only $15 per month. If he decides to do so, he can purchase classified directory advertising for $10 per month. In this case, the sales increase attributable to the telephone itself is three times the increase in expenses, for an increase in profits equal to 20 percent of the expense increase. However, the sales increase resulting from the directory advertising is eight times the increase in expenses, for an increase in profits equal to 220 percent of the expense increase.

Temporary Promotional Expenses

These routines may be classified into two types. One type offers the player the opportunity to stimulate demand for his wares by means of promotional campaigns associated with certain holiday periods. Accordingly, some routines can appear only within a particular month of the game year (e.g., with January 31st report for Washington's Birthday, or with the September 30th report for Columbus Day). The other type of subroutine provides an opportunity to make a small promotional expenditure that is not connected with any holiday and can be made during any game month.

When a determination is made that one of these routines should appear, a search is first made to see if there is a holiday routine that has not previously been used and would be appropriate to introduce that month. If there is none, a general purpose subroutine is selected.[10] For either type, the player is asked whether he wants to spend an amount equal to 1 percent of his current sales (rounded upward to the next $10) for promotional or display purposes sueinf rhw dollowing month. The actual way in which this money is to be used is made known to the player and varies greatly between subroutines. If the player decides to make the expenditure (which he will pay for at the same time he pays his regular monthly expenses the following month), his sales will be higher by an amount equal to 4, 5, or 6 times the amount spent, providing enough merchandise has been stocked.

Permanent Unavoidable Expenses

The periodic introduction of "unavoidable" increases in monthly expenses serves several purposes. One basic purpose is to keep the economic situation of the player somewhat in accord with the model, in which expenses are expected to consume approximately 20 percent of sales revenue. If these unavoidable expense increases did not occur, profit levels could rise to a point (30 percent of sales volume) where the player would have sufficient money available to destroy any incentive for attempting to make rational decisions in the allocation of resources. Another purpose of these expenses is to illustrate circumstances any citizen might face, such as an increase in municipal or school taxes. Not all of these expense increases are "unavoidable" in a true sense, because their appearance is often contingent upon decisions a player has made during the game. The only delivery truck maintenance expense has already been discussed. A similar situation arises for players who install air-conditioning equipment: the increase in profit resulting from air-conditioning is offset by the increase in expenses due to electricity costs. However, virtually all of these expenses *seem* unavoidable to the player; he is simply informed of the increase in expenses, and it is beyond his power to half the increase.

[10] Temporary-expense subroutines are never repeated for a player. Duplication is avoided by storing information as to which random routines remain unused, rather than by selecting the routines in a prescribed order (as is the case with other routines).

In some of the subroutines, the player is able to decide whether or not he wants the increase in monthly expenditures to occur. This is the case when the player is offered the opportunity to take out property and liability insurance. Considering the events that might occur during the game, it will become apparent to the player that the property insurance will more than pay for itself while the liability insurance will not. These routines were included to demonstrate the manner in which risks are shared under an insurance system.

Temporary Unavoidable Expenses

These routines which provide additional expenses for a single month fall into two categories. One set is comprised of events that can occur no matter what the previous decisions of a player have been; examples include necessary cash register repairs and repairs made to a glass display case that is broken. The second set of expenses are those which are contingent upon a player's decisions. For example, a delivery truck accident occurs only if the truck was purchased and chemistry sets catch fire only if the sets have been stocked in the store. Whether or not a player must pay the expenses himself when certain types of damage (e.g., breakage, fire, or theft) occur will depend upon his particular situation with regard to insurance coverage.

When it has been determined that a randomly-introduced expense should occur, the control list is scanned in a random manner for the first previously unused temporary-unavoidable-expense subroutine that is available. If the routine selected is contingent upon the player's decisions and would be inappropriate for introduction (e.g., chemistry sets were not stocked), no expense occurs. Otherwise, the expense subroutine appears. The amount of expense is equal to .01, .02, or .03 times current sales income, rounded upward to the next $10 figure.

THE SCRIPT FOR THE TOY STORE GAME

At this point in the design of the Toy Store Game, a format for a monthly report had been chosen and the model described in the preceding pages had been constructed. Under the terms of the model devised, it was necessary to supply scripts for nearly 100 subroutines, with the game model determining the mathematical characteristics and consequences for each subroutine.

Consider, for example, a subroutine in which a player is offered the opportunity to purchase new kinds of merchandise. In a general form, such a subroutine might appear in the following manner:

Toy Store: A Computer-Based Educational Game

"Your distributor has informed you that he has ________________ availa ble to sell to you. This item has never been available for sale in your store. You could purchase up to $____________worth of this merchandise.

"Do you wish to buy___________________ at this time?
IF YES:

"How much money do you wish to spend to stock this type of merchandise?"

The full script for such a subroutine provides branching back to the main question for a player who answered neither affirmatively nor negatively, forces a player to choose another amount if he chose to purchase more of an item than his distributor had available to sell, and provides feedback to a player *after* his decision is made (within the constraints imposed) in order to prepare him for the nature of the change in sales likely to occur in the next monthly report.

The nature of the item available for sale cannot be chosen without considering the basic model which specifies that there must be a balance in the seasonal applicability of new kinds of merchandise presented to the player. The amount available for purchase is a function of the phase of the game during which this specific subroutine appears and the type of merchandise offered, under the conditions specified by the game model.

The actual wording of the subroutines offering new types of merchandise to the store-owner is extremely flexible: it is simply an exercise in script-writing. However, the nature of the merchandise for sale, the amount available, and the consequences of a player's decisions are all highly dependent upon the model.

Before writing the scripts for the subroutines, I made a decision concerning the style of the computer-controlled visual (slide) displays. In the Sumerian Game and the Sierra Leone Game, graphs and charts are used as visual displays under certain circumstances, but the majority of the displays simply depict some item being mentioned in the computer-controlled printout. Elaborate dioramas were constructed for the Sumerian Game, depicting the manner in which the ancient Sumerians constructed their homes, temples, tools, craft shops, and other matters pertinent to the game. Photographs were made of these dioramas and presented at appropriate points in the play of the game. For the Sierra Leone Development Game, slides were made from published pictorial materials which depicted social, geographic, and economic facts about that country. However, in the Toy Store Game, most of the concrete items alluded to are familiar to the players. For example, in the Sumerian Game a useful purpose is served by displaying a picture of a clay cylinder seal (a Sumerian invention) when that item is under consideration and discussion; whereas in the Toy Store Game it is not necessary to display a photograph of ice skates when a player is asked whether he wished to stock skates in his store.

For the Toy Store Game, I decided to employ cartoon-style displays, to be drawn by a commercial artist, photographed, and used in conjunction with the computer-controlled projector. These cartoons serve a true educational purpose whenever possible, but they are also intended to provide a touch of humor and stimulate the interest of the player in the game. The style employed in the visuals influenced the writing of scripts for the subroutines and the choice of various events that occur during the game. If a computer-controlled cathode-ray display device had been available, better use could have been made of visual displays. For example, the player could be shown a graph indicating his own sales performance or expense levels.

PROGRAMMING AND REVISION

Although this game was designed for delivery on an IBM 7090 time-sharing system, it was eventually programmed for an IBM 1401 system with 16,000 character core-storage capacity and no random-access disk storage capability. Although computer storage limitations made it difficult to program the game as originally designed, these limitations were overcome through the use of various programming methods. Major revisions were made on the basis of results obtained when approximately one dozen fifth-, sixth-, and seventh-grade students played the game as originally designed; these revisions have been described at appropriate points throughout this paper. Most of these changes involved changes in the game script, rather than the game model. The format for the monthly reports went through several revisions, and some subroutines were replaced with others of a similar nature that seemed to accomplish the purpose of the game more suitably.

We found that care had to be taken in assessing the reactions of adults who played the game. Adults appeared to fear "losing face" in front of their peers as a consequence of a wrong decision. Therefore, they would adopt various tactics to delay making a decision in the game. One person actually unplugged the power cord from the wall to disable the terminal. When asked why he took that action, he replied that he "wanted to see what would happen." Reticence of this type was seldom observed in children who tried the game.

I found that the best method for eliciting complaints concerning various facets of the game and determining where improvements were needed was the following process: an individual student would be asked to play the game from beginning to end; then he or she would be asked to assist a friend who would be playing the game for the first time. By monitoring (in an informal manner) the conversation taking place while an "experienced" player and an "inexperienced" player were in partnership competing against the simulated environment, the most valuable suggestions for revision of the game were received.

THE FREE ENTERPRISE GAME: AN OVERVIEW

This paper has placed a great deal of emphasis upon the construction of game models, since, if one strips away the trappings and frills from any successful game, it is the basic model that sustains the game. The model designed for a game, particularly a computerized game in which an attempt is made to utilize many of the features available from a modern data-processing system, may have complex interrelationships between variables. It is up to the game designer to provide some measure of internal consistency to the model, to insure that these interrelationships do not cause improbable or "impossible" circumstances to occur and disrupt play of the game.

Many of the decisions made in the construction of a game appear unrealistic when real-life circumstances are taken into consideration. However, the individuals for which the game was designed are sixth-graders, not business school students. Therefore, no attempt was made to construct a model that would accurately portray the actual circumstances surrounding the operation of a toy store, or any other type of store. If an individual, through playing Toy Store, begins to realize that *any* decisions made involve rewards and costs within a probabilistic framework, and that the best way to attain goals is to minimize probable costs in an effort to maximize probable rewards, then the game has been beneficial to the player.

REFERENCES

LEONARD, JIMMER M., AND RICHARD L. WING
1967 "Advantages of using a computer in some kinds of educational games." *IEEE: Transactions on Human Factors in Electronics* (June).

WING, RICHARD L.
1966 "Two computer-based economics games for sixth graders." *American Behavioral Scientist,* 10 (November), 31–34.
1967 "The production and evaluation of three computer-based economics games for the sixth grade." Final Report, Cooperative Research Project 2841. Yorktown Heights, New York: Board of Cooperative Educational Services.

PHILLIP D. PATTERSON

Chapter 15

The City I Model

In simulation design frequently a set of complex relationships can be influenced by simple devices or transformation schemes. Until these solutions are used, the system can appear hopelessly complicated or unrealistic. Here Patterson demonstrates how one such simple solution—a depreciation scheme—resolved a variety of problems in simulating a man-machine model of urban process.

—The Editors

PART II. CASE STUDIES SECTION B.

The City I Model

The City I operational simulation is a generalized model of an urban system, maintained and changed by the participants through the employment of private and public resources. The participants establish their own individual and group objectives and attempt to accomplish them within the local system. The model was designed to be an educational and elementary research tool which would provide its users with a comprehensive, realistic, dynamic, and multi-disciplinary method of analyzing the effects of macro private and public decisions throughout the system and over time. The participants must consider the total effect of their decisions on the system. Consider, for example, the problem of acquiring school sites. The use of public funds requires the shift of private resources to the public sector; the allocation of these funds to schools denies the money to competing public uses; and the use of the land (a scarce resource) for schools pre-empts it from alternative uses. The payoff to the system is the creation of more and possibly better educational facilities.

To develop such a model, the entire urban system at an aggregate level was simulated, rather than a number of subsystems or a number of roles. Thus, a systemic gaming technique, as contrasted with a role-playing technique, was employed as the major gaming device. (Role-playing methods were used only to add depth to the governmental component of the model.) A systemic game simulates a system or group of systems within which players establish their objectives and strategies to achieve these objectives, using the resources available to them. The players in a systemic game are free to choose similar or dissimilar objectives, and they begin with approximately the same initial resources. In role-playing games a number of roles are simulated, and certain situations are generated for the players, who attempt to achieve the objectives peculiar to the roles they have been assigned. The players in a role-playing game typically have conflicting objectives and dissimilar resources with which to achieve their objectives.

Since all participants in City I perform both private and public functions,[1] many early problems of transforming and simulating the interaction of public and private decisions were eliminated. For example, the demands for school facilities, highways, public utilities, municipal services, etc. are created by participants in their private roles as they build new residences, create new employment opportunities, and establish more transportation nodes and larger densities at these nodes. The

[1] Players as members of a team may own and operate industries, commercial establishments, and residences in the private economy, and teams during any one round may be a county chairman, a councilman, a department head (school) public works and safety, highway, planning and zoning, or finance), the mass media, or all citizens organizations in the public sector.

participants also must solve these public facility deficiencies in their public roles as elected political officials and government bureaucrats.

ONE TRANSFORMATION EMPLOYED IN THE CITY I MODEL

One of the difficulties in the early stages of the development of the City I model was to have the private and public decision-makers take depreciation costs into account in the operation of their developments. In real life, businessmen and public officials must make sure that they maintain their buildings or have a reserve of cash to build new buildings when the old ones wear out. In the original formulation of City I, there was just one reason for players to renovate, and that was to protect their buildings from being extensively damaged if natural disaster struck. But since natural disaster struck so seldom, and when it did strike it had such tremendous effects, we began to explore the actual consequences of not renovating various types of buildings and facilities. Our criterion for condition of buildings and facilities was the *value ratio*, i.e., the ratio of present value to original value. Each year that no renovation is undertaken on a building or facility, its value becomes five per cent less than it was the previous year. Figure I lists the effects of low value ratio by land-use type in the real world and in the model.

In City I there are four socio-economic classes of residences—high-

Figure 1 Transformations Used to Encourage Renovation

If the value ratio declines:

Land use type	*Real world*	*In City I*
Residences	Houses deteriorate and neighborhoods change in composition.	Residences change in socio-economic class when value ratio falls below a certain point.
Commercial Establishments	Stores become outdated, parking becomes inadequate, and customers shift to newer stores.	The capacity of stores to serve customers is reduced in direct proportion to reductions in the value ratio.
Industries	Plant and equipment becomes outdated; industry does not keep up with technological advances.	The income received from the sales of industrial output in national markets declines in relation to the value ratio.
Schools	Facilities and equipment show wear and tear and become outdated.	Quality of education declines.
Municipal Services	Equipment becomes outdated and quality of service falls off.	Level of police, fire and health services declines.
Highways	The road system deteriorates, travel times increase and driver costs increase.	Travel costs increase.

income, middle-income, low-income, and slum. There is not much of an economic reward from building low-income and slum residences, but they tend to appear in the city because teams do not always choose to renovate. In fact, slum residences cannot be built in the City I model: they can appear only after years of deterioration.

The yearly decline in value ratio is five percent of last year's value for all development except roads. In the case of roads, the amount of depreciation and deterioration is a function of the number of users of the road. Thus, the need for renovation will be greatest along those routes receiving the greatest use, which is as it should be. To keep transportation costs low, the Highway Department must renovate the roads receiving the greatest use.

These additions to the City I model resulted in quite realistic responses to the issue of renovation and the need to take depreciation costs into account. Thus, because of the systemic nature of the City I model, a change in one relationship (the effect of declining value ratios) was sufficient to produce the desired changes both in the model and in player performance.

Part III

THE DESIGN PROCESS

"Those who can, do; those who can't, teach."
—Chinese Proverb

Chapter **16**

The Decision to Simulate

PART III. THE DESIGN PROCESS

The Decision to Simulate

As suggested by the case studies, there are three basic uses of simulation: theory-building (e.g., Breznitz and Lieblich), experimentation (e.g., The Gullahorns), and teaching (e.g., Zaltman). Any social scientist is likely to be engaged in one or more of these activities at any point in time, hence, an obvious problem is to identify at what point in these activities simulation would be prescribed as a preferable method. And if simulation is called for, then what mode should be selected?

The few explicit guides for answering this question are primarily matters of practicality. Thus we will begin by reviewing the technical requirements and facilities for developing simulations. Less clearly defined are the substantive directives. At best all we can do in this instance is discuss the rationale for the three uses and let the reader decide how they might fit into his work.

PRACTICALITIES

Time is probably the most basic necessary ingredient before deciding to embark on a simulation development venture. The modal number of years that it took to develop the simulations described in Part II is two years. In some cases a workable or playable simulation was designed well within a year—even weeks—of the initiation of the work; in other cases the work continues after ten years.

In one way designing a simulation is an endless process. No designer seems ever satisfied with his product. Few appear to be able to resist thinking recurrently about improvements either in terms of doing better what the simulation presently aims to do or in terms of doing more things. Apparently as a result of the fascination and open-ended nature of the enterprise, it is the case that several years may pass before a product debuts as a "version." Prior to then it is usually referred to as a "draft," a "trial run," and "attempt," or whatever.

Along with the enticements of endlessly tinkering with the simulation are the time needs simply of debugging the computer simulation or of making the man simulation playable. Computer debugging is a process of unpredictable life, partly a function of the complexity of the simulandum and of the meticulousness of the programmer. Game playability is similarly unpredictable, but Zaltman's paper suggests that it is a function of the number of roles in the game, the heterogeneity of the audience, the complexity of the model, and the number of learning objectives (if any).

Physical facilities and financial resources are the second set of requirements. Let us look first at the case of computer simulation. It will not be sufficient to have access to computing facilities in order to develop a computer simulation. Rather, it is also necessary to assure that the facilities have the *capability* of handling a proposed problem with *efficiency*. Computer facilities with low capability limit the complexity of the simulation one can design. Facilities with low efficiency can result in exorbitant financial expenses.

The most obvious determinant of capability is the memory capacity of a machine. Memory capacity is measured in terms of "words," with each word consisting of "bits" or elementary binary possibilities. Computers come in all sizes, with word lengths ranging from 12 bits to 64 bits. The number of words in the memory core can vary from two thousand to above sixty thousand. Abelson (1969) discusses procedures for estimating whether one's proposed simulation is likely to fit the available machine and describes several techniques for compensating for low capacity.

The second basis for determining the capabilities of local computing facilities is to examine the programs and supporting staff. Large computational centers often have packages of standard programs adapted to the facilities at hand. Such programs can sometimes be incorporated into one's simulation and greatly simplify the programming task, provided there is no language incompatibility. The quality of the supporting staff determines how much of the discrepancy between what one has at hand and what one needs can be effectively resolved.

Finally, the efficiency of local facilities will depend upon machine speed, which can vary in measurement from thousandths of a second to nanoseconds (billionsths of a second). When computer time can run anything between $70 and $400 an hour, several minutes can be critical for funding the research.[1] Thus, if runs are lengthy, funds may run out before sufficient debugging or experimentation has been performed. What can be done if runs are slow and money is limited? As Abelson (1969) has concluded, there is little recourse other than "simplifying the simulation, finding a faster computer, getting a bigger research grant, or praying that the original time estimate was in error."

With regard to games, the physical facilities needed are usually available to anyone. Materials for building the physical parts of a game seldom are more unusual than standard art supplies or duplicating para-

[1] For instance turn-around time, the amount of time between submission of materials and the return of output, is critical. If the machine is slow, or if usage is high, then it may be possible to submit a run only once a day. This laggard pace is irksome during the debugging period, when a long series of computer runs will be necessary to eliminate minor errors in turn. It may be possible at some center to obtain blocks of time in the early morning hours to do these runs. The lesson is that those with low frustration points should brace themselves if their local turn-around time is very long.

phenalia. (Goodman's game, with its hundreds of painted golf tees, is an exceptional case.) A game will also need a setting. Experimental laboratories are perhaps the optimum location because they are well-equipped for observation and recording. (See Noel, 1969, for a description of a laboratory designed for simulation building and research.) In fact, though, the games discussed in this volume were usually tested in any accessible room. To conclude, the essential physical needs for gaming are much less problematic than in computer simulation.[2]

Perhaps the one problematic feature in game design will be locating subjects. Generally a game will have several versions which are modified at every trial of play. Although these first attempts can be tested with literally anyone who is willing—friends, colleagues, and family—it is not advised to do so. Because during this brief period most playability and physical problems take shape and greatly influence future work, it is better to use experimental subjects, who can be more objective in both identifying problems in the game and communicating about them. Once this stage is passed, more systematic tests with the target population will require that larger numbers of subjects be within access.[3]

Except for terminals and special display instruments, computer games require the same facilities as the combination of computer and gaming needs. When interaction with the machine through the game process is not a major feature of the simulation, then even terminals may not be needed.

A third practical feature in deciding to simulate is to consider whether the enterprise is compatible with one's tastes. Technically the designer has the choice among man, computer, and man-computer modes. Man simulations, especially those with gamelike structures, require an investment of tedious hours of work on trivial tasks (such as designing and coloring a game board so that interest in and playability of the game may be enhanced). Similarly, in writing a program one faces the issue of *absolute* accuracy. Without exerting extreme rigor in his work, the designer may spend hours or days in an exasperating

[2] Although facilities are readily available, the costs of game construction may be hidden. One of the writers was astonished to discover that the cost of four sets of a simple game—consisting of a board, chance cards, and score sheets—surpassed sixty dollars. Most of the expense was salary for the assistant who drafted, duplicated, hand-colored, and pasted the pieces on cardboard. About twenty hours was required for the entire task. Ironically, and typical of game research, this version proved worthless after one trial session, and a totally new set of materials was designed.

[3] Simulations designed commercially for teaching purposes may require many hundred players in order to accumulate evidence that the simulation is in fact meeting its objectives. Many fewer test subjects will be required for validating theoretical or experimental simulations, as Chapter Eigtheen makes clear.

search among thousands of symbols to locate an error which turns out to be an omitted comma.

In short, the retrospective view of the case studies may have given simulation design a glamorous aura which is out of perspective compared to the daily round of activities. Simulation is better handled when certain skills and predispositions are present. If the job is not compatible with one's preferences, then the costs can become prohibitive. Attempting a computer simulation might be a devastating experience for somebody who does not have a high tolerance for order, rigor, and sustained application. Likewise, man-simulations might prove frustrating for someone who is not comfortable with the handling of people who are variably sympathetic to the activity.

The moral is that simulation design is not a problem-free endeavor. Unless one is able and willing to spend time, has access to physical facilities, and has the personal predispositions to tolerate the demands of the technique, he might never reach the stage where simulation design becomes intriguing, and even exciting.

SUBSTANTIVE ISSUES

Theory-Building

When simulation serves for data-organization and theory development, it may not be necessary to complete a simulation to the stage of refinement described in the case studies. Simply taking an approach of "What if I simulated this?" may be sufficient in some cases to clarify a problem to one's satisfaction.[4] The reason is that simulation forces the investigator to confront, explicate, and simplify the problem area (Raser, 1969). Also, while attempting to simulate one might discover gaps of information that imply the need for more research before a useful theory can be constructed.

The simulation may actually be carried through to completion, as was the case in Smith's use of simulation for heuristic purposes. Yet it still holds that simulation for purposes of data organization and synthesis need not result in a final operating simulation. The very attempt to simulate is the issue.

If the simulation may never reach completion, does the choice of mode matter? We suggest that it does, partly because the designer may find his casual interest in the simulation turn into a major commitment. Besides practicalities, at least two other criteria deserve consideration.

[4] Manning (1967) and Lyman and Scott (1969) have analyzed a variety of problems from a game-theoretic perspective. Essentially they describe the games underlying interpersonal relations without actually constructing the simulations.

First, if one suspects that one will not be able to be very precise in his attempts to synthesize the mass of information, then one should eschew computer simulation. Game design lends itself better to transformations of more diffusely defined variables. The second criterion is a corollary of the first and relates to the assumptions one wishes to make concerning the psychology or decision-making of the component actors. Computer simulations require that the psychology guiding the actors be explicit; games do not. Hence games would be preferable in building theories where the researcher cannot commit himself or does not yet know the appropriate model underlying the actors' decisions.

Research

Access, control, and replication are the value characteristics of research. Experiments contain all three features and are the prevalent form of empirical research in the physical sciences. Unfortunately large portions of social, political, and economic life are not readily accessible for study, let alone subject to control and replication, because of practical impossibility, cost, or moral objections. The description of international relations by Sullivan could apply to other divisions of social science where experimental procedures have literally been impossible. Instead of experimentation, the phenomena are studied by a variety of methods—personal reports, survey, observation. These methods are weak for the interpretation of results in terms of causal relationships.

The major advantage of simulation is that it provides a means for recursive and controlled observations and manipulation of social interaction or of individual behaviors. Because there is access and manipulability, there can be replication. Simulations produce data, albeit artifically induced, on outputs, behaviors, structures, and processes. Hence it could provide the basis for an experimental sociology and political science (Winter, 1968) as it already seems to have done in economics. (It is impossible to manipulate the entire United States economy, but it was not impossible to simulate it, Duesenberry et al., 1964.)

There is an experimental tradition in terms of small groups research in sociology and game theory in political science and psychology. Those who favor simulation do so on the basis that the technique can correct deficiencies in previous experimental work.

First, it is claimed (Ray and Duke, 1969) that the traditional social experiment too often deals with minutiae. Simple binary choice situations that tell us much about simply structured situations but little about the more common, complex-choice situations predominate. On the other hand, both computer and man simulations can represent complex phenomena and macro-processes bypassed by the traditional experimental approach to date.

Related to this criticism is one that simplistically-designed experiments do not permit extrapolation to other situations (Campbell, 1969). Contrived experiments hold a great many variables constant, while simulations include these background variables. The greater number of variables that are controlled, the greater the probability that the outcome is distorted. Hence extrapolation is more problematic from a traditional experimental setting than from a simulation.[5] Ray and Duke (1969) illustrate this argument with regard to computer games. Complex games, they suggest, require players to take on roles which draw on a large array of cultural cues for behavior, or other bases for deciding what is good, prestigious, and appropriate. Nonsalient laboratory tasks, in contrast, are designed to control away as many as possible of the cultural forms affecting a decision.

Raser (1969) has also raised an important practical point. He has noted that man simulations permit a breakdown of a critical inferential gap in social science, namely between a subject's intrapersonal and interpersonal processes. There is a completely detailed protocol of a process, meaning less need for relying upon post-hoc reports of behavior.

To summarize, the rationale for using simulation in experimental work will be based upon the complexity of the phenomenon and the practical or moral possibility of real-life experimentation. Some investigators furthermore may find that the extrapolation issue and the special data collection features make the technique additionally attractive.[6]

Assuming that the decision has been made, what issues are relevant for selecting the most appropriate mode? First is the issue of the *stability* of the simulation. If there is reason to have control over subsections of the system operations, then computer simulations are preferable. Their outputs over time and across experimenters can be completely comparable. Man simulations, in contrast, are open to contamination by such elements as experimenter suggestion, ecology of the setting, player backgrounds, and so forth. These extraneous influences impede the ability to control features of the runs. If the element of human actors is es-

[5] Extrapolation is not always an issue in one's work, and we do not mean to imply that simpler experiments are without value. For an eloquent defense of the arguments against the extrapolation criterion, and consequently in support of simple experimental situations, see Webster and Kervin (1969).

[6] Deciding to experiment by way of simulation means more than consideration of these reasons. It implies that one has accepted the entire logic underlying the simulation technique; in particular, the assumption that the replicate settings are valid. We shall consider this problem in Chapter Eighteen.

sential to the simulation, then control can be increased by selecting the computer game as the mode.[7]

Second, the more *replicability* (in a sampling sense) is an issue, the more likely computer simulation will prove the efficient choice. This criterion is a corollary to the practicality listing. Game experiments may simply require too many subjects or too much time for a practical set of runs.[8] Computer runs are not only largely insensitive to the size and number of samples needed, but also the special features of some computer simulations mean that a very few runs might be adequate for one's sampling purpose. (See Naylor, 1969, for a discussion of the sampling issue.)

The third criterion is the amount or type of *record-keeping* one desires. Computer simulations can permit a thorough, totally reliable record of the process, including all the minutiae. Game or man simulations rely more upon secondary sources of records: player forms, tape and video recordings, and so forth. Not all activities are covered, nor are they all covered reliably.

Complexity of the phenomenon to be studied is another substantive issue. If numerous steps are required for the transfer and transformation of resources, then the computer has advantages. A process necessitating a lengthy sequencing may be prohibitive based on the real-time constraints of a man simulation.

A final criterion is best introduced by illustration. For simulations of certain processes it is possible to say that at first appearance there would be an equal degree of artificiality in either machine or man mode. For example, while it is probably agreeable to most that macro-economic processes are less artificially represented in computer than in man form, the case is less clear for a model of demographic change. There could be claims for face validity whatever the mode in the latter instance. On the other hand, to conceive of a man simulation in which one says "now we will make babies" is ludicrous. Players do not contribute anything to the process in terms of role-playing or empathy; in fact, role-playing interferes. Indeed, the *face invalidity* of such a game obviates its choice over a computer simulation of the same process.

[7] Raser argues strongly for the use of computer games over pure games in experimental work, regardless of one's purpose. Work on METRO (Ray and Duke, 1969) and Inter-Process Simulation (Smoker, 1969) aptly illustrate the uses of man-machine simulations in research.

[8] Levels of analysis are the main basis for determining one's needs in terms of sampling. Ten games of Consumer will provide data on 170 individual players, on 130 consumer role players, on 30 credit agents role players, but on only 10 groups of credit competition systems.

Teaching

Several theoretical perspectives offer different though converging reasons for the potential value and uses of simulation as a didactic medium. At the present time many of these reasons are best viewed as *claims,* because there has not been sufficient time to verify them through research. Also, it should be understood that these claims are made for games in general, and may not applay in any one case. There is, nevertheless, a surface reasonableness to the various arguments.

First, games come under the category of settings known as "responsive environments" (Moore and Anderson, 1969). These environments are structured to encourage the learner to find a question and then seek the answer to it. We can illustrate the special features of responsive environment with regard to Caribou Hunting, described by Fletcher et al.

One characteristic of these settings is that they permit the learner to explore a system with freedom. A student in the Caribou Hunting game can try many varieties of behaviors in his attempt to beat the herd toward the lake. During this process he will have varying degrees of success, i.e. he will be faced with special problems. The answers to his problems will come from further exploration of the system itself. The game is fully structured to provide answers because it is a representation of the system, not a set of descriptive statements about the system.

Secondly, responsive environments provide feedback on the consequences of actions. Hence the learner can judge the utility of any particular strategy by noting his progress. In games there is continual feedback in several ways. Often scores are cumulated over rounds of play, so a player can see his gains or losses, relative to his other moves in the game. Visual representations are further cues. This happens in Caribou Hunting when the players note how close or distant the herd is, and whether it is heading in the desired direction.

Responsive environments are also characterized as self-pacing. Unless time is a critical feature of the model, players can expand or contract various features of the play. Games can be played where large periods of time, even weeks, separate moves, hence permitting appropriate decision processes to be explored in detail. The importance of time flexibility is the opportunity it gives the learner to consider a problem to the level of detail he himself desires. In a typical Caribou Hunting game, players may play rather quickly at first, making moves without considered planning. Later in the game, when their chances of winning appear less certain, they can protract the discussion period to discuss strategy. Once an algorithm is decided upon, play will go more quickly.

Youngsters may be playing at quite different speeds—their progress is limited only by immediate game partners.

Another feature of a responsive environment is the opportunity it offers for discovering or uncovering a series of interconnected relationships. Unlike drill or memory-developing exercises, games encourage an active experimentation on the system of knowledge. The learner is put in the situation of putting his knowledge to use with consequences bearing upon him in return. He deduces a model from his tinkering with it. To return to Caribou Hunting again, players who have completed several plays of the game are able to answer questions as to how the game would change if the rules (that is, the constraints of the system) were different. They learn, then, not only why Eskimo hunting organization takes a particular form, but also the possibilities for other forms of organization (Fletcher, 1969).

From another perspective, that of the sociology of learning, simulations have been suggested to correct certain existing "structural deficiencies" in the organization of classrooms. These deficiencies consist of social arrangements in the present-day classroom (including many *college* classrooms) that impede learning.

One problem with many classes is that they fail to utilize class peers in the learning process. Much of the learning process is on the individual level, the results of which are visible many times only to the teacher. Learning outside of school typically occurs, however, through the observation, imitation, and criticism of peers. In the classroom, opportunities for free peer-interchange are limited and students often compete on an individualistic, secretive basis.

In contrast, games are contests in which the activity is *visible*. Because others' actions are visible, any student can observe and learn from the opponents' behavior, even copy that behavior. Note that games are probably the one place in the classroom where copying is admissable. Simple copying (or as psychologists would say, modeling) is seldom enough for success in the game. Usually mere repetition of another's strategy will not lead to the best solution, because problems change.

We would also add that simulations provide settings for teaching the *psychological features* of situations. That is, one experiences in the simulation the psychological reactions typically experienced when exposed to given structures. For this purpose symbolic methods of teaching are weak substitutes for enactive methods such as simulation.[9] Reading about the rules of parliamentary debates or reading debates themselves contrasts in so many ways with the experience of participat-

[9] See Bruner (1960) for further discussion of symbolic and enactive modes of learning.

ing in a simulated legislature, that the two activities probably lead to very different forms of knowledge. Averroës, one of the greatest medieval Hellenistic scholars, never understood the meaning of comedy and tragedy, about which he had read so much. Theatre was unknown in Islam, and he had never experienced it.

Another deficiency in classrooms is that teachers are placed in the role of judges. They become evaluators of performance with little time left to contribute directly to the performance. As Boocock and Coleman (1966) have noted, they are judges rather than coaches. Games, however, are self-judging. The scoring system is built into the activity itself, rather than imposed apart from it. The player typically faces a continual series of responses from the game model as his score is affected by various feedbacks. This differs from classroom situations where children get no feedback until all decisions relating to a task are completed, and some time may pass before grades are returned.

Not only is the feedback from simulated environments more lucid and faster than provided in other instructional settings, it is also perceived as less arbitrary. All the processes which determined it are visible. Students can see the basis for the feedback and understand with complete details how it is causally related to their action. As a consequence, attribution of responsibility for doing well or not is to one's own actions, rather than to the idiosyncratic judgments of the teacher.

A third deficiency with some elements of education today is the failure to present material in a manner relevant to real life. There is a difficulty in transferring much of the standard curriculum to daily problems and decision-making. The result is that students become alienated, seeing little relevance in school activities for their "real" life.

Simulations bridge the reality gap by bringing a miniaturized version of some sphere of real-life activity into the classroom. Students can practice consumer decision-making or career planning and so forth *without having the real-life consequences of their actions.* This latter point deserves emphasis because there are seldom opportunities in many actual decisions to try again with a new strategy. Poor career choices, bad marriages, inefficient spending-habits cannot easily, and in some instances ever, be repaired. Simulated life does not have inexorable ends —you can always start a new run.[10]

Finally, games are autotelic activities (Inbar, 1970), in the sense of

[10] Even simulations where the content concerns areas beyond the real-life potential of players, e.g. legislative bargaining, international relations, increase the relevancy of the curriculum material. In these instances the "real" chance to apply content is in the game. Thus no student is likely to ever go on a caribou hunt, but his previous readings on Eskimo life are given relevance through the game hunt.

having the reward for engaging in them built in the activity itself. Being ends in themselves, games generate a motivational force of their own, from within.[11]

The extensive theoretical considerations for simulations in teaching may convince the reader to use simulations in his own classroom instruction. Numerous games and computer games are readily available for all levels of instruction, covering many topics in the social sciences. (See Appendix B for a listing.) But what of the possibility of designing a new teaching simulation? When would such a project be worth undertaking?

A natural approach to this task is to begin by modifying available simulations, perhaps as a class project. From this point it will be easier to attempt to design an original simulation. At the very least there will be the personal, heuristic gains from attempting the task.[12]

Generally, teaching simulations will be games or computer games. The reason is that game structures provide the essential feedback, reward, and motivating structure preferred by specialists in learning. The Zaltman and Fletcher et al. case studies elaborate the basic design principles in detail and should provide an adequate introduction to the criteria to be considered. It is also noteworthy that some pure computer simulations can be readily transformed into computer games for instructional purposes. Sullivan (1970) has described this approach with regard to the teaching of economics.

[11] Although the perspectives suggest many reasons why students should learn through games, early research did not produce startling findings. Cherryholmes' (1966) review of six studies concluded:

> Simulation does produce more student motivation and interest [compared to other teaching techniques] but there are not consistent or significant differences, in learning, retention, critical thinking, or attitude change.

He points out, though, that it is a general feature of education research that there are often ambiguous or no significant differences between new teaching methods and others.

Current evaluative literature on games suggests that the time devoted to playing a game produces an amount of learning equivalent to classroom techniques (Boocock et al., 1967; Fletcher, 1969; Anderson, 1969). Here learning refers to scores on tests typical of those given in a course. There is also evidence that games induce individual skills or traits that are not obtained through conventional teaching methods, e.g. decision-making (Anderson, 1969), sense of efficacy (Boocock and Coleman, 1966), attitudes reflecting realism-cynicism (Cohen, 1969).

In addition, research has uncovered an interesting feature of games. Repeatedly there has been the finding that there is no strong or consistent relationship between performance in a game and academic performance. (Boocock, 1969.) In other words, games apparently mobilize intellectual skills unrelated to verbal skills. Thus the poorest student in a class is as likely to be the winner as the best student. The implication is that games would be especially valuable for the under-achiever, the nonverbal, or the cognitively-deprived student.

[12] And as Breznitz and Lieblich have brazenly admitted, there may eventually be rewards for one's flesh in addition to one's spirit.

REFERENCES

Abelson, Robert P.
1969 "Simulation of Social Behavior." In *Handbook of Social Psychology*. Cambridge, Mass.: Addison-Wesley.

Anderson, Raymond
1969 "The effectiveness of a simulation learning game in teaching consumer credit to senior high school students in comparison to a conventional approach to instruction." Unpublished doctoral dissertation, University of Maryland.

Boocock, Sarane S.
1969 "Instructional games." In *Encyclopedia of Education*. New York: MacMillan.

Boocock, Sarane S. and James S. Coleman
1966 "Games with simulated environments for learning." *Sociology of Education*, 39, 215–236.

Boocock, Sarane S., Erling O. Schild and Clarice Stoll
1967 *Simulation Games and Control Beliefs*. Baltimore: Center for Study of Social Organization of Schools.

Bruner, Jerome
1960 *The Process of Education*. Cambridge, Mass.: Harvard.

Cherryholmes, Cleo H.
1966 "Some current research on effectiveness of educational simulations: Implications for alternative strategies," *American Behavioral Scientist*, 10, 4–7.

Cohen, Karen C.
1969 "The effects of two simulation games on the opinions and attitudes of selected sixth, seventh, and eighth grade students." Baltimore: Center for Study of Social Organization of Schools.

Fletcher, Jerry
1969 "The effects of two elementary school social studies games: An experimental field study." Unpublished doctoral dissertation, Harvard Graduate School of Education.

Herndon, James
1968 *The Way it Spozed To Be*. New York: Simon and Schuster.

Inbar, Michael
1970 "Toward a sociology of autotelic behavior." *La Critica Sociologica*, 14, Summer.

Lyman, Stanford and Marvin Scott
1970 *Sociology of the Absurd*. New York: Appleton-Century-Crofts.

Manning, Peter
1967 "Sociology as a game of games." Department of Sociology, Michigan State University, mimeo.

PART III. THE DESIGN PROCESS

The Decision to Simulate

MOORE, OMAR KHAYYAM AND ALAN ROSS ANDERSON
1969 "Some principles for the design of clarifying educational environments." In David Goslin (ed.), *Handbook of Socialization Theory*. Chicago: Rand-McNally.

NAYLOR, THOMAS (ed.)
1969 *The Design of Computer Simulation Experiments*. Durham: Duke University.

NOEL, ROBERT C.
1969 "The POLIS laboratory." *American Behavioral Scientist*, 12, 30–35.

RASER, JOHN
1969 *Simulation and Society*. Boston: Allyn and Bacon.

RAY, PAUL AND RICHARD DUKE
1968 "The environment of decision-makers in urban gaming simulations." In William D. Coplin (ed.), *Simulation in the Study of Politics*. Chicago: Markham.

SMITH, ROBERT B.
1969 "Simulation models for accounting schemes." *American Behavioral Scientist*, 12, 21–30.

SMOKER, PAUL
1969 "Social research for social anticipation." *American Behavioral Scientist*, 12, 7–13.

SULLIVAN, JAMES
1970 "The economics laboratory: An innovative project in university instruction." *Simulation and Games*, 1, 81–91.

WEBSTER, MURRAY AND JOHN KERVIN
1969 "The problem of artificiality in experimental sociology." Paper presented at the Canadian Sociology and Anthropology annual meetings.

WINTER, J. ALAN
1968 "Simulation games: Tools or toys in research and theory-building." Paper presented at the Eastern Sociological Association annual meetings.

Chapter **17**

Designing a Simulation

Designing a Simulation

We have seen that in general, the larger the number of rules one wants or needs to leave implicit in the simulation, the more computer simulations should be avoided. Human actors can improvise and interpret whenever instructions are missing or ambiguous, whereas computers cannot. Likewise, the more one wants to use the simulation for teaching and training purposes, the more important it is that the form be a man simulation,[1] preferably a game in the strict sense of the term.[2]

Figure 1 diagrams the situation. Each quadrant describes the type of simulation generated by the intersection of the implicit-explicit and research-teaching continua. Note that heuristic simulations, which are solely for the benefit of the designer, can be of any form.

Also bearing on the choice of mode are practical concerns, as discussed in the previous chapter. Assuming that the choice of form has been made, let us now turn to specific design decisions within broad types.

DESIGNING MACHINE SIMULATIONS AND GAMES

The design of simulations involving machines includes two main issues: selecting an appropriate program language and the actual construction of the simulation by means of the language, that is, programming. This second issue is completely beyond the scope of this volume and should be looked into in one of the many available specialized texts (Green, 1963; Meier et al., 1969; Naylor et al., 1968; Gordon, 1969).

One main type of computer language is the general purpose kind, such as FORTRAN, ALGOL, or BASIC. BASIC is a language specially adapted to time-sharing. It allows interaction with the program while it is running and presents advantages for man-machine simulations. ALGOL is most widely used in Europe. FORTRAN is perhaps the most generally available and used. This language permits any variety of operations, being limited only by the memory capacity of the particular machine. It also permits the maximum in output reports, whether graphical or tabular. Finally, there are elaborate diagnostic and error checking programs to insure that the program does not violate the rules of FORTRAN grammar. (There are several variations of FORTRAN, the latest being FORTRAN IV.)

The error checking programs do not often permit a check for logical errors in simulations. Because the identification of logical contradictions

[1] An exception of course, is that of experiments on artificial intelligence, where the objects of the training are computers. See, for example, Samuel (1963).

[2] As the reader will recall, we previously defined a game as a simulation with a *formal* way of determining the winner.

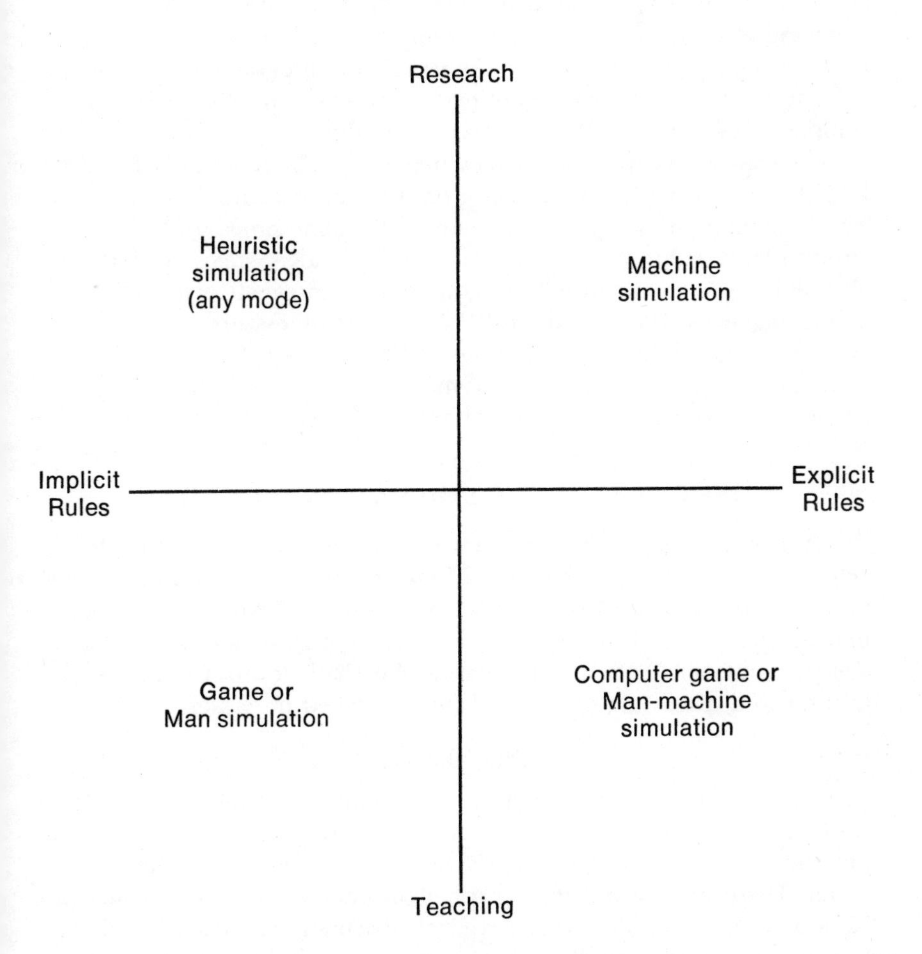

Figure 1: Mode of simulation as a function of the designer's goal and state of available knowledge

is a major part of model development, this problem with FORTRAN can be considerable. A second deficiency with FORTRAN is that the sequencing of steps becomes rapidly complicated, increasing the possibility of minor errors. Special purpose simulation programs have been developed to ease the translation of certain basic complex structures into a computer program and to maximize the ability to modify the program.

The special purpose languages include GPSS, SIMSCRIPT, GASP, DYNAMO, and SIMULATE. The first three are useful when the model can be thought of as a waiting-line and scheduling process. DYNAMO is applicable more for dynamic information-feedback systems. SIMULATE was developed to analyze the large-scale econometric models. Two other languages, IPL-V and LISP 1.5, are list processors, meaning they have a special ability to handle hierarchical lists of items. For descriptions and detailed references on these languages see Naylor (1968), Abelson (1969), and Meier et al. (1969).

DESIGNING A MAN SIMULATION OR GAME

A man simulation is a framework where purposive actors try to achieve a goal through the use of certain resources and while acting under a specified set of constraints. By variously defining and structuring the goals, resources, and constraints the designer can induce numerous forms of behaviors and processes. We shall devote the rest of this chapter to a discussion of a few of these induced processes.

Setting the Goals

The selection of the criteria for winning (in games) or for doing well (in simulations) is a major design decision, because these criteria determine the way in which goal-achievement will motivate the participants. These criteria are more explicit in games because a game must have a winner. For this reason we will discuss goal-setting in the context of games, and we will begin by considering the choices available for structuring the process of winning.

The first choice is between the alternatives of the classic dichotomy of zero-sum versus non zero-sum games.[3] The terminology derives from game theory (see Chapter 3) and refers to situations where the gains of one party equal exactly the losses of the other (i.e. the algebraic sum of the two pay-offs equals zero; hence, zero-sum). Alternatively, zero-sum games are called "games of pure conflict" because one party thrives to the exact extent that the other suffers, and vice versa. Similarly, non

[3] Constant and non-constant sum game would probably be a more accurate terminology.

zero-sum games are often referred to as "mixed-motives games" because they represent degrees of conflict which fall somewhere between the poles represented by completely conflicting interests (pure conflicts) and total absence of conflict. For example, a ten-cent bet between two friends who race each other is structurally a case of pure conflict. On the other hand, a boxing match with two prizes—one of the winner and one for the loser—is of the mixed-motive form. In the racing case one wins exactly what the other loses. In the boxing case both parties stand to win simply by participating in the match. The two parties compete for first prize, but the conflict motive is dampened by the presence of the second prize.

Games of pure conflict are rather easy to structure. They are a case of all or nothing: one winner and one or more losers, with everything which is at stake going to the winner. The more there is at stake, the better. Pure conflicts are, however, an atypical case, both theoretically and empirically.

Conflicts of the mixed-motive form are much more frequent. They are also more difficult to simulate, because there is an infinite gradation of intensities of conflicts between the poles of absolute conflict and no conflict. Varying the values of incentives available to players (e.g. in the form of potential points) is the most apparent solution to this problem, but often it is not sufficient. Instead, different structural arrangements may have to be included to achieve as exact as possible a replica of the precise dynamics of the situation found in the simulandum. In this connection the most interesting structural arrangements found in simulations discussed here and elsewhere seem to involve variations of the following characteristics.

1. Number of criteria for winning. In Simsoc each participant has four objectives to achieve: a personal goal, a group goal, a political-ideological goal, and a societal goal. On the other hand, Leonard's Toy Store game has a single criterion: money earned.

2. Time at which the winning criteria are defined. In Goodman's counseling game the players themselves decide at the conclusion what they feel is the most important criterion for evaluating their performance. In most games, however, the criterion for winning is announced explicitly from the start. An intermediary solution appears in Inbar's Insurrection game, where a winning criterion is set at the start, but can be changed in mid-game by choice of a majority of players.

3. Degree to which the winning criteria are interrelated. In Simsoc there is no formula for translating one's achievements on the four objectives into one over-all score. Thus there is no clear-cut ranking among the participants. By contrast, in the Disaster game, the efficiency criterion and the popularity criterion are linked through the election which takes place at the conclusion.

4. Number of winners. Starting with the polar case of a single winner, a number of arrangements are found. Typically, multi-winner arrangements are produced in one or more of the following ways:

a. Hierarchical Structure. This is the most general and frequent arrangement. The first few players with the highest score on the winning criterion are ranked and declared first, second, third, and so forth. Similarly, the scores of game winners can be compared cross-sectionally or over time, the result being a recursive hierarchy of over-all winners that can be continued endlessly.

b. Group Reference Structure. The principle underlying this arrangement is that the players who are directly competing against each other for gaining points, resources, and such, are *not* competing against each other for winning the game. Parent-Child, discussed in Chapter Two, exemplifies this structural arrangement. Dyads of one parent and one child try to reach agreements about such issues as housework, with both sides having conflicting interests. Each is dependent on the other for earning satisfaction points. There are two winners in the game, a parent and a child. Each one is the player who did best among his role peer groups (among all child players for the child winner, and among all parents for the parent winner). Yet the points earned toward the final score are generated within each parent-child dyad interaction.

The Ghetto game (Toll, 1969) illustrates a similar solution. There is a community of ten role players, with five sets of roles that are matched at the beginning of the game with regard to resources. Each player competes, not against the other nine players, but only against the person whose role is matched to his own. Yet his points are earned through the interactions relating to the entire community of players, not just those interactions involving his matched role partner.

c. Task Structure. This structure essentially creates a dichotomy as follows: success if the task is achieved (no matter the margin of win) versus failure if it is not. The difficulty of the task usually determines the number of winners and losers that the game will yield. Psychologically, the structure is often perceived as one where there are *losers* rather than winners. This is particularly true if the task can successfully be tackled

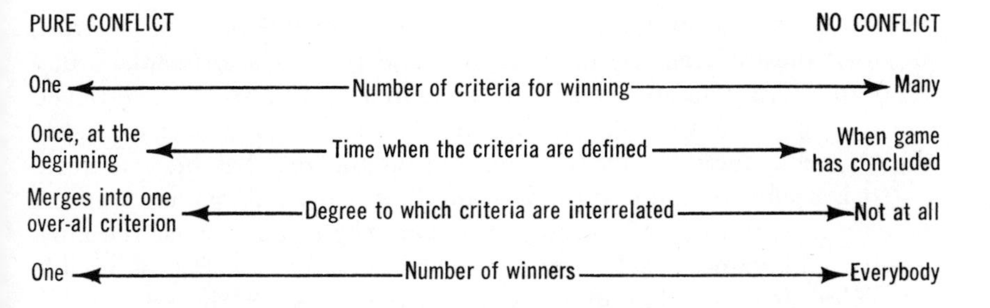

Figure 2: The Conflict Continuum

by a majority of the participants. A good example of this structure is Coleman's (1969) Democracy game. In this game legislators try to get reelected by having the house pass bills which satisfy a majority of their constituents. However, whether a bill is passed with a large majority or a small one is irrelevant. Similarly, being reelected by a large majority may be personally pleasant, but of no consequence in terms of the game outside of "not losing." [4]

By variously combining these selected structures one can generate a great number of types and degrees of conflict. We have seen earlier that games of pure conflict represent an extreme all-or-nothing situation. Conversely, the greater the number of criteria for winning, the later they are defined in the game, the less they are interrelated, and the more winners they yield, the closer one moves toward the other extreme case, the no-conflict pole. Figure 2 summarizes the variables underlying the conflict continuum in graphic form.

Structuring the Constraints

Constraints are elements of both game and non-game man simulations. Among the phenomena and processes of interest that can easily be induced at this level are trust, legitimacy, interdependence, communication, and coalition formation.

Problems of ***trust*** emerge when one party can take advantage of the other by disregarding the terms of an agreement. When there is no punishment for disregard, it is likely to occur more frequently. Structurally it is clear that one can double-cross the other party to an agreement [5] whenever it involves an exchange with sequential rather than simultaneous deliveries of whatever is being exchanged. However, simultaneous

[4] In variations of the game the amount of majority is relevant for the determination of the winner.

[5] The agreement need not be explicit for this discussion to hold.

deliveries can also in special cases be made to involve problems of trust, provided the exchange occurs without inspection.[6] The principle is that in both cases—simultaneous or sequential delivery—the aggrieved player cannot react by withholding part of the bargain, because it has already been delivered by the time the doublecross has been noticed.

It is useful to note that the last round of bargaining games puts one or more players in exactly such a situation. The result is what is known as the "end game effect," through which a large number of double crosses occur in the last round. Ongoing relations, on the other hand, have a built-in mechanism for making a doublecross costly, because the victims always have an opportunity to get even.

This is why end game effects can be minimized simply by withholding from participants exactly when the last round will occur. One can, for example, use a random procedure for terminating the game. If one wishes to avoid problems of trust altogether, a simple solution is to declare that all agreements in the game which meet certain criteria are to be held binding on the players.

Legitimacy is in essence a question of the proper use of role resources. The issue of legitimacy arises whenever there is a delegation of resources such as power or money. In addition, the player delegated the resources should have personal goals as well as role-related goals, *and* he should be able to use directly or indirectly the same scarce resources for meeting both goals. A situation thus exists where the possibility and the temptation to use role-resources for personal ends are present.

Interdependence, which is not to be confused with cooperation, can be elicited by creating the perception of a common fate. In Disaster, if the disaster is not overcome it will spread throughout the system and affect all the players. Cooperation or exchange does not necessarily follow from this circumstance, for reasons to be discussed below. In other words, interdependence can be generated by an event that will affect individuals indiscriminately if some group activity has not taken place.

Patterns of communication are generated by splitting decision-making (task performance) from possession or acquisition of information that is relevant to the decision.[7]

[6] This is what happens in the classical Prisoner's Dilemma (Rappoport, 1966: 128–144).

[7] In another sense, by manipulating the amount of game information one creates a game of strategy as against a game of chance. The less information there is to guide game decisions, the more one approaches a game of pure chance.

Coalition formation requires first that there be available a sufficient number of units for a coalition to form, namely three. In addition, it is a function of the definition of winning, especially with regard to the distribution of resources. Because of this fact we shall have more to say on this topic below when we discuss how resource allocation can generate various social processes.

Allocating the Resources

This is a means for structuring various degrees of equality or inducing feelings of fairness or injustice. It is also a mechanism for introducing randomness in a setting or for keeping it deterministic. But above all, the designer molds a *process of exchange* through the way in which he selects and allocates the resources in the simulation. Indeed, the essence of an exchange is always a transfer of resources.

The existence of a process of exchange implies that parties found it reciprocally advantageous to surrender control over one type of resource in order to gain control over another. In other words, the process requires that the distribution of resources and interests should not overlap completely. At the same time the distributions should not be totally independent.

Overlap can occur in two senses:

1. Overlap for each player between his needs and his resources: There is no scarcity. Each player has all the means that are needed to achieve his goals. Hence there is no motivation to exchange.
2. Overlap between the goals and the scarce resources among the players: Here all the actors are pursuing a goal with the same scarce resources. They cannot exchange—they must compete.

Independence, on the other hand, occurs whenever actors have resources which are neither adequate to reach their goal (e.g. they have money when they need water) nor helpful for reaching the goal, however indirectly (e.g. nobody in the system needs money—or nobody has water).

The range of situations where exchanges can develop must consequently have the following characteristics:

1. The participants have insufficient or inadequate resources for reaching their goals.
2. The actors possess *other* resources which are useful to some other participants in the simulation.

3. The distribution of resources and needs in the system are such that either directly, or through a chain of exchanges, it will be possible for some mutually-complementary deals to be made.

Let us consider extreme cases to see what is the range of processes that various allocations of resources can induce. Consider the case of an all-to-the-winner game where there is a single pay-off that can be shared with participants if desired. If no one actor can achieve the goal individually, forces for coalition formation arise among the same subset of actors who can muster the required amount of resources. This coalition will either increase the probability of reaching a goal or guarantee it, depending upon the rules that set whether the goal is achieved probabilistically or deterministically, once the required amount of resources are gathered. The more a certain amount of resources is a deterministic condition of goal attainment, the stronger the forces of coalition formation will be. Correlatively, those left out of coalitions will be all the more alienated (in the sense of powerlessness).

Alienation can also be structurally induced by varying the characteristics of the resources rather than their quantity and distribution. Thus, holding distributions of interest constant, a system based exclusively on transitive resources, such as money, is more likely to generate cases of alienation (participants left without any resources) than systems based at least in part on non-transitive resources, such as voting rights.

Another extreme type of situation takes either of two forms as follows. An actor has resources in a subsystem where he has no interests (goals), but he does have interests in another subsystem. Or, the actor has interests in a subsystem in which he has no resources, but he does have resources in another subsystem. These structures are conducive to the appearance of the related processes of resource conversion across boundaries, and of a cellular-type growth of previously unrelated groups.

Consider first the case of a collective decision to be reached in a simulation involving a small committee where an actor has a voting right but no interest whatsoever one way or another in the outcome of the issues. The dynamics of this situation are such that the other members of the committee cannot offer support to the actor on an issue in exchange for his support on another one, because the actor has interest in none. Thus, the only way to induce him into an exchange is to look for some other system where the actor does have interests (e.g., the moral or financial spheres). The members can then offer him resources that he can use either directly or indirectly in this other system in exchange for his resource (the vote) that is needed in the committee.

The second case is as follows. The actor has a great deal at stake in the committee decisions, but has no voting right or other resource in the committee. In this case the actor who wants to gain some influence in the committee must find a direct or chain path to transfer or make available to interested committee members resources that he has in another system where they have interests.

The dynamics of both situations generate forces which relate together previously independent groups in interlocking/intersecting social systems of increasing size and complexity. Indeed, the situation can be characterized essentially as one of a constant search for third systems where otherwise uninvolved actors have interests and otherwise powerless actors have resources.

QUALIFICATIONS

A few warnings about the quality, quantity, and order of presentation of the structural arrangements discussed in the previous section are now in order.

First, the order in which we have presented a number of choices which are open to the simulation designer was chosen not for its realism but for its clarity. It does not represent the real design process—in fact, any attempt to order the process, either in progress or in retrospect would distort its essential heuristic nature. As the simulation progresses, numerous and interdependent changes occur, not only those resultant from procedural decisions on the part of the designer, but even some which bear on the very nature of the enterprise. That is, as the simulation progresses, its focus may shift, to the effect that even the topic simulated might be affected, sometimes drastically.

In quantitative terms the number of decisions that we have discussed are but the top of an iceberg. Likewise the list of relationships between structures and processes that we have presented is incomplete. For instance, we have left untouched the processes which develop in structures such as teams. Also, the relations between structures and processes that we discussed are not of the "necessary condition" type. At best the structure mentioned is a sufficient condition for the occurrence of a given process, "all other things being equal."

In short, we have presented only a very partial branching tree of decision choices and some elements of a transformation scheme relating a set of structure to processes. A complete and comprehensive set of guidelines must await a greater accumulation of knowledge and experience than is presently available in the field.

Boocock and Schild (1968) recently stated that "game design is not only not a science, it is hardly a craft," and could best be described as "an 'art' in the sense that we have no explicit rules to transmit." We have tried to show that this need not be the case indefinitely.

REFERENCES

Coleman, James S.
1969 *Democracy*. New York: Western.

Gordon, G.
1969 *System Simulation*. Englewood Cliffs, N. J.: Prentice-Hall.

Green, Bert F.
1963 *Digital Computers in Research*. New York: McGraw-Hill.

Meier, Robert C., William T. Newell, and Harold L. Pazer
1969 *Simulation in Business and Economics*. Englewood Cliffs, N. J.: Prentice-Hall.

Naylor, Thomas H., Joseph L. Balintfy, Donald S. Burdick, Kong Chu
1966 *Computer Simulation Techniques*. New York: Wiley.

Rappoport, Anatol
1966 *Two-Person Game Theory*. Ann Arbor, Michigan.

Samuel, A. L.
1963 "Some studies in machine learning using the game of checkers." In E. A. Feigenbaum and J. Feldman (eds.), *Computers and Thought*. New York: McGraw-Hill.

Toll, Dove
1969 *Ghetto*. New York: Western.

Chapter **18**

Validation

Validation

A major issue when examining the results of an inquiry is their meaning. In part this interpretation depends on the validity and reliability of the instruments used to obtain the results. The strategies for devising valid and reliable instruments, particularly measurement instruments, form an important section of any course or text on research methods.[1] However, because simulation is a recent technique, the procedures for establishing its reliability and validity are not yet widely agreed upon. Consequently systematic treatment of the question is yet to come.

RELIABILITY

Questions of reliability logically precede those of validity. If a measurement is not reliable, then there is no use in considering whether it is valid. It is futile to ask what something is measuring if the answer is inconsistent.

Interestingly, none of the authors of our case studies mention the term reliability. This is not an oversight because many of them discuss what are in fact problems of reliability and procedures for handling them. The reason is that reliability in simulation design is a relatively easy problem to cope with, though there are yet aspects of the issue which are difficult to handle.

The basic principle for establishing the reliability of a simulation is that *successive runs should give similar results.* In practice this means that the mechanics of the model should be free of unplanned-for effects. Thus there should not be divergence in the operations and outputs of the model over a series of runs with the same initial conditions.[2]

Reliability is not of great concern in computer simulations. Because computers are such demanding beasts, they accept no less than their own stringent requirements for reliability in order to operate. If instructions are vague, contradictory, or unstructured, the debugging process will force the designer to correct these errors. During debugging the investigator has unusual access to the scope of his decisions. He obtains not only printouts of the program instructions, but also of diagnostic clues as to what is wrong with the instructions.

[1] A valid measurement is one which measures what it was intended to measure; e.g. measuring feminity with regard to questions concerning artistic inclinations is of questionable validity. A reliable measurement is one which can be reproduced when the same object is measured in another comparable situation; e.g. respondent's date of birth should be the same from one interview to another if the information has been collected reliably.

[2] This statement should be qualified, for in the case of models that are not deterministic, the additional task of controlling the random distributions of events must also be attended to.

With only rare exceptions a computer simulation, once it is operating, is unreliable. One such exception is the unlikely occurrence of error in the computer machinery itself. There are also infrequent instances where a program may appear debugged, yet the later entry of extreme values on some variable causes problems. Neither of these cases is likely to be of concern in most computer experiments.[3]

On the other hand, making games reliable is a major source of their protracted development time. A game can be considered reliable when it develops along similar paths when played with separate but comparable sets of subjects and administrators. As intuition suggests, there are many sources of variation between game runs.

Playability

Probably the most controllable source of variance is basic playability: The game must operate smoothly. Playability depends in large part on the following characteristics.

1. The physical equipment should not be cumbersome or impractical. The problems with the Caribou Hunting game were to a great extent involved with finding the most manageable playing pieces. The first map was so big that the players could not reach all points of it to place markers. At a later stage little ball markers fell out of their resting places and scattered. The adventures of this case, highlight how decisions about seemingly trivial parts of a game may substantially impede its final development. (And we know of some games which never materialized simply because the physical equipment problem could not be solved.)

When equipment is cumbersome pieces may be misplaced, lost, or even worse, overlooked. Players may be so preoccupied by managing piles of paper, pawns and other tokens that portions of the game procedure are missed. If various parts are similar in shape, and cannot be immediately identified (e.g. by color-coding) they may be misused.

2. The rules should be as clearly and simply stated as possible. Much of Boocock's early difficulty with Life Career rested here. Her game and basic playing pieces were workable. Rather, her problem was to reduce the voluminous instructions to players enough that the target audience—poorly skilled high school students—could follow the instructions. Observation and questioning during the field tests helped her to develop work through to a concise, better-programmed instruction book.

[3] Of course, there is also always the possibility of human error in preparing the materials for the program runs, but such errors are very unlikely to go unnoticed.

If rules are not clear, players may perform in ways contrary to the designer's intentions. If players are not certain of the kinds of relationships they can have with other players, they improvise according to their own personal inclinations and experiences. Similarly, if the sequencing of activities is not well stated, the game activities could change from one round to the next.

Related to the issue of rule-clarification is the standardization of game administration procedures. Oftentimes the game administration problem is solved simply by making technical or substantive modifications in the teacher's manual or experimenter's guide. On another level, though, the source of variance is less under the designer's control. As the Caribou Hunting designers discovered, the teachers were often an obstacle to proper game operations. For example, some refused to accept the degree of their students' freedom and hence intruded on the game activities. This source of a game's unreliability is not easily handled much beyond careful training of administrators.[4]

3. The rules should be complete and self-contained. Breznitz and Leiblich's framework for simulation showed that it is not enough to have rules in the game relevant only to the simulandum. Rather, it is necessary to recognize that the game is a system of its own and needs complete procedural rules for its complete operation. Some of these rules give such simple specifications as the order in which players may take turns. Others are police and adjudication rules for handling instances of game rule-violations or cheating. As Zaltman explains in some detail, the absence of police or adjudication rules can conceivably reduce the game to chaos.[5]

4. The game should not overtax the player's span of attention. There are two ways in which this can be avoided. One is to insure that there is not too much information and too many decisions to handle per play. Otherwise player reactions may just be a function of some hapless sampling among an unmanageable set of possibilities. The

[4] This is a more serious problem for experimental games than for teaching games. There is of late some literature on experimenter bias and techniques for overcoming it (Friedman, 1967; Baldwin, 1969). Administrator variability has been shown to be a factor in the degree to which students enjoy and learn from a game (Inbar, 1966). But since games are structured with feedback systems so as to be self-contained learning environments, the administrator effect, though real, can be tolerated.

[5] These policing rules are somewhat analogous to the computer's requirement that all activities have a definite termination point. So long as any degree of freedom is left to players above and beyond the computer form of the simulation, man simulations will have a built-in source of unreliability.

point is not that games cannot be complex, but that the structuring of the rules should not incur an unintended playing complexity. Second, the game should not last so long as to be physically exhausting. (Conversely, turn around time should not be so long as to fail to engross the player.[6]) In all of these cases player interest and motivation will be adversely affected, generating erratic behaviors.

VALIDITY

While reliability is necessary if a simulation is to simulate anything at all, it is not sufficient evidence that the simulation has any merit. A designer can easily delude himself into thinking that, because his game is playable or his program is debugged, he has a worthwhile simulation. He may just be using a glorified name for an entertaining activity or for a statistical analysis. To have merit a simulation must bear some relationship to an external empirical or theoretical reality. This relationship determines the degree of validity of the enterprise.

Validation Procedures

Correspondence between simulation and simulandum can be defined in several ways.

1. The simulation appears reasonable or has face validity. This is the easiest and least dependable method of validation. (And few of our case studies went beyond this stage.) In this method the investigator addresses such questions as:

Are the purposes those expected? (E. g. in a simulation of conflict, people compete.)

Do any untoward events occur? (E. g. there were too many "suicides" in the early version of Simsoc.)

Do players find the environment in games realistic? (E. g. Life Career players expressed that they identified with their game roles.)

In a computer simulation, does the output look sensible given the input? (E. g. in an early version of one computer simulation, the average education level for the population was 98 years.) The problem with this type of evidence, as the Gullahorns aptly explain, is that it is merely plausible that the simulation is valid. It is akin to "eyeballing the data" in research without paying reference to statistical decision standards.

Why is this procedure so ineffective? Ray and Duke (1969: 151)

[6] The best theoretical discussion of the issue of player engrossment is Goffman (1964). His discussion focuses upon those variations in game structure that influence player interest in and enjoyment of the game.

brusquely summarize its deficiencies with regard to computer simulation. It fails to tell us:

> How many of the variables and parameters that have been introduced are rigorously justifiable in theory and verifiable from empirical evidence? How many "fudge factors" and "computational conveniences" have been introduced in lieu of solid knowledge, or even at the behest of the computer programmer? And how many models or sub-routines depend on knife-edge equilibrai of certain variables that must be accurate, say, within 1 per cent of the variance, when we know that the probable errors in our data sources (and not least in our measures) must exceed 5 to 10 per cent? Or how many variables have been translated into ratio scales for the computer program, when the most one is certain of is a weak rank-order scale?

And we would add as parallel the following criticisms not addressed by a simple face validation of man simulations:

> How many of the payoff structures are rigorously justifiable in terms of theory, and, where relevant, research? Have some rules been introduced for convenience only? How much of the game processes as observed in field-testing were due to special characteristics of the trial subjects? To what degree did administrator suggestion rather than the game structure itself provoke expected game responses?

There is a philosophical position current that you are what you appear to be.[7] This cannot be said for simulations. Unless the designer provides evidence that his simulation is what it is intended to be, then it will be presently a misrepresentation with potentially-damaging implications for theory development, teaching, social planning, or whatever its purported use.

2. Another validation procedure is to compare gross output of simulation to simulandum. The comparison may be to a theoretical distribution or an empirical distribution. Data from the simulation would be treated similarly to data in the real world, that is, by means of observation, categorization, and statistical analysis.

Smith utilized this method of validation in the early simulation of recruit disobedience. The output indicated that intensive non-duty behavior was highest among simulated recruits who were high in anxiety and subjected to an arbitrary leadership climate. This finding corresponded with the original survey data.

[7] See Vonnegut's (1961) novel. Lyman and Scott (1970) discuss the history of this idea in social science and discuss the implication of taking it seriously with regard to social theory.

Another variation on this type of validation occurred in Zaltman's simulation. He expected that by late plays the consumers would be shopping selectively for credit. Observation and study of record sheets verified his hypothesis. (Zaltman was not systematic in the sense of counting these behaviors. Presumably he could have set up a decision-rule, for example, that seventy per cent of the consumers would shop for credit in round eight, and test the hypothesis with a systematic count of game samples.)

A related type of validation check is based upon predictions concerning the intermediary internal processes and outputs. The dynamics can be studied in two contexts. One involves changes in outputs over time, such as the increasing rate of credit-shopping by consumers through rounds of the game. Another involves specific time-ordered or causal relationships, such as a prediction that bankers in Consumer will be increasingly selective in granting loans as their funds decrease. Smith used the latter approach for testing the myriad relationships of his first simulation. He examined each of the separate relationships against comparable ones in the survey data and located many instances of poor correspondence. This poor validation led to reconceptualization of his theory, and in turn, of the simulation.

3. Component units and their characteristics as defined in the simulandum should parallel those entered in the simulation. This strategy addresses the question of whether all the appropriate actors are included and whether their resources, predispositions, motivations, and so forth are distributed as prescribed by the simulandum. Consider, for example, the Parent-Child simulation game, in which there is only one parent and one child. If an important resource for a parent in controlling his child is the possibility of coalition with the other parent, then the game, which may be valid as a parent-child simulation, is not valid as a family simulation.

4. Correspondence also demands non-interference with the simulation process of the additions or omissions required by the simulation mode. The previous points have been to examine the parallel between elements stated to exist in the simulandum and those that should exist in the simulation. Another aspect of the correspondence strategy is to search for undesirable elements in the simulation. In other words, are foreign structures, outputs, or processes present that violate the assumptions of the model? These elements are what Breznitz and Lieblich refer to as "simulation-specific," being features that were introduced into the simulation because of the requirements of the simulation mode.

Consider, for example, the Caribou Hunting game. It is likely that this simulation would score high in a systematic validation of its output, structure, and interrelationships. However, at one point in game development the game map was greatly reduced in size and the number of players cut from nine to three. These changes made the game more playable and manageable in the classroom setting. Yet they also introduced features of face-to-face interaction that do not occur in real-life situations, in which Eskimos are diffused geographically over a large area. The designers had to satisfy themselves that these changes from the simulandum brought on by the needs of the game itself were minor with regard to their overall aims.

With regard to computers, as Ray and Duke indicated, it is necessary to impose numbers on processes because computers need clear cutting points in order to make decisions.

We turn now to a practical question: Which validation strategy should one select in his own work? Breznitz and Lieblich have suggested that the primary consideration is the goal for which the simulation has been designed. If the simulation is for teaching purposes, then correspondence of structures is most important because there is a strong argument for maximizing the amount of information that is available to the player. In the case of simulations for research, correspondence of outputs is argued to take precedence. We would suggest, however, that these guidelines at best set a priority ranking of strategies to use in validation. An example from one validation study will illustrate the use of several of the strategies, as well as point to some problems underlying their use.

An Illustration

Hanneman et al. (1969) developed a computer simulation of innovation diffusion in a peasant village, SINDI I. The basis for the simulation was generalizations about the diffusion process available from previous empirical research. Parameter estimates and input data for the simulation were developed from Rogers (1965) research of a Colombian peasant village. There were two types of output data: the number of people who had knowledge of the innovation at the time of the final run, and a curve representing the cumulation of knowers over time.

Looking only at final output, the simulated data approached to within five per cent the number of real-world knowers at the time of data collection. On the other hand, the process data, i. e. the cumulative increase in the number of knowers over time, did not adequately replicate the real-world cumulative adoption curve. In real life the adoption of innovations is generally S-shaped, while the simulated curve was linear.

Hanneman et al. discussed possible reasons for the lack of validity. One suggestion was that the simulation was not conceptually equivalent to the simulandum. Lack of equivalence may stem from different sources. A crucial component of the model may be missing. In this case, the psychological processes involved in accepting information has been ignored although the designers were aware of them. Another reason can be that a relationship may be incorrectly defined in the simulation. For example, in SINDI I it had been assumed that tellers randomly contact others. In fact, it is well known that tellers seek out certain types of individuals and that the information exchange is therefore not random.

The authors also suggested faulty parameter estimation. Assuming that the basic innovation model selected was in fact adequate, then its transformation into simulation form may have been faulty. In SINDI I the authors admit that "most of the general parameter values were arbitrarily set." For instance, the probability of accepting new information from one of the innovators in the model had been set at .50 with little preconceived rationale for this decision.

Another possibility they suggested—and one ignored by simulators who insist upon reality-tests of validity—is that the data base itself was perhaps invalid. For example, a serious deficiency that they found in their Colombian survey data was that it was recall information, not information gathered through time. Hence, they concluded that the poor correspondence between the reality and the simulated diffusion curves could have been the fault of the reality measure, and not the simulation.

Clearly, then, the validity issue is both a complex and open-ended problem. It is possible to point to strategies and priorities for establishing the existence of some correspondence between a simulandum and its simulation. Ultimately, however, the significance of the result must remain ambiguous, because no strategy is infallible.

REFERENCES

BALDWIN, JOHN

1969 "Influences detrimental to simulation gaming." *American Behavioral Scientist* 12, 14–21.

FRIEDMAN, NEIL

1967 *The Social Nature of Psychological Research*. New York: Basic Books.

HANNEMAN, GERHARD J., TOM W. CARROLL,
EVERETT M. ROGERS, J. DAVID STANFIELD, AND NAN LIN

1969 "Computer simulation of innovation diffusion in a peasant village." *American Behavioral Scientist*, 12, 36–45.

INBAR, MICHAEL

1966 "The differential impact of a game simulating a community disaster." *American Behavioral Scientist*, 10, 18–27.

Validation

LYMAN, STANFORD AND MARVIN SCOTT
1970 *Sociology of the Absurd*. New York: Appleton-Century-Crofts.

RAY, PAUL AND RICHARD DUKE
1968 "The environment of decision-makers in urban gaming simulations." In William Coplin (ed.), *Simulation in the Study of Politics*. Chicago: Markham.

ROGERS, EVERETT
1965 "Mass media exposure and modernization among Colombian peasants." Public Opinion Quarterly, 29, 614–625.

VONNEGUT, KURT
1961 *Mother Night*. New York: Avon.

Appendices

Appendix A ANNOTATED BIBLIOGRAPHY

This list was prepared for those who desire to explore special areas of simulation in detail. The first part includes review articles, anthologies, and texts. The remaining sections are devoted to separate sections on economic, political, sociological and psychological processes. The listing does not approach totality—over 2,000 entries are eligible for a thorough bibliography of social science simulations. (See Werner and Werner, 1969, listed below.) Many of these references are difficult to obtain, because they are limited-circulation technical reports, symposia proceedings, or out-of-print books. Therefore, general availability is one criterion for entry here, as well as the writers' displays of competence and sophistication in their presentations.

Besides the sources below there are other places to locate current work in social science simulations. One is *Simulation and Games,* a social science journal devoted to research, design, methodology, and evaluation of computer and game simulations. Papers on simulation also appear frequently in *Behavioral Science.*[1] Finally, anyone working in the area, especially with regard to simulations for teaching, will find Project SIMILE's Occasional Newsletter useful for the most recent information on new simulations, availability of unpublished research reports, and workshops. Project SIMILE is located at Western Behavioral Sciences Institute, 1121 Torrey Pines Road, La Jolla, California 92037.)

A. GENERAL REVIEWS, ANTHOLOGIES, AND TEXTS

Abelson, Robert P. "Simulation of Social Behavior," pp. 274–356 in G. Lindsey and E. Aronson (eds.), *Social Psychology,* Cambridge, Mas-

[1] *Simulation and Games* and *Behavioral Science* should be available in college libraries.

sachusetts: Addison-Wesley, 1969. A practical introduction to computer simulation, along with a review of social-psychological models.

BOOCOCK, SARANE S. and ERLING O. SCHILD (eds.) *Simulation Games in Learning*. Beverly Hills: Sage, 1968. Readings on the application and evaluation of simulations used for teaching purposes.

COHEN, KALMAN J. and ERIC RHENMAN. "The Role of Management Games in Education and Research," Management Science 7 (January, 1961): 131-66. Review and critique of management games.

COHEN, KALMAN J. and RICHARD M. CYERT. "Simulation of Organizational Behavior," pp. 305–334 in *Handbook of Organizations*, James G. March (ed.), Chicago: Rand-McNally, 1965. Reviews examples of descriptive. quasi-realistic, and normative models of business organizations; also surveys problems associated with simulation procedures.

COLEMAN, JAMES S. "Mathematical Models and Computer Simulation," pp. 1027–1062 in *Handbook of Modern Sociology*, R. E. L. Faris (ed.), Chicago: Rand-McNally, 1964. Reviews and illustrates uses of simulation for the study of social organization.

COLEMAN, JAMES S., SARANE S. BOOCOCK, and ERLING O. SCHILD (*eds.*). *Simulation Games and Learning Behavior*, Parts I and II, special issues of *American Behavioral Scientist* 10 (October and November, 1966). Papers on the rationale and evaluation of teaching simulations.

COPLIN, WILLIAM D. (ed.). *Simulation in the Study of Politics*. Chicago: Markham, 1968. A collection of papers explaining and discussing models of political processes.

GREEN, BERT F. *Digital Computers in Research*, New York: McGraw-Hill, 1963. A text on computer technology for behavioral research.

GUETZKOW, HAROLD (ed.). *Simulation in Social Science*, Englewood Cliffs, New Jersey: Prentice-Hall, 1962. Useful source materials on early work with social simulations.

GUETZKOW, HAROLD and PHILIP KOTLER. *Simulation in Social and Administrative Science*, Englewood Cliffs: Prentice-Hall, 1970. An anthology of review articles.

HYMES, D. (ed.). *The Use of Computers in Anthropology*, The Hague, Netherlands: Mouton, 1965. Includes a number of papers on computer simulation of anthropological theories.

MEIER, ROBERT C., WILLIAM T. NEWELL, and HAROLD L. PAZER. *Simulation in Business and Economics*. Englewood Cliffs, N. Y.: Prentice-Hall, 1969. An introduction to simulation, with emphasis on computer techniques.

NAYLOR, THOMAS H., JOSEPH L. BALINTY, DONALD S. BURDICK, and KONG CHU. *Computer Simulation Techniques*. New York: Wiley, 1968. A text on computer simulation techniques presented in a clear style which presumes only moderate acquaintance with computer technology. Also reviews numerous models of economic simulations in its examples.

NAYLOR, THOMAS (ed.). *The Design of Computer Simulation Experiments*, Durham, N. C.: Duke, 1969.

NESBITT, WILLIAM A. *Simulation Games for the Social Studies Classroom*, revised edition, New York: Foreign Policy Association, 1968. A brief, reasoned introduction to academic simulations. Bibliography lists resource persons, available games, and evaluative literature.

RASER, JOHN R. *Simulation and Society*, Boston: Allyn and Bacon, 1969. Explains the rationale behind scientific gaming. Useful in its review of many unpublished reports.

SIMON, HERBERT A. *Sciences of the Artificial*, Cambridge, Mass.: M.I.T. Press. Discusses the ontology of simulation and rationale for its use in scientific advances.

"Simulation," *International Encyclopedia of the Social Sciences*, 1968, XIV, pp. 262–81. A set of three essays: "Individual Behavior," by Alan Newell and Herbert A. Simon; "Economic Processes," by Irma Adelman; "Political Processes," by Charles F. Hermann.

STARBUCK, W. A. and J. M. DUTTON (eds.). *Computer Simulation in Human Behavior*, New York: Wiley, 1970. Collected papers on a wide range of simulations of social process.

TOMKINS, SILVAN S. and SAMUEL MESSICK (eds.). *Computer Simulation of Personality*, New York: Wiley, 1963. Psychological simulations.

WERNER, ROLAND and JOAN T. WERNER. *Bibliography of Simulations: Social Systems and Education,* La Jolla, California: Western Behavioral Sciences Institute, 1969. This 178-page listing is the most complete bibliography available. Not annotated, but grouped by basic themes. Includes non-published materials and symposium presentations.

B. ECONOMIC PROCESSES

ADELMAN, IRMA and FRANK L. ADELMAN. "The Dynamic Properties of the Klein-Goldberger Model," Econometrica 27 (October, 1959): 596–625. One of the first digital computer simulations in economics.

AMSTUTZ, ARNOLD E. *Computer Simulation of Competitive Market Response,* Cambridge: M. I. T., 1967. Based on a behavioral model of market interactions.

BALDERSTON, FREDERICK E. and AUSTIN C. HOGGATT. *Simulation of Market Processes,* Berkeley: Institute of Business and Economic Research, 1962. A computer simulation of the West Coast lumber industry.

BONINI, CHARLES P. *Simulation of Information and Decision Systems in the Firm,* Englewood Cliffs, New Jersey: Prentice-Hall, 1963. A computer simulation of a hypothetical firm based upon a synthesis of decision theory, economics, accounting, and organization theory.

COHEN, KALMAN J. *Computer Models of the Shoe, Leather, Hide Sequence,* Englewood Cliffs, New Jersey: Prentice-Hall, 1960. A computer simulation of the leather industries for the time period 1930–1940.

COHEN, KALMAN J., WILLIAM R. DILL, ALFRED A. KUEHN, and PETER R. WINTERS. *The Carnegie Tech Management Game,* Homewood, Illinois: Irwin, 1964. A description of perhaps the best-known game used in graduate schools of business.

CYERT, R. M., E. A. FEIGENBAUM, and J. G. MARCH. "Models in a Behavioral Theory of the Firm," *Behavioral Science* 4 (April, 1959): 81–95. A highly detailed computer simulation to study the classical theory of duopoly using the tin can industry as an illustration.

DUESENBERRY, JAMES S., GARY FROMM, LAWRENCE R. KLEIN, and EDWARD KUH (eds.). *The Brookings Quarterly Econometric Model of the*

United States, Chicago: Rand-McNally, 1960. A massive macroeconomic computer simulation of the U. S. economy.

HOLLAND, EDWARD P. and ROBERT W. GILLESPIE. *Experiments on a Simulated Under-developed Economy,* Cambridge, Massachusetts: M.I.T. Press, 1963. A large computer simulation of a stylized underdeveloped economy.

ORCUTT, GUY H., MARTIN GREENBERGER, JOHN KORBEL, and ALICE M. RIVLIN. *Microanalysis of Socioeconomic Systems,* New York: Harper, 1961. A computer simulation of demographic and economic changes in households for the U. S., 1950–1960.

THORELLI, HANS B. and ROBERT L. GRAVES. *International Operations Simulation,* New York: Free Press, 1964. The development and use of a business management game that focuses upon international trade.

WING, RICHARD L. "Two Computer-Based Games for Sixth Graders," *American Behavioral Scientist* 10 (November, 1966): 31–34. Economics games.

C. POLITICAL PROCESS

ABELSON, ROBERT P. "A Computer Simulation Model of Community Referendum Controversies," *Public Opinion Quarterly* 26 (Spring, 1963): 93–122. A computer simulation of the dynamics of community fluoridation referenda.

BALDWIN, JOHN. "The Economics of Peace and War: A Simulation." *Journal of Conflict Resolution,* 11 (December, 1967): 383–397. Description and analysis of a game of trade and war.

BENSON, OLIVER. "A Simple Diplomatic Game," pp. 504–511 in *International Politics and Foreign Policy,* James N. Rosenau (ed.). New York: Free Press, 1961. A computer simulation of the contemporary international system.

BOGUSLAW, ROBERT, R. DAVID, and E. GLICK. "A Simulation Vehicle for Studying National Policy Formation in a Less Armed World," *Behavioral Science,* 11 (1966), pp. 48-61. Research on PLANS, a pressure group game.

CHERRYHOLMES, CLEO and MICHAEL J. SHAPIRO. *Representatives and Roll Calls,* Indianapolis: Bobbs-Merrill, 1969. Computer simulation of roll call votes in the U. S. Legislature.

COLEMAN, JAMES S. "Collective Decisions," *Sociological Inquiry,* 34 (1964), pp. 166–181. Discusses basis of a legislative game (later an instructional game for high school students).

CRECINE, JOHN P. *Governmental Problem Solving,* Chicago: Rand-McNally, 1968. A computer simulation of municipal budgeting.

GOLDHAMER, HERBERT and HANS SPEIER. "Some Observations on Political Gaming," pp. 498–503 in *International Politics and Foreign Policy,* James N. Rosenau (ed.). New York: Free Press, 1961. A description of one of the early international relations games developed at RAND.

GUETZKOW, HAROLD, CHADWICK F. ALGER, RICHARD A. BRODY, ROBERT C. NOEL, RICHARD C. SNYDER. *Simulation in International Relations,* Englewood Cliffs, New Jersey: Prentice-Hall, 1963. Papers on the development of Inter-Nation Simulation, a game used for both research and teaching.

HERMANN, CHARLES F. *Crises in Foreign Policy,* Indianapolis: Bobbs Merrill, 1969. Experiments with Inter-Nation Simulation.

MCPHEE, WILLIAM N. "Notes on a Campaign Simulator," *Public Opinion Quarterly,* 25 (July, 1961): 184–193. A computer simulation of voting behavior.

POOL, ITHIEL DE SOLA, ROBERT P. ABELSON, and SAMUEL POPKIN. *Candidates, Issues, and Strategies,* Cambridge, Massachusetts: M. I. T. Press, 1964. Discussion of the Simulmatics Project, a computer simulation of the 1960 U. S. Presidential election.

RAY, PAUL H. and RICHARD D. DUKE. "The Environment of Decision-Makers in Urban Gaming Simulation," pp. 149–175 in *Simulation in the Study of Politics,* William D. Coplin (ed.), Chicago: Markham, 1968. Report on the assumptions of man-machine models, with special reference to METRO, an urban game.

SMOKER, PAUL. "Social Research for Social Anticipation," *American Behavioral Scientist* 12 (July–August, 1969): 7–13. Experiment on Inter-Process Simulation, an international relations computer game.

D. SOCIOLOGICAL PROCESSES

BOOCOCK, SARANE S. and JAMES S. COLEMAN. "Games with Simulated Environments in Learning," *Sociology of Education* 39 (Summer, 1965: 215–236. Experiments in three games for high school social studies (Life Career, Democracy, Community Disaster).

COLEMAN, JAMES S. "Analysis of Social Structures and Simulation of Social Processes with Electronic Computers," Pp. 61–69 in H. Guetzkow (ed.), *Simulation in Social Science*, Englewood Cliffs, N. J.: Prentice-Hall, 1962. Description of computer models of (1) reference group behavior, (2) interactions in triads.

DUKE, RICHARD D. *Gaming Simulation in Urban Research*, East Lansing, Michigan: Institute for Community Development and Services, Michigan State University, 1964. History of the development of Metropolis, a game modelling the decision processes for the allocation of land resources.

ENVIROMETRICS. INFORMATION FOLDER. Washington, D. C.: Envirometrics, 1969. Describes City I and City II, computer games for urban research.

FINDER, N. V. and W. R. MCKINZIE. "On a computer Program that Generates and Queries Kinship Structures," *Behavioral Science* 14 (July, 1969), pp. 334–340.

FREEMAN, LINTON. *Patterns of Residential Segregation*, New York: Schenkman, 1969. Reports on construction and research with a computer simulation of housing patterns.

GILBERT, J. P. and E. A. HAMMEL. "Computer Simulation and Analysis of Problems in Kinship and Social Structure," *American Anthropologist* 68 (February, 1966), pp. 71–93.

GULLAHORN, JOHN T. and JEANNE E. GULLAHORN. *Explorations in Computer Simulation*, New York: Free Press, 1970. The continuing odyssey with HOMUNCULUS, a computer simulation of elementary social behavior.

HANNEMAN, GERHARD, TOM W. CARROLL, EVERETT M. ROGERS, J. DAVID STANIELD, and NAN LIN. "Computer Simulation of Innovation Diffusion in a Peasant Village," *American Behavioral Scientist* 12 (July–August, 1969): 36–45.

RANIO, KULLERVO. "A Study of Sociometric Group Structure: An Application of a Stochastic Theory of Social Interaction," Pp. 100–123, in *Sociological Theories in Progress,* Volume 1, Joseph Berger et al. (eds.). Boston: Houghton-Mifflin, 1966. Computer simulation of friendship structures.

ROME, BEATRICE and SYDNEY ROME. "Leviathan, and Information Handling In Large Organizations," Pp. 161–192 in Harold Borko (ed.), *Computer Applications in the Behavioral Sciences.* Englewood Cliffs, N. J.: Prentice-Hall, 1962.

SMITH, ROBERT B. "Simulation Models for Accounting Schemes," *American Behavioral Scientist* 12 (July–August, 1969): 21–30. Computer models of residential mobility, military authority and recruit behavior, prison riots, and collective disturbances.

E. PSYCHOLOGICAL PROCESSES

BREZNITZ, SCHLOMO, and AMIA LIEBLICH. "The Unconscious Play Patience: An Attempt to Simulate Dream-Work," *Simulation and Games* 1 (1970), 5–17.

CLARKSON, GEOFFREY, P. E. *Portfolio Selection: A Simulation of Trust Investment,* Englewood Cliffs, New Jersey: Prentice-Hall, 1963. A computer simulation of the decision-making processes of investment counsellors.

COLBY, KENNETH. "Computer Simulation of a Neurotic Process," pp. 165–179 in *Computer Simulation of Personality,* Silvan S. Tomkins and Samuel Messick, (eds.), New York: Wiley, 1963. Computer simulation of therapeutic manipulation of patient emotions.

COE, RODNEY M. "Conflict, Interference, and Aggression: Computer Simulation of a Social Process, *Behavioral Science* 9 (April, 1964: 186–197. Computer simulation of emotional responses to frustration and conflict.

FEIGENBAUM, EDWARD A. "The Simulation of Verbal Learning Behavior," Pp. 297–309 in *Computers and Thought,* Edward A. Feigenbaum and Julian Feldman, (eds), New York: McGraw-Hill, 1963. A computer simulation of verbal rote memorization.

APPENDIX A

NEWELL, ALLEN and HERBERT A. SIMON. "GPS: A Program that Simulates Human Thought," Pp. 279–293 in *Computers and Thought*, E. A. Feigenbaum and J. Feldman (eds.), New York: McGraw-Hill, 1963. A computer simulation of problem-solving such tasks as puzzles or geometric proofs.

REITMAN, WALTER R., RICHARD B. GROVE, and RICHARD G. SHOUP. "Argus: An Information-Processing Model of Thinking," *Behavioral Science* 9 (July, 1964): 270–281. A Hebbian model of thinking, remembering, and forgetting.

Appendix B GAMES

Samuel A. Livingston

The entries in this list consist only of games readily available. Many other games have been produced in limited editions for experimental use or have simply never been published on a large scale. Business management games have been excluded because they are on the borderline of social science simulations.[1] Some of the games cannot be obtained separate from the larger curriculum units of which they are a part. Unless otherwise identified, the entry is an all-man simulation.

The stated purpose of a game is that of the original designer. However, the potential range is in most cases greater. Games developed for high school can typically be played at the college level or with adults. (The lower age limit of a game is an indicator of the complexity of the simplest version of that game.) Similarly, an investigator may find that a game developed for pedagogical purposes matches the role structure, power distribution, and social process of the type that he wishes to study through experimentation.

There was difficulty in obtaining details for some of the entries, such as the preferred size range, whether the game can be broken up over time periods, or even the original designer. We have ourselves played a majority of these games, seen virtually all the others, and consulted with others who have played them. From this experience it can be said that the entries are probably satisfactory at least with regard to playability and adequacy of instructional materials.

American Government Simulations

DESIGNERS: Leonard Stitelman and William D. Coplin

Five simulation exercises (both games and paper-pencil simulations) on the American Constitutional Convention, budgetary politics,

[1] The reader interested in these games should consult Kalman J. Cohen and Eric Rhenman, "The Role of Management Games in Education and Research," Management Science 7 (January, 1961): 131–66.

presidential election campaigning, decision-making committees, the congressman at work. Intended for college level courses. The simulations are brief (a class period) and flexible to class size. Available from: Science Research Associates, 259 East Erie Street, Chicago, Illinois, 60611.

C & O/B & O (formerly Dispatcher)

DESIGNER: Charles S. Roberts

The operations of modern railroad dispatching. No research or pedagogical aim stated. Available from: Avalon-Hill Company, 4517 Harford Road, Baltimore, Maryland, 21214.

City II

A *man-machine* simulation of the economic, governmental, and social activity in a hypothetical metropolitan area. For teaching high school, college, and graduate students; also for research on decision-making processes and on the effects of public policy. Requires at least two full days or four 3-hour sessions. Requires access to a large-scale computer (such as the GE 635) either directly or via teletype. For further information contact Applied Simulations International, Inc., Suite 900, 1100 Seventeenth Street N. W., Washington, D. C. 20036.

Caribou Hunting; Seal Hunting

Two games which simulate the processes by which the Netsilik Eskimos hunt caribou and seals. Available *only* as part of the total fifth-grade social studies curriculum, *Man, A Course of Study,* from Education Development Center, Social Studies Curriculum Development Program, 15 Mifflin Place, Cambridge, Mass. 02138.

CLUG: Community Land Use Game

DESIGNER: Allan Feldt

The processes of urban economics and land development in a metropolitan area. For teaching college and graduate students; also for research in city management. Requires 4 to 10 hours; can be played in one-hour sessions. A desk calculator or slide rule is recommended. Available from The Free Press 866 Third Ave. New York, N.Y. 10022. Player's Manual $4.95, Instructors Manual $2.95. Complete game kit available from Systems Gaming Associates, A 1–2 Lansing Apts., 20 N. Triphammer Rd., Ithaca, N. Y. 14850.

Consumer

DESIGNER: Gerald Zaltman

The problems and economics of installment buying. For ages 12 through adult. Requires about two hours; can be played in shorter sessions. Available from Western Publishing Company, Inc., School and Library Department, 850 Third Avenue, New York, N. Y. 10022.

Crisis

An international conflict model. For classroom use with students from 6th grade through graduate school. Available from Simile II, P. O. Box 1023, 1150 Silverado, La Jolla, Calif. 92037.

Dangerous Parallel

DESIGNER: Foreign Policy Association

Conditions leading to the outbreak of the Korean War. For classroom use with high school and college students. Requires about 3 hours; can be played in 40-minute periods. Available from Scott, Foresman & Co., College Division, Glenview, Illinois.

Democracy (formerly "Legislature")

DESIGNER: James S. Coleman

An eight-level game simulating the legislative process. For classroom use with students from junior high school through graduate school; also for research on group decision-making. Each level requires about 40 minutes. Available from Western Publishing Company (see listing for "Consumer").

Destiny (and other historical simulations)

The American political situation during the Cuban crisis which led to the Spanish-American War. For high school classes in history. Contains all materials necessary for a two-week classroom unit. Available from Interact, P. O. Box 262, Lakeside, Calif. 92040. Other games produced by this group include:

Disunia: on the politics of the Articles of Confederation
Division: on U. S. politics of the 1850's
Mission: on domestic conflict relating to the Vietnam war
Panic: on the economic crisis of 1929

Dig

The process by which archeologists reconstruct ancient civilizations from artifacts. For use with high school classes in history or anthropology. Contains all materials necessary for a two-week classroom unit. Available from Interact (see listing for "Destiny").

Diplomacy

The military and diplomatic power structure of Europe before World War I. No research or teaching purpose stated. It is a game of pure strategy for up to 7 players. Has been used in various college courses to illustrate the dynamics of diplomacy and war, or as an example of an enticing simulation. Time required 4–8 hours; can be divided into two-hour sessions. Available from Games Research, Inc., 48 Wareham Street, Boston, Mass. 02118 (also in many stores).

Disaster (formerly "Community Response")

DESIGNER: Michael Inbar

The response of communities to local natural disasters (fire, flood, tornado, etc.). Used to teach emergency preparedness to high school students and adults; also for college classes in sociology. Requires 3–5 hours; can be played in shorter sessions. Available from Western Publishing Company (see listing for "Consumer").

Economic Decision Games

DESIGNER: Erwin Rausch

A series of games which teach eight aspects of economics: the market, the firm, collective bargaining, the community, scarcity and allocation, banking, the national economy, international trade. For high school or introductory college classes in economics. Each game requires about 45 minutes. Available from Science Research Associates (see listing for "American Government Simulations").

Economic System

DESIGNERS: James S. Coleman and T. Robert Harris

Basic principles of economics in a competitive society (supply and demand, marginal utility, interdependence of industry and agriculture). For high school or junior high school students. Time required is indefinite; recommended time is 2–3 hours; can be played in shorter sessions. Available from Western Publishing Company (see listing for "Consumer").

The Free Enterprise Game

DESIGNER: Jimmer Leonard

A *computer game* which teaches basic economic concepts. For students in grades six and up. Divided into "The Toy Store Game" (8 hours), in which the player takes role of a retailer; and "The Surfboard Game" (2 hours), in which he becomes a manufacturer. Both games can be played in 40-minute sessions. Programmed for IBM 1050 with random-access audio-visual unit. Also available in Autocoder for IBM 1401 (12K) and in Coursewriter for IBM 360/30. For further information contact Board of Co-Operative Educational Services, 845 Fox Meadow Road, Yorktown Heights, N. Y. 10598.

Generation Gap (formerly "Parent-Child")

DESIGNERS: E. O. Schild and Sarane S. Boocock

The conflict between an adolescent's desire for independence and a parent's desire for control. For teaching basic strategies of negotiation and compromise to older children and younger adolescents; also for research into children's attitudes toward authority. Requires about 30 minutes. Available from Western Publishing Company (see listing for "Consumer").

Gettysburg

DESIGNER: Charles S. Roberts

One of a series of games which simulate famous battles and military campaigns. The series includes "Waterloo," "1914," "Stalingrad," "Midway," and others. Intended primarily for entertainment. Time required varies from game to game. Available from Avalon-Hill Company (see listing for "C & O/B & O").

Ghetto (formerly "Poor People's Choice")

DESIGNER: Dove Toll

Teaches players the problems of the urban poor, including economic and personal satisfaction, participation in illegal activities. For adults and high school students. Requires about 2½ hours; can be played in shorter sessions. Available from Western Publishing Company (see listing for "Consumer").

High School Geography Project

Six classroom units which contain simulation games and activities, including "Portsville," "Metfab," "Farming," "Section," "Point Roberts," and "Flood Hazards." Each unit requires from 4 to 8 weeks (five periods per week). Available from the Macmillan Company, School Dept., 866 Third Avenue, New York, N. Y. 10022.

Inter-Nation Simulation

DESIGNERS: Harold Guetzkow and Cleo H. Cherryholmes

Simulates the main political, economic, and military aspects of an international situation. Used to teach international relations to college students; also for research into the dynamics of decision-making on an international scale. Time required is indefinite; minimum recommended time is 5 hours; can be divided into one-hour periods. Can be played in several small rooms or one large room. A typewriter and duplicating machine are strongly recommended. Available from Science Research Associates, Inc. (see listing for "American Government Simulations").

Life Career

DESIGNER: Sarane S. Boocock

The marriage, education, and labor markets in the U. S. as they affect social mobility and personal satisfaction. Minimum recommended time is two hours; a complete game requires about four hours; can be played in 40-minute sessions. Available from Western Publishing Company (see listing for "Consumer").

Management

DESIGNER: Charles S. Roberts

Top-level management decision-making in a competitive industry. Intended primarily for entertainment; can also be used to teach high school or college students. Time required is indefinite; recommended minimum of one hour. Available from Avalon-Hill Co. (see listing for "C & O/B & O").

Market

Based on the grocery business; used to teach basic principles of economics (profit and loss, supply and demand) to elementary school students. Requires three class periods of about 40 minutes each. Furniture in the room must be movable; 8 marking crayons are required. Available from Industrial Relations Center, The University of Chicago, 1225 East 60th Street, Chicago, Illinois 60637.

Marketplace

Teaches principles of economics (factors of production, supply and demand, circular flow of money and goods, ownership of stock). For high school and college classes in economics. Requires 2 to 12 periods of one hour each. Furniture in the room must be movable. Available from Security Pacific National Bank, Bankers' Equipment Department, 1307 South Alvarado Street, Los Angeles, Calif. 90006.

NAPOLI (NAtional POLItics)

The legislative process as influenced by party and regional affiliation. For classroom use with students from 6th grade through graduate school. Requires 3 to 6 hours. Available from Simile II (see listing for "Crisis").

PLANS

Conflicts between powerful interest groups in American society. For classroom use with students from 7th grade through graduate school. Available from Simile II (see listing for "Crisis").

The Railroad Game

Reproduces the conflicts among railroads and their customers during the 1870's in the United States. For high school classes in American history. Can be played in one 45-minute period. Part of a complete unit, *The Railroad Era*. Available from American Education Publications, Education Center, Columbus, Ohio 43216.

The Sierra Leone Game

DESIGNER: Walter Goodman

A *computer game* which places the player in the role of an American economic advisor in a developing nation. For students in grades six and up. Requires six hours; can be played in 40-minute sessions. (For computer requirements and availability, see listing for "The Free Enterprise Game.")

SIMSOC

DESIGNER: William A. Gamson

Requires players to create their own social order in a mock society. For college classes in sociology or political science. Requires 12 one-hour or 6 two-hour periods. Can be played in one large room with movable furniture; four small rooms with a common adjacent hallway are ideal. Available from The Free Press, 866 Third Ave., New York, N. Y. 10022.

Simulation, the Decision-making Model

The international decision-making process. Used to teach international relations to high school and college students. Requires five periods of approximately 45 minutes each. A blackboard and wall chart are required; five separate rooms are desirable but not necessary. Available from The World Affairs Council of Philadelphia, The John Wanamaker Store, Third Floor Gallery, 13th and Market Streets, Philadelphia, Penna. 19107

SITTE

The conflicts among powerful interst groups in an American city. For classroom use with students from 7th grade through graduate school. Available from Simile II (see listing for "Crisis.").

Starpower

Simulates, in abstract form, the relationship between wealth and power in human societies. For use with classes or groups of any age; 18 to 35 participants are required. Available from Simile II (see listing for "Crisis").

The Sumerian Game

DESIGNER: Mabel Addis

A *computer game* which teaches basic economic principles. The player takes the role of the ruler of a primitive agrarian society. For students in grades six and up. Requires eight hours; can be played in 40-minute sessions. (For computer requirements and availability, see listing for "The Free Enterprise Game.")

Trade and Develop

DESIGNER: Samuel A. Livingston

Teaches basic concepts of international trade and economic development. For students in grades 6 through 10. Requires about 40 minutes. Available from Academic Games Associates. 430 East 33rd Street, Baltimore, Maryland.

Index

INDEX

INDEX

INDEX

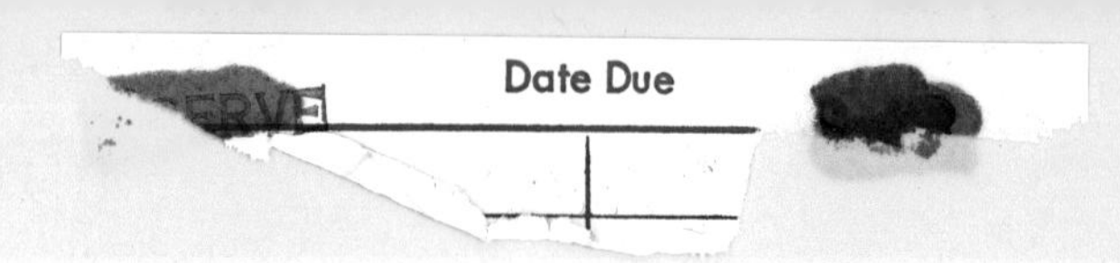
Date Due